AF519305

Impact of Irrigation on Indian Farm Economy

Impact of Irrigation on Indian Farm Economy

A. N. Pawar
V. B. Bhise

SERIALS PUBLICATIONS
NEW DELHI (INDIA)

© A. N. Pawar & V. B. Bhise

First Published - 2011

ISBN: 978-81-8387-443-4

All rights reserved with the Publisher, including the right to translate or reproduce this book or parts thereof except for brief quotations in critical articles or reviews.

Published by

SERIALS PUBLICATIONS
4830/24, Prahlad Street, Ansari Road
Darya Ganj, New Delhi-110002 (India)
Phone : 23245225 Fax : 91-11-23272135
E-mail: serials@sify.com

CONTENTS

PREFACE

Irrigation is the most important Instrument for the development of agriculture, because it enhances both agricultural productivity and production and brings stability in them. It helps in stabilizing agriculture prices and increases marketable surpluses of agricultural product it also helps for improving returns to the farmers and for reducing rural poverty.

The present book focuses on the development of irrigation in India as well as Maharshtra state. It gives a detailed outline of irrigation development in India during the pre - and post independence period. Just about 18 per cent of the cropped area was under irrigation in India at the time of independence. At present, the irrigation level has increased to 40 per cent. This book also reviews the irrigation development in Maharshtra state after the formation of the state in 1960.The ultimate irrigation potential in Maharshtra is 126 lakh ha. Out of which 40 lakh ha. Irrigation potential is created so far. The irrigation benefit was to the found of 1.2 million ha. In 1961 , the corresponding benefits near about tripled by the year 1999-2000 to reach 3.4 million ha. in Maharshtra state.

The book presents the macro–level and micro–level impact of irrigation on agriculture in the study area. The macro level analysis reveled that the growth of irrigation has positive effect on the cropping intensity, which increased from 4 per cent to 25 per cent. Irrigation has made favorable shift in cropping pattern form low value crops to high value crops such as sugar cane, oilseeds and fruits and vegetables. The study has intended the positive correlation between irrigated area and crop production. The micro level analysis reveled that the irrigated farmers are more efficient in land utilization than the farmers of un irrigated area. The index of overall crop intensity in irrigated area was significantly higher than that in the un irrigated area. The cropping pattern in irrigated area was favorable with more diversification of high value crops overall net return per ha in irrigated area was found to be 19 times higher than that in un irrigated area. The per hector employment was three and half times higher on the irrigated farms in the study area.

We are thankful to all concerned for providing us with the required information.We acknowledge with thanks the cooperation received from the librarian and staff of the Dr. Babasaheb Ambedkar Marathwada University, Aurganbad, Water and land management institute, Aurganabd and Ghokhale Institute of politics and Economics, Pune.

Lastly, we are thank full to Mr. Murleedharan for long hours typing and this man script and large number of tables contained in it and data processing within a short period of time.

A. N. Pawar
V. B. Bhise

CHAPTER 1

INTRODUCTION

INTRODUCTION

Irrigation is the most important instrument of the development of agriculture. The agriculture of different regions and countries in the world enjoying high productivities in different crops are found to be mainly depended on irrigation. Irrigation in an agrarian economy assumes the same importance as blood in human body. In the earlier times, when there was no pressure of population, water flowing in the rivers, supported by the rainfall was adequate to meet the needs of human life and for cultivation of the required crops. As the pressure of population increased and standard of living of human being raised, necessity of increased water resources has been felt. This led to the concept of storing water through the construction of dams and using it through a canal system in other seasons.

Development in India is synonymous with rural development because more than 60 per cent of its population live in rural areas with nearly 40 per cent below the poverty line. Agriculture is the main occupation of these people. Near about 70 per cent of the population are in agriculture, it engages 60 per cent of work force. And it contributes around 26.8 per cent in 1998-99[1]. 80 per cent of farmers are small and marginal farmers and 75 per cent of the poor are in rural areas. Acceleration of agricultural production and productivity has become the primary objective to meet the increasing demands, both food and employment, of the population and also boost the national economy on a sustained basis. For realising this full potential of agriculture, water is the most critical input and efforts to harness it in the form of irrigation are being done extensively both by the central and state governments of India[2].

Irrigation is defined as the artificial application of water to soil, for the purpose of supplying water essential to plant growth. It is a means by which water is conveyed to arid areas from rivers, reservoirs or wells to increase the fertility of the land. Scientific irrigation involves a knowledge of the available water supply, its conservation and application to the land, the characteristics and needs of the different types of the soil and requirements of various crops to be produced. It is the science of harnessing the source of water and distributing the same for agriculture[3].

Irrigation is becoming more and more important from the point of view of the development of the whole world's agricultural economy. The impact of irrigation is all pervading as it leads to change in cropping pattern, increased yield rates and labour utilisation and ultimately it brings prosperity to the areas, hence irrigation is regarded as a catalyst for socio-economic change that sets in motion the productive forces in the agricultural sector[4].

The term "irrigation" includes all operations or practices in artificial supply of water to the soil for growing crops. In Indian planning, since April 1978, the cultivated area is being considered as the basis for the classification of irrigation projects. According to new criterion, the following are the definitions of different irrigation projects:

(a) Major irrigation projects: An irrigation project which covers more than 10,000 hectares as the cultivated command area.

(b) Medium irrigation project: An irrigation project which covers area between 2,000 hectares and 10,000 hectares as the cultivated command area.

(c) Minor irrigation project: An irrigation project which covers less than 2,000 hectares as the cultivated command area.

Thus an attempt is made in first chapter to assess the importance of irrigation in agrarian economy, research methodology and objectives.

Importance of irrigation with different socio-economic and developmental aspects are shown in Figure 1. This figure shows the importance of irrigation in the agrarian economy of developing countries like India.

Agriculture would continue to be the backbone of Indian economy in the near future. A developed agriculture is a prerequisite for sustained and rapid economic and social development in India. An introduction of improved agricultural practices and technological improvements with irrigation water will increase agricultural productivity and generate surpluses for capital accumulation. Agriculture continues to hold the key to the progress of the economy as well as means for individual welfare.

IMPORTANCE OF IRRIGATION IN AGRARIAN ECONOMY

It becomes clear from the points indicated in the Figure 1 that the irrigation is important for the development in agriculture. The importance of irrigation in agrarian economy is interpreted comprehensively as follows:

IRRIGATION →

→ (1) Removes uncertainty of agricultural production.

→ (2) Increases in agricultural production

→ (3) Helps for agricultural price stability

→ (4) Increase in marketable surplus

→ (5) Increase in money return on high value cash crops

→ (6) Provides employment opportunities

→ (7) Enables adoption of modern agricultural technology

→ (8) Reduces rural poverty

→ (9) Promotes rural development

→ (10) Inputs utilisation

Figure 1 : Importance of Irrigation

Irrigation and Uncertainty of Agricultural Production

One of the greatest defects in the structure of Indian agriculture is the unreliability of rainfall, which is marked by its wide variations in different parts and also variation from year to year in its quantity, incidence and duration. Most of the rainfall (i.e. about 80 per cent) occurs during June-September, while winter rains amount to only 20 per cent.

The rainfall over the country is unequal, irregular and quite often liable to complete failure. With such a wide difference in rainfall between one part and another (such as 1270 cm at Cherrapunji and only 25 cm in Western Rajasthan), famines have occurred several times in the past. The areas generally affected by variations in the rainfall are those which receive a rainfall of 127 cm (50") and less per annum. Whenever rain fails, i.e. when it is less than 80 per cent of the average, or when it does not occur at the proper crop season, production falls. If deficiency of rainfall is 40 per cent or more, famines result and crops do not even grow. To banish famines, the only remedy is artificial supply of water to the lands through irrigation[5]. Thus, irrigation is the means of making the country's agriculture relatively independent of the vagaries of rains. Irrigation helps to remove uncertainty of agricultural production, even in drought prone area.

Irrigation and Food Problem

Irrigation development is highly correlated with population growth and is a primary means of providing additional food for increasing population. So food problem can be solved to a considerable extent, with irrigation development. The development of irrigation has a very important role in the growth of Indian agriculture to meet the rising demand for food and fibre of rapidly growing population. Irrigation possesses significant area effect. It increases the net area cultivated and more importantly, the gross cropped area which enhances food production.

Irrigation and Cropping Pattern

Irrigation changes cropping pattern by absorbing modern inputs such as high yielding varieties of seeds, fertilisers, pesticides etc. High value crops like cotton, sugarcane, oilseeds and other food crops like rice, wheat etc. would be found in place of inferior food crops like jowar, bajra, etc. Availability of water throughout the year enables the farmers to take at least three crops in a year amounting to three hundred per cent cropping intensity. Thus, by promoting multiple cropping, irrigation breaks the rhythm of traditional crops cycle.

Irrigation and Crop Yield

Irrigation is a proven means for increasing crop yields and farm income. Crop yields and farm incomes are usually three to four times higher in irrigated agriculture as compared with rainfed agriculture.

The Famine Enquiry Commission (1945) has rightly emphasised that among the measures that may be adopted to increase the area under cultivation and the yields per acre, the first place must be given to the works for the supply and conservation of water.

Irrigation is deemed necessary for the maximum production of most farm crops. According to the Indian Council of Agricultural Research (ICAR), the output of irrigated crops is, on an average, 50 to 100 per cent higher than that of unirrigated crops in the same locality. The average yield of irrigated fields have shown a wide difference over the unirrigated fields, such as in the case of rice it has been of the order of 52.5 per cent higher, wheat 53.1 per cent and maize 53.0 per cent higher.

Improved water management can probably do more towards increasing agricultural production in the irrigated area of the world than any other agricultural practice[6].

Irrigation is every thing in India. Water is more valuable than land, because when water is applied to land it increases its productiveness at least six fold and renders great extents of land productive, which otherwise would produce nothing.[7]

Irrigation development in the past had mostly taken place as a measure of famine relief. In fact, famines gave birth to the idea of artificial irrigation in India. Now, with the population multiplying rapidly, irrigation has assumed greater importance for augmenting agricultural production[8]. The importance of irrigation may be viewed from two aspects viz., 'protective aspect' to make up the moisture deficiency in soils during the cropping season so as to ensure proper and sustained growth of crops grown, 'additional land use aspect' to enable a second or third crop being raised on lands provided with irrigation which could otherwise not be cultivated efficiently more particularly during the past or pre-monsoon period. While the protective aspect helps in stabilising agricultural production against droughts, the second facility cannot be neglected by an alert agriculturist. Irrigation has also a third aspect. It helps in augmenting and preserving the properties of soils by application of adequate supply of water.

Irrigation and Price Stability

Irrigation contributes substantially to price stability of agricultural produce by removing, to a large extent, the elements of uncertainty in an agricultural production system.

Besides, the sixth Five Year Plan also emphasised the importance of irrigation, since it is helpful in bringing price stability in agricultural goods. The plan said, irrigation contributes substantially to the agricultural price stability, by removing to a large extent the elements of uncertainty in an agricultural production. Therefore, expansion in irrigation would be envisaged as a part of price stabilisation policy[9].

Irrigation Increases Money Return and Marketable Surplus

Irrigation changes the cropping pattern of the farmers in irrigated area by absorbing modern inputs like seeds, pesticides, fertilisers, etc. The high value crops like cotton, sugarcane, fruits etc. and other food crops like paddy, etc. (which are of higher commercial value) would be found in place of inferior food crops like jowar, bajra etc. in the command area[10]. Besides, it supports not only long duration crops like cotton, sugarcane, groundnut, etc. but also those of high yielding varieties of short duration. In addition to this, it paves the way for double and multiple cropping. Diversification of cropping pattern results in an increase of marketable surplus of agricultural commodities.

The increase in agricultural production and marketable surplus raises farm income of the farmers with assured irrigation facility combined with the use of modern inputs can grow double or multiple crops in their same piece of land every year. This enhanced agricultural production is not wholly consumed by the farmers but a portion of it is sold in market resulting in increase in their farm income. Further, if they reinvest the increased farm income on farm improvements, their gross income can further be raised substantially. In this way, irrigation assists the process of capital formation in the economy.

Irrigation Increases Employment Opportunities

Irrigation responds favourably in the generation of additional employment opportunities for rural masses. Irrigation operation itself creates farm level employment through increased cropping intensity and adoption of improved and labour-intensive cultural practices such as transplantation, line sowing, application of manures, fertilisers and pesticides. Further, irrigation also leads to enhanced employment opportunities in activities whose linkages with the agricultural sector are high. William Sander[11] observes that agricultural modernization (primarily due to irrigation development) helps to stimulate non-farm employment of a region. The activities like rice milling, cotton ginning, vanaspati, sugar industry, repairing or maintenance activities of improved agricultural implements and other agro-based activities, which have forward linkage with the agricultural sector generate additional employment opportunities in the economy. On the other hand, backward linkage effects with the agricultural sector are industrial activities pertaining to the production of fertilisers, pesticides, improved agricultural implements, etc. also lead to an increase in employment opportunities. Thus, increased activities relating to raising of different crops, processing units and agro-based industries and industrial activities concerning to the production of modern inputs provide ample opportunities for utilizing both uneducated and educated man-power. Irrigation, therefore, reduces the resource of unemployment, under employment and seasonal unemployment in the economy considerably.

In an agrarian economy, irrigation may be a good source of employment as well. Irrigation raises both the employment and income content of land and thus adds to capital formation. The construction and maintenance of an irrigation project have far reaching effects on the economic life of the community living within a region and also to some extent on the community living without it. Investment in an irrigation project leads to the creation of new or additional productive activity and new or additional production. The utilisation of the opportunities created by such capital work needs further investment in order to launch new productive activities or for expanding old activities in the area affected by the project[12]. This additional investment involves the employment of additional capital and labour resources which in turn will lead to an increase in production.

In this way irrigation generates employment and capital formation. It may supplement the slender income of poor farmers by providing side jobs. It encourages farmers to adopt more scientific techniques. It also permits them to go in for more intensive cropping which creates new opportunities for gainful employment[13].

Irrigation and Modern Agricultural Technology

Sufficient irrigation facilities is a prerequisite for adopting modern agricultural technology. Modern agricultural implements, machinery, equipments viz. tractor, power tillers, etc. can be efficiently used only with ensured availability of water. These capital intensive techniques increase agricultural produce, requires less time for completion of agricultural activities and reduces unit cost of production. With irrigation, modern agricultural practices such as multiple cropping, mixed cropping, crop rotation etc. can be implemented and use of high yielding varieties, modern seeds, fertilisers can be made possible. Thus, with adequate irrigation facility modern agricultural technology and practices can be adopted which increases cropping intensity of the land.

Irrigation Helps in Poverty Alleviation

While suggesting the measures of the eradication of poverty, however, we agree with the approach of the Fifth Plan which categorically states that "Employment is the surest way to enable the vast numbers, living below the poverty level, rise above it. However, the conventional fiscal measures for redistribution of income cannot by themselves make a significant impact on the problem[14]. Out of the suggested measures, extension of minor irrigation works can be helpful to enlarge employment in the process which leads to removal of poverty.

It has been observed that extension of irrigation facilities and especially minor irrigation works are helpful in creating employment opportunities as well as the level of product of per unit of land and labour. Besides, it will be more useful to provide water to dry lands by extending minor irrigation works. Thus, the provision of irrigation facilities in dry land areas will help to eradicate poverty.

The irrigation has a favourable effect on wage rate in agriculture. There are evidences to support this that the irrigation improves the wage in agriculture. The increased wage rate would lead to increase in incomes of the poor labourers. The experience of Punjab and Haryana supports this path of development. On the other hand, the states like Bengal and Kerala which claim highly progressive land ceiling laws, have failed to reduce rural poverty[15].

Irrigation and Other Resources

Irrigation alone does not help to achieve optimum production. Irrigation is looked upon as a system in which optimum utilisation of water along with other agricultural inputs, helps to increase agricultural incomes. Irrigation, with proper combination of other agricultural inputs viz. land, labour, seed, fertiliser, pesticides, agricultural implements, capital etc. increase marginal productivity of water as well as of other inputs.

Among several inputs water content in the soil is most important input for the growth of plant. This water content is even more important than soil for if the soil is the store house of plant nutrients, water content is its carrier. In the absence of this carrier plant nutrients remain unused and seeds do not germinate well. Hence, supply and maintenance of moisture in the soil is essential for the growth of crops.

Charles Threvelyan rightly pointed out that "Irrigation is every thing in India, water is more valuable than land, because when water is applied to land it increases its productiveness and renders great extent of land produce, which otherwise would produce nothing or next to nothing"[16].

Irrigation and Rural Development

Irrigation is an important pre-requisite for the agricultural and ultimately the rural development. Well managed irrigated agriculture contributes to economic growth. Irrigation works have made life secured, major irrigation projects act as anti-famine, and anti-flood measures. They have increased the yields and value of land and even revenue to government. Similarly, the minor irrigation projects act as beneficial to marginal farmers and increases their income. It provides higher level of income and creates additional employment opportunities in rural areas. Irrigation is useful to reduce the poverty of rural people to some extent. Irrigation increases capital formation and is considered as a primary engine of rural development in developing countries, self sufficiency, stability and prosperity of agriculture in India depend on irrigation more than on any other single sphere of activity. And agricultural prosperity is the key to the general prosperity in the country.

Irrigation and Advantages of Soil, Sunshine and Climate

The need of irrigation also arises from the fact that inspite of considerable advantages of the soil, sunshine and climate, crop production in India is not so efficient as in other parts of the world specially because of lack of moisture in the soils. Sandy soils require frequent water than the alluvial or black soils. And it cannot be over emphasized than to state that "a sadder commentary on our economic situation cannot be found than the close, direct correspondence between harvests and mortality"[17] and the security of harvests depends primarily upon the adequate supply of water.

Vital Role of Irrigation

Irrigation has proved beneficial to the country. In fact, irrigation forms the datum line for sustained successful agriculture. It alleviates suffering, preserves life, averts famines and advances the material prosperity of the country. Dr. Knowles writes that the irrigation works have made security of life, they have increased the yields, and the value of land and the revenue derived from it. They have lessened the cost of famine relief and have helped to civilize the whole region. In addition, they yield handsome profits to the government[18].

In this way, irrigation plays a very crucial role in agricultural and economic development of a country. Well managed irrigated agriculture contributes to economic growth on substantial scale. Irrigation works have made life secured, major irrigation projects act as anti-famine and anti-flood measures. Irrigation facilitates modernization process of the agricultural sector by adopting new technology. With proper combination of other inputs, irrigation increases marginal productivity of water as well as of other inputs of agriculture. Irrigation is a proven means for increasing crop yields and farm income. It has increased yields/hectare and has provided higher levels of income to the farm families. Introduction of irrigation facilities is likely to result in higher employment opportunities and improve the economic conditions of labourers. Irrigation also leads to the improvement of infrastructural facilities and living standards of rural people. Thus, irrigation is considered as a primary engine for rural development in developing countries.

CHOICE OF THE SUBJECT

Water is one of the strategic inputs for the agricultural transformation. The predominant source of water in India is rainfall. But it is erratic and unevenly distributed over time and space. This temporal and spatial variations in the occurrence of rainfall very often result in drought and flood-drought situations. In view of this the need for the development of water resources, in the country was well recognised, more particularly, after the launching of planning process. Irrigation assumes a key role in the strategy for agricultural transformation in developmental planning of Indian economy. From the launching of the first Five Year Plan till to date the irrigation along with agriculture has been accorded the highest place in our developmental schemes and investment priorities.

As in other parts of the country, agricultural operations in Maharashtra are also subject to the vagaries of rainfall. Drought and scarcity conditions are very common. It has been assessed by the Memorandum Commission that the scarcity areas were increased to cover 147,262 sq. km that is 48 per cent of the total geographical area. It included 112 talukas of which 62 wholly and 50 partially fell in the category of scarcity areas[19]. The above factual analysis clearly emphasizes the need for making all our efforts to tap irrigation facilities. The soil, topography, rainfall and climate in Maharashtra are in general not very conducive to agriculture, resulting in relatively low yields of the important crops in the state as compared with these in India. Nearly one-third area of the state fall in the rain shadow region where rains are not only scarcity but also erratic. The level of irrigation in state is lower than country. The percentage of gross irrigated area to gross cropped area in the state being only 15.41 per cent as compared with 38 per cent for the country as a whole in 1999-2000[20]. The agriculture in the state is thus largely dependent on monsoon. The investment on irrigation schemes creates favourable impact on economic life of rural households. From this point of view, it is necessary to assess irrigation development and its impact on agriculture. The study is undertaken with this view.

SCOPE OF THE STUDY

The present study aims at analysing the impact of irrigation on farm economy. The study covers irrigation development and proposes to quantify the extent to which it has increased agricultural production and productivity, farm income favourable cropping pattern and cropping intensity. It also intends to find its role as the generator of employment opportunities. In view of the difficulties involved in covering the entire country and also the entire farming community as unit of the study, and also with a view to achieve the greater accuracy, Osmanabad district (of Marathwada region) in Maharashtra state is selected as a unit of the study. In brief, the study aims at evaluating the impact of irrigation on farm economy of Osmanabad district.

Agriculture is the most dominant sector in the selected district. The economy of the district is primarily depends on agriculture as supported by the fact that cultivators (40.51 per cent) and agricultural labourers (41.07 per cent) together constitute (81.60 per cent) of the total workers in the district as against the state average of 59.62 per cent[21]. The agricultural sector has thus absorbed a predominant proportion of the total main workers in the district. This is so because there are no alternative employment opportunities available in the district. Less than 20 per cent of main workers are engaged in non-agricultural activities. So, agriculture is the main occupation of the people in Osmanabad. More than 80 per cent of the district's work force depend on farm sector for their livelihood. The district has by and large a dry agricultural terrain, having scarce and uncertain rainfall. The whole district may well have been completely "a gamble in monsoon. The average rainfall of this district is 588 mm to 771 mm and there has been no assured supply of water and at present irrigation covers near about 17 per cent of its gross cropped area. Moreover, the impact of irrigation on agriculture in this district is evident because most of the area of agricultural sector depends on the uncertainty of the monsoon.

OBJECTIVES OF THE PRESENT STUDY

In the present work an attempt has been made to study the irrigation development and its role in agricultural development in Osmanabad district. The present study has the following specific objectives:

1. To review the development of irrigation in India and Maharashtra state during the plan period.

2. To assess the season-wise and crop-wise growth in irrigation and to find out the intensity of irrigation in the study area.
3. To assess the impact of irrigation on agricultural development i.e. land use, cropping pattern, intensity of cropping, and crop production in the study area.
4. To assess the impact of irrigation on costs and returns of sample farms in the study area.
5. To assess the impact of irrigation on employment in sample farms in the study area.

LIMITATIONS OF THE STUDY

At this stage, it is necessary to emphasise the limitations to which a study like this is subjected to. As stated earlier in the scope of the study, the study pertains only to analyse the broader areas of impact of irrigation on agriculture in Osmanabad district during the period 1999-2000. Thus the study excludes a deeper inquiry into other important aspects such as consumption pattern, saving and investment, marketing, literacy, debt position assets and influence of socio-cultural factors on sample farms. Further, the study does not cover the districts other than Osmanabad district in Maharashtra.

RESEARCH METHODOLOGY

The adoption of sound methodology in any economic investigation forms a vital part of the study. Hence, an attempt has been made here to describe the different aspects of methodology adopted in the study under report.

Measurement of Irrigation Impact

Impact of irrigation on farm households can be measured by either of two approaches: (i) Before-After Approach, and (ii) With-Without Approach - 'before' and 'without' serving as the control and 'after' and 'with' serving as the command. The first approach compare the existing irrigated condition with that which was there prior to the advent of irrigation. On the other hand, the second approach compares the irrigated (command) situations with unirrigated (control) situation at a point of time. The 'with – without' approach in effect provides a better estimation since interaction aspects of various other programmes operating in the command area over a period of time make it difficult to isolate the impact of irrigation under the 'before – after' approach. Hence, the present study adopts the 'with – without' approach which can be said to satisfy the ceteris paribus conditions quite closely. The evaluation of benefits of irrigation is based on with-without principle under which Regan and Witzel have shown two situations, such as the development of economy with the project and development that would accrue without it are compared[22]. Thus, survey data on both 'with' (command) and without (control) irrigation situations have been used to measure the impact of irrigation during the agricultural year 1999-2000.

Sources of Data

This study is the outcome of field work done by the writer during the year 1999-2000. The data were collected both from the primary and secondary sources.

To study the impact of irrigation on agriculture in study area the secondary data was collected from various publications of the state and local government offices such as-

(i) Socio-Economic Review and District Statistical Abstract of Osmanabad District.

(ii) District-wise Agricultural Statistical Information of Maharashtra Part II, Commissionerate of Agriculture, Maharashtra State, Pune 1997-98.

Since the period for macro-level study is considered from 1982, taluka level published data were available for Osmanabad district. Before 1982, the taluka Latur was one of the parts of Osmanabad district and which was formed as new district in 1982. So the taluka-wise data for Osmanabad district has been taken from 1982 onwards. So all the analysis has been done for selected Osmanabad district and its six talukas viz. Osmanabad, Tuljapur, Omerga, Bhoom, Paranda and Kallam.

To study the impact of irrigation at micro-level, a socio-economic survey is conducted in selected district. Data from primary sources have been collected through (i) field survey, (ii) interviews with farmers and (iii) discussion with the government officials. For getting accurate information, the farms were visited frequently. The agricultural year 1999-2000 was a normal year, in the sense, that there was normal rainfall received in irrigated and unirrigated area. Hence the year 1999-2000 was selected as the year for finding the impact of irrigation in the present research investigation.

Statistical Methods

The study is attempted to make use of the following statistical methods.

(a) The intensity of irrigation and cropping both were computed by the following formula.

$$\text{Irrigation Intensity Index} = \frac{\text{Gross irrigated area}}{\text{Net irrigated area}} \times 100$$

$$\text{Cropping Intensity Index} = \frac{\text{Gross cropped area}}{\text{Net cropped area}} \times 100$$

(b) Correlation coefficients were calculated between total irrigated area and total crop production, irrigated area under foodgrains and foodgrains production and irrigated area under non-foodgrains and non-foodgrains production with the following formula :

Correlation coefficient or

$$r = \frac{\Sigma xy - N\,\bar{x}\,\bar{y}}{N\,6x\,6y}$$

Where $\bar{x}$ = Actual mean of x values.

x = Total irrigated area/irrigated area under foodgrains/ irrigated area under non-foodgrains.

$\bar{y}$ = Actual mean of y values.

y = Total crop production/foodgrains production/ non-foodgrains production.

6x = Standard deviation of x values.

6y = Standard deviation of y values.

Estimation of Farm Cost and Farm Income

In micro level analysis, an attempt is made to study the impact of irrigation on costs and returns of crop enterprises. To estimate the farm costs and returns, the tool of farm management procedure has been used in the study[23]. The different cost concepts such as cost A_2, cost B and Cost C and return concepts like farm business income and net returns are discussed in the following paragraphs.

Cost A_2 includes (a) value of hired human labour, (b) value of hired bullock labour or own bullock or machine labour, (c) value of both farm produced and purchased seed, (d) value of pesticides, (e) value of farm yard manures (owned and/or purchased and chemical fertilisers), (f) depreciation on fixed capital (implements and farm building), (g) hire charges for implements, (h) interest on working capital, (i) irrigation charges, (j) land revenue, (k) cost of transportation and (l) miscellaneous expenses. Cost B includes cost A_2, plus the rental value of owned land and interest on owned fixed capital (excluding land), cost C includes cost B plus the imputed value of family labour.

The costs of hired labour have been evaluated at wages prevalent in different seasons for agricultural year 1999-2000. The cost of family labour has been evaluated at the wage rate for casually hired labour. The working cost of owned bullock labour (8 hours work done by a pair of bullocks) has been evaluated at a rate of Rs. 60 per pair per day, the prevalent rate for hiring a pair of bullock in view of the differences involved in correctly ascertaining the maintenance cost of owned bullocks by interview method.

For computing the value of seeds, the prices of different seeds prevalent in the village at the time of sowing have been taken into account. The value of chemical fertilisers and pesticides have been taken according to their market value. The farm yard manure has been evaluated at prices prevalent in the villages. Depreciation on fixed capital has been evaluated on the basis of straight line method. Wherever the implements have been hired, actual hire charges have been added. Irrigation charges and land revenue have been calculated on the basis of actual payments made in different sample villages. The rental value of own land is considered as equal to $^{1}/_{6}{}^{th}$ of the total gross value of output obtained from all crops during the year. Such an approach is in conformity with the latest farm management procedure currently in force in India and has also used in studies such as that of Singh and Govindarajuly[24]. Interest on fixed capital has been charged as per the rates charged by primary co-operatives during the survey period 1999-2000. Interest on working capital has been worked out for a period of 6 months at an interest rate of 12 per cent per annum on the total cost of seeds, manures, fertilisers and pesticides.

Output includes the value of both main and by-products of crops evaluated at the prices prevailed in the village within the two months of harvest.

The following income concepts have been used in the study;

(a) Farm business income (FBI) = Gross value of output – Cost A_2

(b) Return to Family labour and Management (RFLM) = Gross value of output – Cost B.

(c) Net income or net return (NI) = Gross value of output– Cost C.

Analytical Tools

Simple tabular analysis based on percentages and averages has been adopted wherever they are necessary. The aggregate and ratio measures, such as farm business income, return to family labour and management, net return, have been used to compare the efficiency of the farms with and without irrigation.

Selection of the Field (Talukas)

Since the micro-level study pertains to impacts of irrigation, Tuljapur taluka having good irrigation incidence was purposively selected for the study is consider the taluka-wise irrigated area in the district. The talukawise net irrigated area and the percentage of gross irrigated area to gross cropped area during 1986-87 to 1995 has been calculated and is presented in Table 1. It is seen from this table that in period 1986-87, Tuljapur taluka was enjoying highest both in net irrigated area (28.06 percentage) and gross irrigated area (22.68 percentage) in the district. Similarly, in period 1995-96, again this taluka has the highest in net irrigated area (31.69 percentage) and gross irrigated area (23.34 percentage) in the district. It is clear that, Tuljapur taluka is highest developed in irrigation compared to other talukas in Osmanabad district. So, Tuljapur taluka was purposely selected for the present study.

The Sample Design

Present study conducted a micro level field survey in a homogeneous region of Osmanabad district. The study was based on with and without principle. The sampling technique adopted for field investigation was based on three stage stratified random sampling with farm household as the ultimate unit samples. At the first stage Tuljapur taluka was purposely selected based on the concentration of taluka-wise irrigation development in Osmanabad district. It is seen from the Table 1 that during period 1986-87 to 1995-96, Tuljapur taluka was the highest (31.69) in percentage share of net irrigated area as compared to other talukas in district. At the second stage, three villages were selected based on the concentration of source-wise irrigation development in Tuljapur taluka. At the third stage for the selection of the sample unit, a list of all the farm households in selected villages with and without irrigation was prepared from the records of local revenue officer Talathi. And each village has divided into three strata of size group I, II and III i.e. small, medium and large operational holdings. From each stratum 10 per cent sample households were selected at random.

Table 1
The Taluka-wise Net Irrigated Area, Gross Irrigated Area and Percentage of Gross Irrigated Area to Gross Cropped Area in Osmanabad District

(Area in '000 hectares)

		Irrigated area			
Taluka / District	*Year*	*Net irrigated area*	*Gross irrigated area*	*Gross cropped area*	*Percentage of gross irrigated to gross cropped area*
1	2	3	4	5	6
Osmanabad	1986-87	19.49 (23.93)	21.58	116.20	18.57
	1995-96	17.66 (17.66)	21.17	123.70	17.11
Kallam	1986-87	12.14 (14.97)	17.22	97.50	17.66
	1995-96	11.59 (11.59)	12.90	98.20	13.14
Omerga	1986-87	7.20 (8.88)	11.61	150.30	7.72
	1995-96	12.17 (12.17)	19.33	150.40	12.86
Tuljapur	1986-87	22.76 (28.06)	25.79	113.70	22.68
	1995-96	31.69 (31.69)	34.45	147.60	23.34
Paranda	1986-87	11.02 (13.58)	14.21	109.50	12.98
	1995-96	18.94 (18.94)	23.39	124.80	18.74
Bhoom	1986-87	8.58 (10.58)	11.56	67.90	-
	1995-96	7.95 (7.95)	9.45	95.50	9.90
District	1986-87	81.11 (100.00)	101.98	655.10	15.56
Total	1995-96	100.00 (100.00)	122.07	740.20	16.49

Figures in brackets show the percentage to total

Source: Socio-Economic Review and District Statistical Abstract, Osmanabad District, Directorate of Economics and Statistics, Government of Maharashtra, Mumbai, 1995-96, p. 35.

Therefore, total 142 farm households were selected for the study. Out of this, 39 small, 23 medium, 18 large farm households selected with irrigation and remaining 34 small, 16 medium, 12 large farm households were without irrigation.

Village-wise sample-size of the farms selected in the irrigated and unirrigated sources in study area is shown in Tables 2 and 3. The selected households were studied with a structural questionnaire and the heads of the households were interviewed personally by the author for the purpose. As usual with survey methods, in the absence of farm record books, the respondents had to rely on the collections from their memory. However, all efforts were made to elicit as accurate information as possible.

Table 2
Village-Wise Distribution of Sample Farmers with Irrigation

Name of the village	*No. of sample farmers according to land holding*			
	Group I 1-2 hectares (small)	*Group II 2.01 to 4 hectares (medium)*	*Group III more than 4 hectares (large)*	*Grand total*
Andur	26	16	12	54
Khudawadi	8	4	4	16
Babhalgaon	5	3	2	10
Total	39	23	18	80

Source : Field survey.

Table 3
Village-wise Distribution of Sample Farmers without Irrigation

Name of the village	*No. of sample farmers according to operational land holding*			
	Group I Small 1-2 hectares	*Group II Medium 2.01 to 4 hectares*	*Group III Large more than 4 hectares*	*Grand total*
Andur	25	12	8	45
Khudawadi	6	3	3	12
Babhalgaon	3	1	1	5
Total	34	16	12	62

Source: Field survey.

SCHEME OF CHAPTER

The present study is divided into seven chapters. The importance of irrigation in agrarian economy and the essence of the present study are explained in first chapter. The objectives of the study, methodology adopted in study them and scheme of chapters are also given in this introductory chapter.

In the second chapter, an attempt is made to take a historical review of irrigation development. This chapter is divided into two sections. Section A deals with the irrigation development in India during pre and post independence periods and section B discusses the irrigation development in Maharashtra.

In third chapter an attempt is made to take the review of literature. In the present study, important aspects like development of irrigation and its impact on cropping pattern, cropping intensity, per hectare yields, employment and on costs and returns have been dealt with.

The fourth chapter throws light on macro-level impact of irrigation on agriculture in Osmanabad district. In this chapter, various macro–level irrigation impacts such as crop-pattern, cropping intensity, productivity and production in Osmanabad district have been assessed.

The fifth chapter is devoted to discuss irrigation impact on agriculture in Osmanabad district. In this chapter micro–level irrigation impact on crop-pattern, cropping intensity, land-use pattern, employment and cost and returns in the study area have been highlighted.

The sixth and final chapter summarises the findings of the present study and suggests suitable policy measures.

References

Thamarajakshi R. (2000), National Agricultural Policy, Confusion on Ends and Means, Economic and Political Weekly, August 26– September 2, p. 3237.

Jajam Iyengar M.K. (1951), Text Book of Irrigation, Allied Books Stall, Pune.

Vijaya Shyamala C. (1994), Current Approach to Irrigation Management. *Yojana*, Vol. 38, No. 10, June 15, p. 8.

Sivarama Krishnarao C. and Mohammad Iqbal Ali (1986), Impact of Irrigation on Cropping Pattern, *Kurukshetra*, August-September, p. 37.

Famine Enquiry Commission, Final Report, 1945, p. 129.

Jha U.M. (1984), Irrigation and Agricultural Development, Deep and Deep Publisher, p. 18.

Mukherjee R.K. (1993), Economic Problems of Modern India, Vol. 1, p. 167.

Nath Baleshwar (1966), Irrigation, *Yojana*, December, p. 10.

Sixth Five Year Plan, Government of India, p. 147.

Anand, O.P. (1960), Some Aspects of Optimum Benefits from Utilization of Irrigation Potential of Chambal Valley Project,

Indian Journal of Agricultural Economics, Vol. 15, No. 4, October-December, pp. 19-33.

William Sander (1983), Irrigation Development and Non-Farm Employment Changes in Communities in the Philippines, *Indian Journal of Agricultural Economics,* Vol. 38, No.1, January-March, p. 14.

Gadgil, D. R. (1948), Economic Effects of Irrigation–Report of a Survey of the Direct and Indirect Benefits of Godavari and Pravara Canals, Pub. No. 17, Gokhale Institute of Politics and Economics, Pune, p. 18.

Clark Colin (1970), The Economics of Irrigation, Pergamon Press, Oxford, London and Edinburgh, New York, First edition, 1967, Second edition, p. 21.

Planning Commission - Approach to the Fifth Plan (1974-79), January 1975, p. 5.

Bhattacharya C.B. (1983), Micro-Irrigation in Rural India, *Yojana* (16-30) September.

Mukherjee R.K., *op. cit.*, pp. 16-76.

Mukherjee R.K., *op. cit.*, p. 9.

Knowles, Economic Development of British Empire Overseas, Vol. 1, pp. 367-68.

Government of India, Report of the Irrigation Commission, Vol. II, 1972.

Government of Maharashtra, Economic Survey of Maharashtra, 1999-2000, p. T31.

District Census Handbook Osmanabad, Census of India 1991, Maharashtra Census Directorate Published by the Director, Government Printing and Stationery, Maharashtra State, Mumbai, 1995, pp. 18-36.

Regan, M.M. and Wietwell, E.G. (1947), "Economic Valuation of Soil and Water Conservation - Measures and Programmes", *Journal of Farm Economics,* November, pp. 1275-1294.

Government of India, Report on the Studies in Economics of Farm Management in Cuttack District, Orissa, Directorate of Economics and Statistics, Ministry of Agriculture, 1967-68, p. 68.

Singh J.P. and Govindarajulu K.V., "New Technology of Paddy Adoption and Yield Differentials", V.K.R.V. Rao(ed.) New Seeds Adoption and Yield, Sterling Publishers Limited, New Delhi, 1979, p. 89.

Chapter 2

Irrigation Development – A Historical Review

In the preceding chapter we have examined the importance of irrigation in the context of economic development of an agrarian economy. An attempt has been made in this chapter to review the development of irrigation system in India and Maharashtra. This chapter is divided into two sections. Section A deals with the irrigation development in India Section B discusses the irrigation development in Maharashtra.

SECTION–A

IRRIGATION DEVELOPMENT IN INDIA

The picture during pre-independence era, and picture during planning era are fundamentally different at least in one respect, whereas the first picture emerged out of negligence and apathy on the part of both Government and farmers, the second picture is replete with instance of intense activity in this sphere. The planning era has bid good bye to the attitude of apathy and as a consequence, development of irrigation has occupied place of pride among the various schemes of agricultural development. The extent of irrigation, the sources of irrigation as well as investment in irrigation schemes / multi-purpose projects have undergone a sea-change during planning era. In order to spread the benefits of irrigation to a vast mass of scattered farmers, the schemes of minor irrigation have been undertaken on a massive scale and new vistas has been opened for small and marginal farmers.

Thus, an attempt is made to analyse irrigation development in India during plan period.

Water Resources of the World and India

Total water on earth is about 1.4 billion cubic kilometers, which is enough to cover the United States to a depth of 150 kilometers[1]. Out of total world's water resources, 97.5 per cent is salty water accumulated in oceans which is not useful for human beings, and the only 2.5 per cent is global fresh water. All this 2.5 per cent global fresh water is not renewable but its mere 0.3 per cent is renewable which is in the form of lakes and river flows i.e. surface water. About 69 per cent of the fresh global water is glaciers and under covers of permanent snow, also called polar ice caps. Remaining 30.7 per cent of fresh water is ground water (including soil moisture, swam water, etc.).

The annual renewable water supply in the world is about 47,000 cubic km. Corresponding figure for India is 1,869 cubic km., which is about 4 per cent of the world's supply. The per capita annual availability of water in India is about 2,200 cubic meters (1991), which is lower than the world average (i.e. about 8,500 cubic meters). Principal consumptive use of water has traditionally been for irrigation. Globally 3,240 cubic km. of fresh water are withdrawn and used annually. Out of this 3,240 cubic km, 69 per cent is used for agriculture, 23 per cent for industry and 8 per cent for domestic use. Water use varies considerably around the world. India uses 83 per cent of its water for agriculture[2]. Out of the total water resources potential of the country about 690 cubic km. of surface water and 450 cubic km. of ground water per year is available for use through conventional structures. With this it will be possible to irrigate 113.5 mha. of area each year. Utilization of water for different purposes and availability of water is given in the Table 1.

It is seen from this table that presently utilization of water in the country is about 550 cubic km. (1990 A.D.). This includes 460 cubic km. (83 per cent) used for irrigation. By the turn of this century (2000 A.D.), the utilization of water will be about

750 cubic km. which is likely to go up to about 1050 cubic km. (700 cubic km. from surface and 350 cubic km. from ground water) by the year 2025 A.D. This includes 52 cubic km. (5 per cent) for domestic use, 770 cubic km. (73 per cent) for irrigation, 71 cubic km. (6.76 per cent) for energy, 120 cubic km. (11.43 per cent) for industry and remaining for other purposes. Thus almost the entire utilizable water resources of the country would be required to put to use by the year 2025 A.D.

Table 1

Purposewise Utilization and Availability of Water in India

(In cubic km.)

Particulars	*1990 A.D.*	*2000 A.D.*	*2025 A.D.*
A. Utilization of Water			
Domestic	25 (4.53)	33 (4.40)	52 (4.95)
Irrigation	460 (83.33)	630 (84.00)	770 (73.33)
Power	19 (3.44)	27 (3.60)	71 (6.76)
Industry	15 (2.72)	30 (4.00)	120 (11.43)
Others	33 (5.98)	30 (4.00)	37 (3.53)
Total	552 (100.00)	750 (100.00)	1050 (100.00)
B. Availability of Water			
Surface water	362 (65.58)	500 (66.67)	700 (66.67)
Ground water	190 (34.42)	250 (33.33)	350 (33.33)
Total	552 (100)	750 (100)	1050 (100)

Note: Figure in the parentheses indicate percentage to total.

Source: Data compiled from Ghosh R. "Water Resources Development and Management in 2025 A.D. – A Perspective", *Journal of Indian Water Resources Society*, Vol. 13, No. 3 & 4, July-October, 1993, pp. 168–169.

Water on the earth is in motion through the hydrological cycle. The utilization of water for most of the users i.e. human, animal or plant involve movement of water. The dynamic and renewable nature of the water resources and the recurrent need for its utilization requires that water resources are measured in terms of its flow rates. Thus water resources have two facets. The dynamic resources measured as flow is more relevant for most of development needs. The static or fixed nature of the reserve, involving the quantity of water, the length or areas of the water bodies is also relevant for some activities like pisciculture, navigation, etc.

Rivers

India is a land of many rivers endowed with large water resources. As many as 12 of them are classified as major rivers whose total catchment area is 252.8 million hectares (mha.) of the major rivers, the Ganga, Brahmaputra-Meghna system are the biggest with catchment area of about 110 mha., which is more than 43 per cent of the catchment area of all the major rivers in the country. The other major rivers with catchment area more than 10 mha. are Indus (32.1 mha.), Godavari (31.3 mha.), Krishna (25.9 mha.) and Mahanadi (14.2 mha.). The catchment area of other medium rivers is about 25 mha. and sidbernararckha with 1.9 mha. catchment area is the largest river among the medium rivers in the country[3].

India has 12 major river basins (having drainage area exceeding 20,000 sq.km.). The remaining have been combined together so as to form 8 other basins, making a total of 20 basins. In addition, there are a few desert rivers which flow for some distance and are lost in the desert. Major and medium river basins contribute over 90 per cent of the total run off in the country[4].

Water Resources Potential in India

The resources potential of the country which occurs as natural run off in the rivers is about 1,869 cubic km. as per the latest estimate of Central Water Commission, considering both surface and ground water as one system. Ganga-Brahmaputra-Meghna system is the major contributor to total water resources potential of the country. Its share is about 60 per cent in total water resources potential of the various rivers. Based on 1991 census, the per capital availability of water works out to 2,208 cubic metre. Due to various constraints of topography, uneven distribution of resources over space and time, it has been estimated that only about 1122 cubic km. of total potential of 1,869 cubic km. can be put to beneficial use, 690 cubic km. and 432 cubic km. due to surface and ground water-resources[5].

Potential and Utilizable Water Resources in India

Average run-off in the river system of the country has been assessed as 1869 cubic km.. Of this, the utilizable portion is estimated as about 690 cubic km. In addition, there is a substantial replenishable ground-water potential in the country estimated at 432 cubic km. The sourcewise picture of potential and utilizable water resources is shown in Figures 1(A) and 1 (B).

Basin-wise
Water Resources Potential
1,869 cubic kilometre

Figure 1(A) : Potential Water Resources

Basin-wise
Utilizable Water Resources:
690 cubic kilometre

Figure 1(B) : Utilizable Water Resources

Potential and Utilizable Ground Water Resources

As per present estimates, the total groundwater resources in the country have been assessed as 432 cubic km. keeping a provision of about 71 cubic km. (i.e. 16 per cent of total potential) for domestic, industrial and other uses, the availability for irrigation is 361 cubic km. of which the utilizable quantity is 325 cubic km.

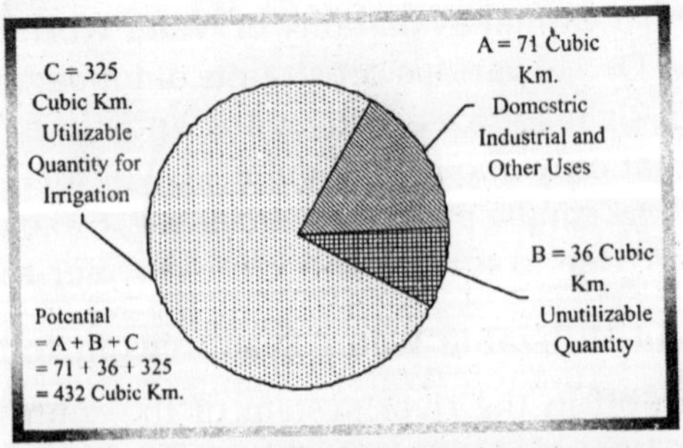

Figure 2: Potential & Utilizable Ground Water

Based on the crop water requirements and availability of culturable land, the total area that can be irrigated from ground water is of the order of 64.05 million ha, out of which the potential from natural rainfall recharge is 50.82 million ha. and the balance 13.23 million ha. is from augmentation from canal irrigation systems.

Ultimate Irrigation Potential in India and Maharashtra State

According to official statistics, the area which can be provided with irrigation if the potential of water resources is fully exploited is estimated at present, to be 148.5 million hectares as shown in the Table 2.

Table 2
Revised Estimate of Ultimate Irrigation Potential

Items	*Irrigation potential*		
	First estimate	*Expected potential*	*Total*
From major and medium irrigation projects	58.5	+ 25.0	98.5
Minor irrigation projects	15.0		
Minor ground water	40.0	+ 10.0	50.0
Total	113.5	+ 35.0	148.5

Sources: Government of India, Planning Commission, Seventh Five Year Plan, 1985-90 Vol. II, p. 72.

As per present estimates, out of a total geographical area of about 329 million hectares, the cultivable area is about 186 million hectares[6]. As shown in the Table 2, the ultimate irrigation potential of the country has been estimated to be 113.50 mha., comprising of 58.50 mha. from major and medium irrigation schemes, 15 mha. from surface minor irrigation schemes and 40 mha. from ground water exploitation. However, the national perspective for water resources development having two components viz. Himalayan River Development and Peninsular River Development for inter-basin transfer of water envisages an additional benefit of 25 mha. by surface water and 10 mha. by increased use of ground water which is expected to raise the ultimate irrigation potential from 113.5 mha. to 148.5 mha.[7]. Further, the Central Ground

Water Board provisionally puts the revised estimate of ground water at 80 mha., as against the previous estimate of 40 mha. Pending firming up of these estimates, the ultimate irrigation potential is taken as 113.5 mha.

Even taking into account this revised estimate of ultimate irrigation potential, an area of 37.5 mha. of cultivable area will be without irrigation. To modernise the agricultural practices in this dry-farming region, a more scientific method of utilizing and conserving rain-water will have to be adopted.

According to Central Water Commission of July 1998, the total ultimate irrigation potential (UIP) of country stands at about 139.9 mha. comprising 58.5 mha. (41.81 per cent of total ultimate) from major and medium irrigation schemes, 17.4 mha. (12.44 per cent of total) from minor irrigation schemes (surface) and 64.00 mha. (45.75 per cent of total) from minor ground water.

Table 3 shows the statewise ultimate irrigation potential from major, medium and minor irrigation schemes in India. It is seen from this table that Uttar Pradesh has highest ultimate irrigation potential (30.4 mha.), followed by Madhya Pradesh (17.9 mha.), Bihar (13.3 mha.), Andhra Pradesh (11.2 mha.) and fifth is Maharashtra state (8.9 mha.). The ultimate irrigation potential of Maharashtra state is estimated as 8.9 mha., comprising 4.1 mha. from major and medium irrigation projects, 1.2 mha. from minor irrigation schemes (surface) and 3.6 mha. from ground water (minor) schemes.

The share of minor irrigation is higher by 22.95 mha. as compared to that of major and medium irrigation. Ground water schemes contribute more than 78 per cent of the total ultimate potential through minor irrigation. Uttar Pradesh and Bihar are first two states as regards potential due to major and medium sector. These two states along with Madhya Pradesh, Andhra Pradesh and Maharashtra account for 58 per cent of the total ultimate potential of major and medium irrigation in the country. The largest ultimate irrigation potential for minor irrigation (groundnut water) exists in Uttar Pradesh. Andhra Pradesh and Madhya Pradesh are two major states in which potential of minor irrigation (surface water) is far greater than

Table 3
Statewise Ultimate Irrigation Potential

(Area in thousand hectares)

State/Union Territories	*Major and medium*	*Minor irrigation*			*Grand total of (major, medium and minor)*
		Surface water	*Ground water*	*Total*	
Andhra Pradesh	5000	2300	3960	6250	11260
Arunachal Pradesh	(a)	150	18	168	168
Assam	970	1000	900	1900	2870
Bihar	6500	1900	4947	6847	13347
Goa	62	25	29	54	116
Gujarat	3000	347	2756	3103	6103
Haryana	3000	50	1462	1512	4512
Himachal Pradesh	50	235	68	303	353
Jammu & Kashmir	250	400	708	1108	1358
Karnataka	2500	900	2574	3974	5974
Kerala	1000	800	879	1679	2679
Madhya Pradesh	6000	2200	9732	11932	17932
Maharashtra	4100	1200	3652	4852	8952
Manipur	135	100	369	469	604
Meghalaya	20	85	63	148	168
Mizoram	(a)	70	-	70	70
Nagaland	10	75	-	75	85
Orissa	3600	1000	4203	5203	8803
Punjab	3000	50	2917	2967	5967
Rajasthan	2750	600	1778	2378	5128
Sikkim	20	50	-	50	70
Tamil Nadu	1500	1200	2832	4032	5532
Tripura	100	100	81	181	281
Uttar Pradesh	12500	1200	16799	17999	30499
West Bengal	2310	1300	3318	4618	6928
Total of States	58377	17337	64045	81382	139759
Total of Union Territories	98	41	5	46	144
Grand total	58475	17378	64050	81428	139903
Percentage	41.81	12.44	45.75	54.25	100.00

Source: Water and Related Statistics, Central Water Commission, 1998, p.49.

those in remaining states. Uttar Pradesh again occupies the first place among the states so as to have maximum potential due to all types of schemes.

Uttar Pradesh, Bihar, Madhya Pradesh and Andhra Pradesh account for more than 52 per cent of the total potential of the country. The ultimate irrigation potential per thousand persons for the country as a whole is about 165 hectares. Punjab, Haryana, Madhya Pradesh, Orissa and Manipur have much higher than national average per capita potential. Other states where per capita potential is more than the national figure are Andhra Pradesh, Arunachal Pradesh, Jammu and Kashmir, Sikkim and Uttar Pradesh. A study of per capita potential due to major and medium irrigation reveals that Haryana and Punjab again are in the forefront where the respective figures work out to 182 and 148 hectares per thousand persons. In Orissa the per capita availability is 114 ha per thousand persons whereas the national average is 69 ha. only.

Table 3 and Figures 3(A) and 3 (B) show the proportionate share of different sources of irrigation in the ultimate irrigation potential of India and Maharashtra. It is seen that out of 139.9 mha., over all ultimate irrigation potential of India, 58.5 mha. (41.81 per cent) is from major and medium, 17.4 mha. (12.44 per cent) and 64.0 mha. (45.75 per cent) from minor (surface) and minor ground water schemes. It means that 75.90 mha. (54.25 per cent) can be irrigated by surface water and remaining 64.00 mha. (45.75 per cent) by ground water after full development of irrigation potential in India. This potential may, however, increase significantly by adopting modern irrigation methods like drip and sprinkler methods and optimum development of our river systems by fuller inter-state cooperation and cooperative development of international rivers with neighbouring countries. For optimum development of our river system, there is a need of inter-basin transfer of water from surplus to the deficit and the drought-prone areas.

In case of Maharashtra state, it is seen from Figure 3(B) that out of 8.9 mha., 4.1 mha. (46.07 per cent) is from major and medium projects, 1.2 mha. (13.48 per cent) and 3.6 mha. (40.45 per cent) are from minor surface and minor ground water irrigation schemes respectively. It means after full exploitation of irrigation potential in Maharashtra state, it is possible to irrigate 5.3 mha. (59.55 per cent) by surface water and 3.6 mha. (40.45 per cent) by ground water.

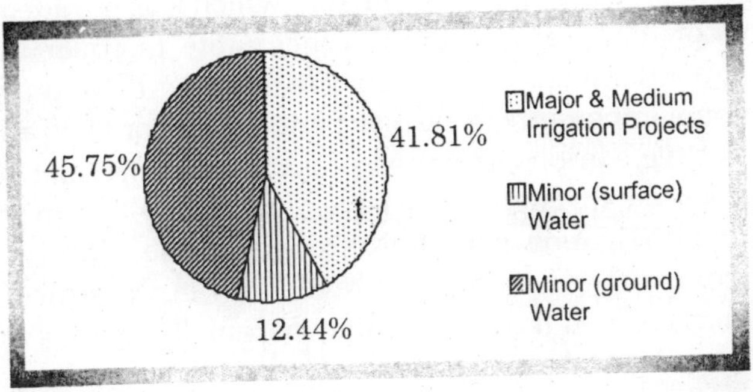

Figure 3(A) : Ultimate Irrigation Potential of India (139.9 mha.)

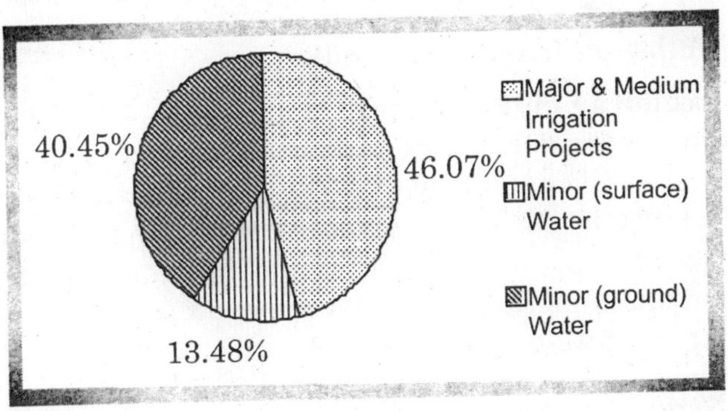

Figure 3(B): Ultimate Irrigation Potential of Maharashtra (8.9 mha.)

Irrigation Development During Plans

In the initial phase of irrigation development during the plan period after independence, rapid harnessing of water resources was the prime objective. Accordingly, the state governments were encouraged to expeditiously formulate and develop water resource projects for specific purpose like irrigation, flood control, hydropower generation, drinking water supply, industrial and various miscellaneous uses. As a result of large number of projects comprising dams, barrages, hydropower structures, canal net work, etc. have come up all over the country in successive five year plans.

At the time of commencement of the First Five Year Plan in 1951, population of India was about 361 million and annual foodgrain production was 51 million, which was not adequate. Import of foodgrains was then inevitable to cover up the shortage. Attaining self-sufficiency in food was therefore given paramount importance in the plan period and in order to achieve the objective, various irrigation projects were formulated and implemented through successive five year plans to create additional irrigation potential throughout the country. This drive compounded with green revolution in the agricultural sector has enabled India to become marginally surplus from a deficit one in foodgrains. In 1996-97 foodgrains production in the country has been 198 million tons for a population of about 900 million[8].

Plan Outlay on Irrigation in India

From beginning of the first plan, a sustained and systematic programme for development of irrigation facilities in the country was taken up. Irrigation programmes were accorded high-priority in our development schemes and investment priorities. The planwise public sector investment on major, medium and minor irrigation development schemes in India and expenditure on Command Area Development (CAD) programme in successive plan periods (1951-97) is shown in Table 4. It is seen from this table that the average expenditure on development of irrigation schemes is progressively increasing throughout the planning period i.e. from 1951 to 1997.

There has been a consistent increase in the planwise financial expenditure on irrigation sector over different plan periods. However, it has failed to match with the growth of total plan expenditure on all sectors as is evident from the share of expenditure on irrigation to the total which declined from 23 per cent during first plan to about 6 per cent in the annual plan of 1995-96.

Command Area Development (CAD) programme primarily aims at the speedy utilization of irrigation potential

Table 4
Planwise Outlay on Irrigation Development in India

(Rs. in crores)

Plan periods	Major, medium, minor and CAD							
	Major and medium	*Minor*	*Command Area Develop-ment*	*Total*	*Cumulative*	*Average expenditure per year*	*Total Plan expenditure in all sectors*	*Percentage of expenditure on irrigation to total*
1	2	3	4	5	6	7	8	9
1st plan (1951-56)	376.2	65.6	-	441.8	441.8	88.4	1960	23
2nd plan (1956-61)	380.0	161.6	-	541.6	983.4	108.3	4672	12
3rd plan (1961-66)	576.0	441.5	-	1017.5	2000.9	203.5	8577	12
Annual plans (1966-69)	429.8	556.0	-	985.8	2986.7	328.6	6625	15
4th plan (1969-74)	1242.3	1167.3	-	2409.6	5396.3	481.9	15779	15
5th plan (1974-78)	2516.2	1426.3	147.6	4090.1	9486.4	1022.5	28653	14
Annual plans (1978-80)	2078.6	976.6	215.3	3270.5	12756.9	1635.3	22950	14
6th plan (1980-85)	7368.8	3416.9	743.1	11528.8	24285.7	2305.8	109292	14
7th plan (1985-90)	11107.3	6192.9	1447.5	18747.7	43033.4	3749.5	218730	9
Annual plan (1990-91)	2634.8	1487.8	285.6	4408.2	47441.6	4408.2	58369	8
Annual plan (1991-92)	2824.0	1518.1	333.8	4675.9	52117.5	4675.9	64751	7
Eighth plan (1992-97)	22414.5	11096.8	2510.1	36020.9	88138.4	7204.2	434100	8
Annual plan (1992-93)	3047.1	1806.1	322.8	5176.0	57293.5	5176.0	72852	7

Contd...

(Rs. in crores)

Plan periods	Major, medium, minor and CAD							
	Major and medium	Minor	Command Area Develop-ment	Total	Cumulative	Average expenditure per year	Total Plan expenditure in all sectors	Percentage of expenditure on irrigation to total
1	2	3	4	5	6	7	8	9
Annual plan (1993-94)	3571.4	1923.9	374.9	5870.2	63163.7	5870.2	88081	7
Annual plan (1994-95)	4159.1	2188.7	422.1	6769.9	69933.6	6769.9	106204	6
Annual plan (95-96) (Anticipated)	4499.6	2100.7	437.3	7037.6	76971.2	7037.6	119898	6
Annual plan (1996-97) (Target)	7081.3	3156.4	506.1	10743.8	87715.0	10743.8	144798	7
1951-52 to 1996-97	53892.5	28586.4	5236.1	87715.0	87715.0	10743.8	144798	7

Note: Totals may not tally due to rounding off.

Source: Water and Related Statistics, Central Water Commission, Ministry of Water Resources, New Delhi, 1999, p. 257.

created. It is a centrally sponsored scheme started in 1974-75. Central Government offers assistance to the state governments for implementation of various activities like land leveling, field channels, warabandi, etc. Beginning with the CAD share of 3.6 per cent of the total combined expenditure on major and medium, minor and CAD during fifth plan (1974-78), the expenditure on CAD increased progressively during subsequent plan periods and constituted 7.7 per cent of the total in the seventh plan. There has, however, been a slight decline in the percentage of CAD likely expenditure to 6 per cent in the eighth plan. From a level of central financial assistance to the tune of 36 per cent of the total expenditure on different CAD programmes up to sixth plan, there has been a marginal decline in this percentage during seventh plan to 34 per cent which further declined to 28 per cent in the year 1995-96. The targeted central assistance to states for CAD programmes during 1996-97 is likely to be around 27 per cent of the total expenditure on different CAD programmes in the country.

Share of Expenditure on Irrigation in Major and Medium, Minor and CAD Projects

Figure 4 shows that out of the total expenditure incurred in irrigation sector during 1996-97, major and medium sector

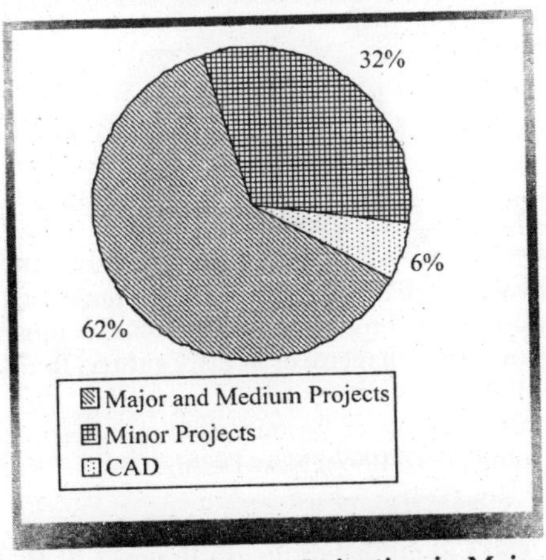

Figure 4: Share of Expenditure on Irrigation in Major & Medium, Minor and CAD Projects

accounted for 62 per cent and remaining was shared by minor irrigation sector and command area development programme (CAD), accounting for 32 per cent and 6 per cent respectively. Even in terms of the cumulative expenditure since first plan, the share of these sectors broadly remains the same.

Planwise Status of Irrigation Projects

It is seen from Table 10 that the average expenditure on development of irrigation schemes is progressively increasing throughout the planning period from 1951-52 to 1996-97. With the massive investment on irrigation, it became possible to undertake 292 major projects and 944 medium projects during last 46 years of planning period (i.e. from 1951-52 to 1996-97).

Table 5
Planwise Status of Irrigation Projects Completed in India (Cumulative)

	Major Projects		*Medium Projects*		*E.R.M. (+)*	
Plan period	*Under-taken*	*Comple-ted*	*Under-taken*	*Comple-ted*	*Under-taken*	*Comple-ted*
1st Plan (1951- 56)	44	5	169	35	12	3
2nd Plan (1956–61)	77	25	271	121	17	9
3rd Plan (1961–66)	109	35	315	181	25	15
Annual plans (1961- 69)	120	40	345	226	26	18
Fourth Plan (1969–74)	152	55	418	288	32	22
Fifth Plan (1974--78)	222	61	718	354	53	22
Annual Plans (1978–80)	235	63	770	371	56	24
Sixth Plan (1980–85)	265	65	861	519	101	29
Seventh Plan (1985–90)	277	111	894	655	146	43
Annual Plans (1990–92)	278	120	894	668	146	51
Eighth Plan (1992–97)	292	158	944	768	162	96

+ ERM = Extension Renovation and modernization.

Sources: (1) Navalawala B.N., "Irrigation Development in India – Issues and Approaches" Proceedings of National Seminar on India: Water Resources Management in 21st Century, Roorke, December 27-28, 1996, p. 25.

(2) Ministry of Water Resources, Water Resources Development in India (1947-1997), New Delhi, 1998.

Table 5 shows planwise status of irrigation projects completed (cumulative) in India. This table indicates that the number of major proejcts, medium projects and work of extension, renovation and modernization (ERM) undertaken and completed by the end of each plan period. It is seen from this table that during First Five Year Plan (1951-56), 44 major and 169 medium projects were undertaken, out of which 5 major and 35 medium projects were completed. By the end of Eighth Five Year Plan (1992-97), 292 major and 944 medium projects were undertaken, out of which 158 (54 per cent) and 768 (81 per cent) major and medium projects respectively were completed. However, number of both types of projects completed is very low as compared to projects undertaken during respective plan period.

Major Projects Taken up and Completed

Graph 1(A) shows that a total of 158 major irrigation projects have been completed during the post-independence period (1947-1997). Emphasis is being laid on the completion of the remaining 119 projects during the next decade.

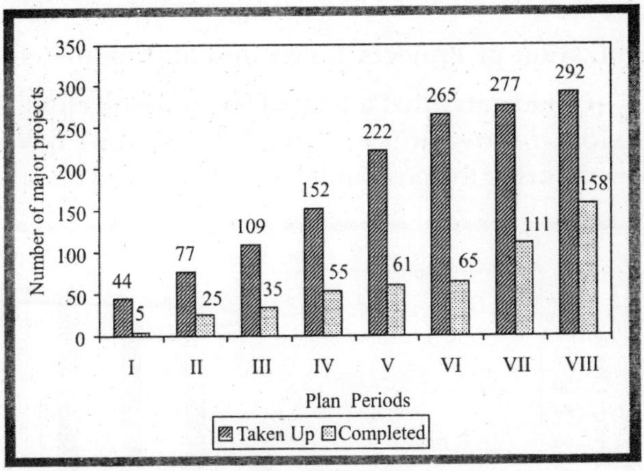

Graph 1(A): Major Projects Taken up and Completed

Medium Projects Taken up and Completed

Graph 1(B) shows that a total of 768 medium irrigation projects have been completed during the post-independence period (i.e. 1947–1997). Completion of medium irrigation projects during the post independence era has been significantly higher. Emphasis is being laid on the completion of remaining projects during the next five years.

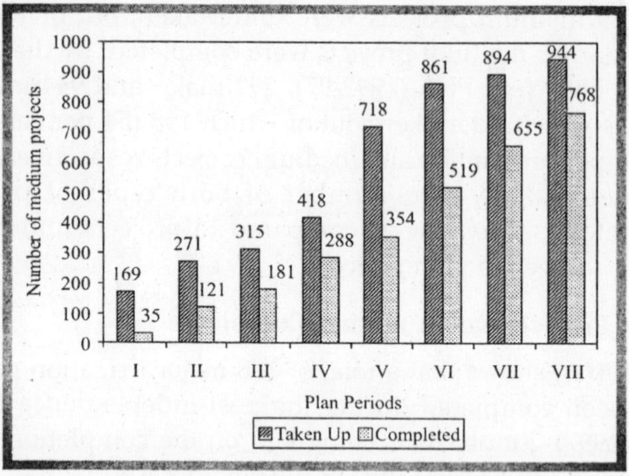

Graph 1(B) : Medium Projects Taken Up and Completed

Modernization of Projects Taken up and Completed

Graph 1(C) indicates that a total of 96 modernization projects (extension, renovation and modernization) have been completed during the post-independence period (i.e. 1947-97).

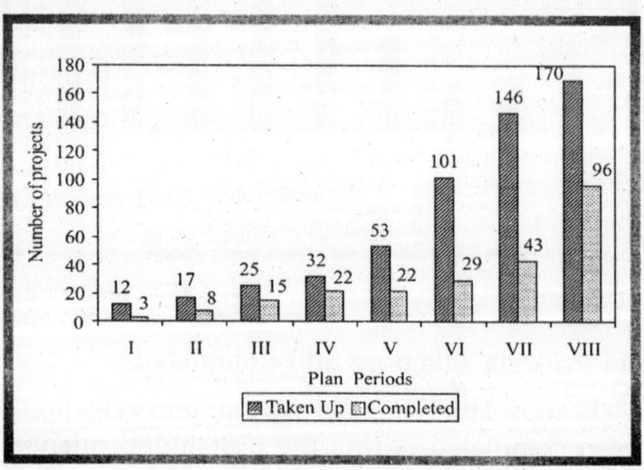

Graph 1(C) : Modernisation of Projects Taken Up and Completed

Modernization of projects includes extension, renovation, rehabilitation of the major and medium projects which have deteriorated with the passage of time. The objective is to achieve the designed as well as the enhanced potential.

Growth of Major and Medium Irrigation Projects

Against 74 major and 143 medium projects were completed in the pre-plan period, 158 major and 768 medium projects have been completed up to 1997. In addition, 119 major and 176 medium projects taken up in earlier plan period are in different stages of completion which is clearly indicated in Graph 2.

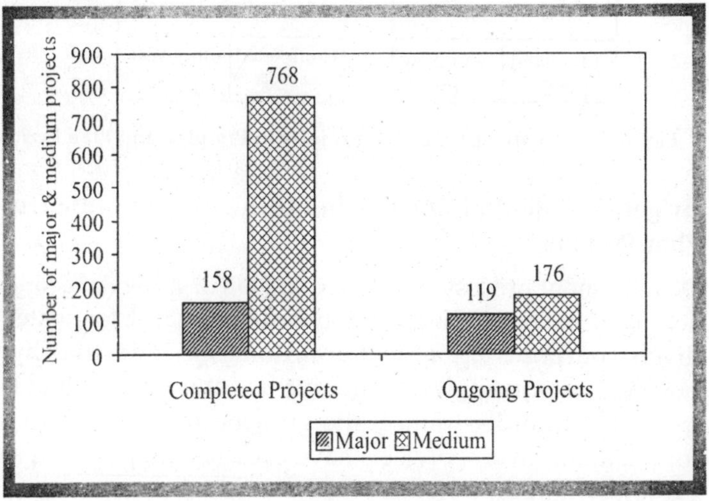

Graph 2 : Growth of Major and Medium Irrigation Projects

Addition of several projects since pre-plan period is not only an indication of the committed policy towards improving irrigation facilities but the impressive growth is also responsible for unleashing a sense of reliability in water availability for different uses, particularly irrigation and drinking water. Figure 5 shows the picture of growth of major and medium irrigation projects in pre-plan and plan periods of India.

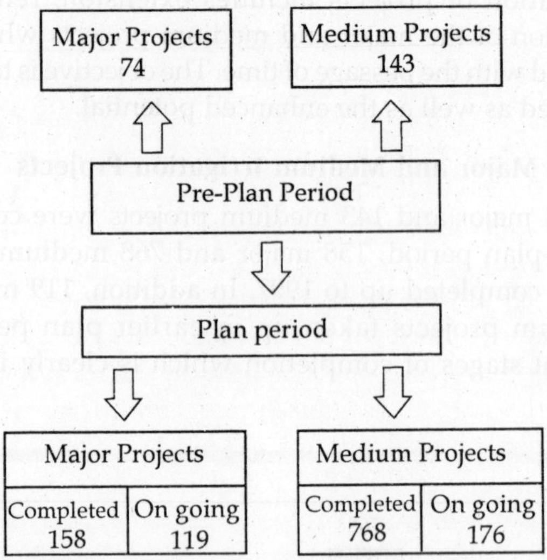

Figure 5 : Growth of Irrigation Projects in Pre-plan and Plan Periods

Irrigation Potential Created and Utilization in India During Plan Periods

Development process and the expansion of sphere of economic activities inevitably lead to increased demand for water for diverse purposes e.g. agricultural, domestic, industrial, hydro-power. The principal consumptive use of water in India is for irrigation. In order to meet the growing requirement of food for palation, several projects have been taken up in the past to exploit irrigation potential in the country. From about 22.6 million ha, at the time of independence, the irrigation potential created in the country multiplied and rose to 91.79 million ha. by the end of the year 1996-97.

Let us now turn to the discussion of the development of irrigation potential and utilization in India during the planning period (i.e. 1951 to 1997). The data about the irrigation potential created and utilization during the successive plans by all sources is presented in the Table 6. It is seen from this table that the total area irrigated from all sources (projects) during the pre-plan period (i.e. prior to 1951) was 22.60 million ha. Out of this 9.70 million ha. was from major and medium projects and 12.90 million ha. from minor irrigation schemes which accounts for around 16.16 per cent of the ultimate irrigation potential of the country. After independence of the country, as a massive investment has been made on irrigation development, irrigation potential has increased substantially. It is seen from Table 6 that irrigation potential created since launching of the First Five Year Plan in 1951, has increased from 9.70 mha. to 30.74 mha. from major and medium irrigation schemes at the end of annual plans 1990-92 and from 12.9 mha. to 50.34 mha. during the same period from minor irrigation schemes. Thus, the country's irrigation potential rose from 22.60 mha. to 81.08 mha. i.e. rose about three and half times in four decades.

It is seen from this table that by the end of the Eighth Five Year Plan (1992-97), the irrigation potential created stands at 91.79 mha. of which, 33.82 mha. (36.84 per cent) potential created is from major and medium projects and remaining 57.97 mha. (63.16 per cent) from minor projects. Thus during last five decades, the irrigation potential in the country rose from 22.6 mha. to 91.79 mha. i.e. rose more than 4 times.

Thus the net irrigated area is 37 per cent of net sown area and 29 per cent of total cultivable area. As stated earlier the ultimate potential due to major and medium projects has been assessed as 58 mha. of which 60 per cent estimated to be developed by 1996-97. Total potential created by 1996-97 (as targeted) is 91.8 mha. which is 81 per cent of earlier assessed ultimate potential of 113 mha.

Now let us turn to the discussion about the utilization aspect of irrigation potential in India. Because the creation of irrigation potential and its utilization are equally important, the aspect of utilization of irrigation potential has direct bearing with agricultural development. The Table 6 and Graph 3 indicate that irrigation potential created by all projects was 22.6 mha. in pre-plan period (1950-51) and this potential was fully utilized. But from beginning of the first plan and up to end of the eighth plan (1992-97), the difference between the irrigation potential created and its utilization has been increasing. After the Fourth Five Year Plan, this gap became wider. The

Table 6
Plan-wise Irrigation Potential Created and Utilized in India (Cumulative)

(Area in million hectares)

Plan period	*Major/medium irrigation*			*Minor irrigation*			*Total (major, medium & minor)*		
	Potential Created	*Utilized*	*Per-centage of utilization*	*Potential Created*	*Utilized*	*Per-centage of utilization*	*Potential Utilized*	*Utilized*	*Per-centage of utilization*
1	2	3	4	5	6	7	8	9	10
Pre-plan (up to 1951)	9.70	9.70	100.00	12.90 (6.5)	12.90 (6.5)	100.00	22.60	22.60	100.00
1st Plan (1951-56)	12.19	11.00	90.2	14.06 (7.63)	14.06 (7.63)	100.00	26.25	25.06	95.50
2nd Plan (1956-61)	14.34	13.30	98.8	14.75 (8.30	14.75 (8.30)	100.00	29.08	28.05	96.45
3rd Plan (1961-66)	16.57	15.20	91.7	17.00 (10.52)	17.00 (10.52)	100.00	33.57	32.20	96.00
Annual Plan (1961-69)	18.10	16.80	92.8	19.00	19.00 (12.50)	100.00 (12.50)	37.10	35.80	96.50
Fourth Plan (1969-74)	20.71	18.70	90.3	23.50 (19.80)	23.50 (19.80)	100.00	44.21	42.20	95.45
Fifth Plan (1974-78)	24.72	21.20	85.8	27.30 (19.80)	27.30 (19.80)	100.00	52.02	48.50	93.20
Annual Plans (1978-80)	26.61	22.70	85.3 (22.00)	30.00 (22.00)	30.00	100.00	56.61	52.70	

Contd...

(Area in million hectares)

Plan period	*Major/medium irrigation*			*Minor irrigation*			*Total (major, medium & minor)*		
	Potential Created	*Utilized*	*Per-centage of utilization*	*Potential Created*	*Utilized*	*Per-centage of utilization*	*Potential Utilized*	*Utilized*	*Per-centage of utilization*
1	2	3	4	5	6	7	8	9	10
Sixth Plan (1980-85) (original)	30.01	25.33	84.4	37.33	35.25 (27.80)	94.42 (26.2)	67.53	60.58	89.70
Sixth Plan (1980-85) (Reappraised)	27.70	23.57	85.1	37.52 (27.82)	35.24 (26.23)	94.28	65.22	58.82	90.18
Seventh plan (1985-90)	31.52	27.77	87.7	46.60 (38.95)	43.12 (32.50)	94.60	78.12	70.89	90.7
Annual plans (1990-92)	30.74	26.31	85.58	50.34 (38.89)	46.53 (36.24)	92.43	81.08	72.85	89.85
Eighth plan (1992-97) (Target)	33.82	29.22	86.40	57.97 (45.73)	52.80 (41.99)	91.08	91.79	82.02	89.36

N.B. : Figures in brackets indicate the created potential/utilized under ground water.

Sources: 1. Water and Related Statistics, Central Water Commission, July 1999, p. 117.

2. B.N. Navalawala, "Indian Perspective Water Resources Planning", Seminar on Irrigation Water Management, New Delhi, 1992, p. 39.

3. Bhagirath, Vol. XXXXVI, Central Water Commission and Ministry of Water Resources, New Delhi, 1999, p . 80.

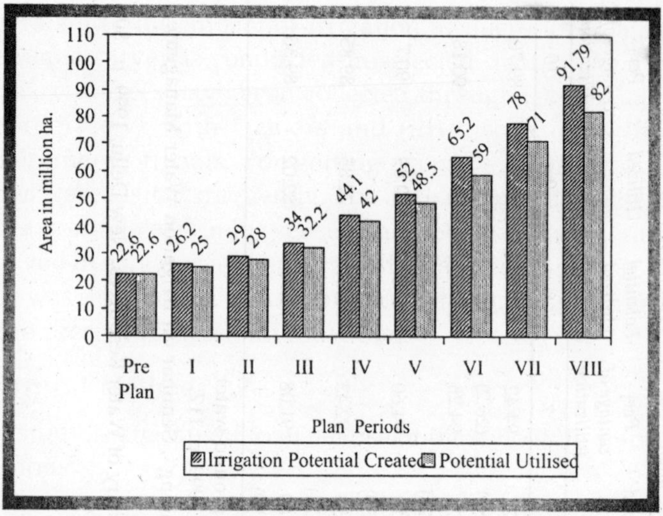

Graph 3 : Irrigation Potential Created and Utilised (Cumulative) From All Projects (1951-1997)

percentage of utilization to the potential created was found to be steadily increasing around 95.4 per cent up to fourth plan. But after the fourth plan this percentage of utilization has been declining and at the end of eighth plan (1992-97), percentage of utilized irrigation potential is found to be 90 per cent indicating more under utilization of irrigation potential created. It is seen from Table 6 that there is cent per cent utilization of potential created from minor irrigation schemes up to 1980.

The problem of under utilization of created potential applies to almost all major and medium irrigation schemes. In respect of minor irrigation schemes the potential created is found to be fully utilized, because minor projects are small in size, have smaller gestation period and have limited local irrigation potential which can be easily fully utilized. The irrigation potential created from minor irrigation schemes is found to be fully utilized, while capacity so far created is short of the aggregate requirement for Indian agriculture, it is paradoxical that even the available capacity itself is not fully utilized[9].

Graphs 4(A) and 4(B) indicate the picture of ultimate irrigation potential, potential created and its utilization of major and medium irrigation projects and minor projects in India up to 1996-97. These figures show that the country's irrigation potential up to 1996-97 is 91.79 mha. (81 per cent of ultimate irrigation potential of 113 mha.). Out of this 33.82 mha. (36.84 per cent of potential created) is from major and medium projects

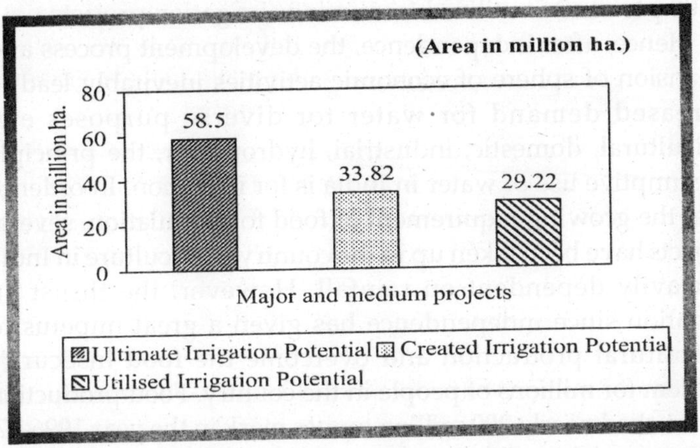

Graph 4(A) : Irrigation Potential - Ultimate, Created and Utilised up to 1996-97 (Major & Medium Projects)

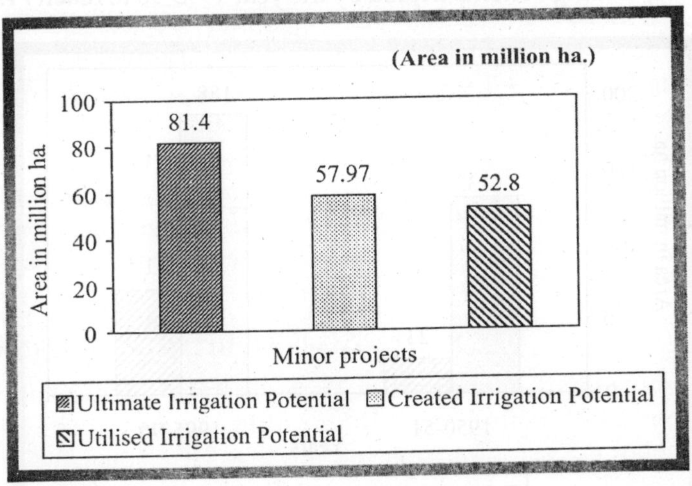

Graph 4(B) : Irrigation Potential - Ultimate, Created and Utilised up to 1996-97 (Minor Projects)

and 57.97 mha. (63.16 per cent of potential created) is from minor projects. Similarly it is seen from these figures that country's utilization from all projects is 82.02 mha. (89 per cent of potential created), out of which 29.22 mha. (86.40 per cent) is utilized from major and medium projects and 52.80 mha. (91.08 per cent) is utilized from minor irrigation projects.

Hence, after independence, the development process and expansion of sphere of economic activities inevitably lead to increased demand for water for diverse purposes e.g. agricultural, domestic, industrial, hydropower, the principle consumptive use of water in India is for irrigation. In order to meet the growing requirement of food for population, several projects have been taken up in the country. Agriculture in India is heavily dependent on rainfall. However, the thrust on irrigation since independence has given a great impetus to agricultural production and overcome the food insecurity problem for millions of people in the country. Food production has touched nearly 200 million tonnes mark in the year 1996-97.

It is seen from the Graph 5 that just about an equivalent of 23 million ha. of irrigation benefits in 1950-51, the corresponding benefits tripled by the year 1995-96 to reach 71.5

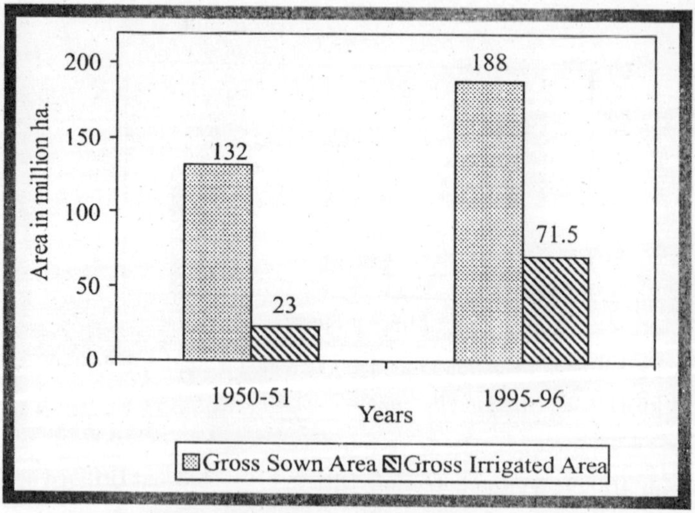

Graph 5 : Growth in Irrigation (million ha.)

million ha. As compared to just about 18 per cent of the cropped area under irrigation at the time of independence, the irrigation level has since increased to 38 per cent in 1995-96 though there has been an increase of nearly 42 per cent in cropped area.

SECTION–B

IRRIGATION DEVELOPMENT IN MAHARASHTRA STATE

Irrigation occupies a place of prime importance in any strategy to increase agricultural production and in the state like Maharashtra, with more than a third of its area prone to frequent droughts, the development of irrigation assumes great importance. After assessing the irrigation development in country as a whole, an attempt has been made in this section to discuss the irrigation development in Maharashtra State.

The linguistic state of Maharashtra was politically evolved on the first of May 1960 as a late consequence of the states reorganization - schemes of the Government of India. Commanding a amore or less central situation in the Republic of India, Maharashtra is the third largest state in republic both in population and in area[10]. The total geographical area of the state is 307.58 lakh hectares and net sown area of 179.11 lakh ha. (58.23 per cent of geographical area). The gross cropped area in the state comes to 218.97 lakh hectares and the percentage of gross irrigated area to gross cropped area is found to be 15.40 per cent by the end of the year 1999-2000[11]. According to the 1991 population census, the total population of the state stood at 789.36 lakhs, out of which 61.31 per cent lives in rural areas and remaining 38.69 per cent lives in urban areas. In Maharashtra there is very limited scope for an increase in cropped area. It is through intensive agriculture alone that only marked increase in food production can be achieved. The agro-climatic conditions of the state are favourable to maximising yields through irrigation[12].

The main feature of the Maharashtra state is that agriculture continues to be the major source of income of the state. The distinctive feature of the state is that it is situated in a relatively low rainfall tract, 33 per cent of the state area is the drought prone. The rainfall in the state varies from 700 cm in the Konkan area (coastal belt) to 50 cm in the drought prone areas. The rainy days are 45 in a year. The lack of adequate rain underlines the need for irrigation. Culture and history of irrigation also indicates that civilization in the state has developed and flourished on the banks of major rivers in the state like Godavari, Krishna, Bhima, Panchganga, Nira, Tapi, Purna, Wainganga, Painganga, etc. Agriculture of Maharashtra state to a large extent depends on the rainfall which is uneven. The rainfall is unevenly distributed among the regions in Maharashtra. About 33 per cent of population of Maharashtra State is suffering from scarcity.

During the pre-independence period little attempts were made for the development of irrigation schemes in Maharashtra. British Government appointed Famine Commission in 1880 and the Commission reported that protective irrigation schemes should be undertaken by government. At the same time the Commission was of the opinion that the government should give first priority to irrigation schemes and should not think how much profit in terms of money is back to it from these schemes. But it should think that how much protection to famine area is getting from irrigation. Yet railway department was in loss, it was given much outlay and irrigation schemes were neglected. In 1901, famine was intolerable, hence government appointed Irrigation Commission in 1901. This commission stated that farmers should dug more wells and when it was not possible then only government should undertake irrigation schemes. In 1902, Bombay Government appointed Shri F.H. Bill for suggesting measures to face the water problem in famine areas in Maharashtra. As per recommendation of F.H. Bill, the Bombay Government gave sanction to Pravara, Bhandara and Girna irrigation projects. These schemes benefited to Western Maharashtra up to 1940, one lakh hectares of land came under irrigation through these schemes.

Irrigation development in Maharashtra gained momentum after the formation of the state. Thus, before the formation of state i.e. up to 1960, the achievement on the irrigation front in

Maharashtra on the whole remained considerably poor. The gross irrigated area of the state was amounted to a mere 6 per cent of gross cropped area and the irrigation potential in the state amounted to a mere 2.16 per cent of net sown area in 1960[13]. The efforts for the development of irrigation in state started since the formation of Maharashtra State in 1960. The first and immediate action of the Maharashtra Government was the appointment of State Irrigation Commission. This Commission made a comprehensive study of the irrigation potential in the state and submitted its report to government in 1962. The commission hoped that near about 30 per cent area can be irrigated by river water and after completion of all proposed large, medium and minor irrigation projects.

On the basis of the first irrigation commission's recommendations a number of new works including the Godavari canal, the Girna left bank canal, the Chankapur tank and its distribution channels were taken up. Simultaneously works were carried out on remodelling, improving and extending the Pravara and Nira canals.

No irrigation work of any significance was taken up during the pre-independence period in the vulnerable Marathwada region. However, a large number of tanks were excavated during the first two decades of century in the Vidharbha region, which then formed part of the erstwhile central province. The Ramtek tank in Nagpur district, the Chandrapur, Khairbhanda, Chol Khamara and Bodulkasa tanks in the Chanda district were excavated during this period. Then followed a period of inactivity lasting nearly three decades up to the partition of the country, which no new works were taken up[14].

Water Resources in Maharashtra

In Maharashtra, five major river basins viz. Godavari, Krishna, Tapi, Narmada and Konkan constitute the major water resources. The basinwise distribution of available water is shown in the Table 8 and it is seen from this table that distribution of total water being 31.06 per cent, 20.77 per cent, 5.57 per cent, 0.35 per cent and 42.25 per cent in Godavari, Krishna, Tapi, Narmada, and Konkan river basins respectively.

Table 7
Basin-wise Water Availability in Maharashtra

Geographical area : Thousand sq.km.
Cultivated area : Lakh hectares
Water : Million cubic meters.

River basin	*Total geographical area covered by the basin*	*Percentage of basin area covered to total geographical area (of 3)*	*Cultivable area*	*Percentage of cultivable area to total geographical area (of 5)*	*Average water availability*	*Permission for utilization of water*	*Percentage of permission to level of availability*
1	*2*	*3*	*4*	*5*	*6*	*7*	*8*
Godavari	152.81	46.71	112.56	49.94	50880	34185	67.19
Krishna	69.03	22.45	56.27	24.96	34032	16818	49.42
Tapi	51.3	16.69	37.31	16.55	9118	5415	59.39
Narmada	1.05	0.34	0.06	0.28	580	308	53.1
Konkan	33.23	10.81	18.64	8.27	69210	69210	100.00
Total	307.42	100.00	224.83	100.00	163820	125936	76.87

N.B.: Small part of Mahanadi basin in Maharashtra has not to think over its geographical area is 90 square km.
Source: Government of Maharashtra, Second Irrigation Commission, Vol.1, July 1999, p. 205.

Government of Maharashtra had recently established Second Irrigation Commission under the chairmanship of Dr. M. A. Chitale in December 1995. This commission has submitted its report to State Government in October 1999 and made comprehensive study of the irrigation in Maharashtra. The commission has estimated that 9.7 mha. is to be the ultimate irrigation potential for the state and out of which 4.1 mha. to be from the ground water and 5.6 mha. to be from the surface water. This commission has also expected that, by using the modern irrigation technique and improving water management distribution on land, the ultimate irrigation potential in the state would be increased up to 12.6 mha.

Potential and Utilizable Water Resources in Maharashtra

Potential and utilizable water Resources for the state has been recently assessed by the Second Irrigation Commission (1995) and is presented in Table 7. Table 7 reveals that, average run-off in the river system of the state has been assessed as 1,63,820 million cubic meters (163.82 cubic kilometers) while 1,869 cubic kilometers has been estimated for the country, and it is 9 per cent of the estimate for the country. Based on 1991 census per capital availability of water in the State works out to 2,076 cubic meters and 1,967 cubic meters for the country in the year 1997. But due to limit of the inter-state water distribution, 12,596 million cubic meters (77 per cent of total potential) would be utilisable water available in the state.

The potential and utilisable water resources are explained in the Figures 6(A) and 6(B). Out of the 125.94 cubic km. the 10 per cent (12.6 cu. km.) is available for other purposes and 90 per cent (113.3 cu. km.) is available for irrigation purpose.

Plan for the Utilization of Water for Different Purposes in the Year 1996 and 2030 A.D.

Second Irrigation Commission has worked out a plan about the utilization of the water for different purposes in the year 1996 and in the year 2030 A.D. It is seen from the Table 8 that the total of 39484 million cubic meter water has been utilized in the year 1996 for the different purposes. Out of this, 79 per cent was utilized for irrigation purpose and remaining 21 per cent for other purposes viz. (i.e. 9 per cent for drinking and 12 per cent for industry). This fact shows that only 28.3 per cent of the total available water was utilized for difference purposes in this year (i.e. 22.4 per cent for irrigation and 5.9 per cent for other purposes).

Basin-wise

Water Resources Potential :

163.82 cubic kilo-meters

Figure 6(A) : Potential Water Resources

Basin-wise

Utilizable Water Resources :

125.94 cubic kilo-meters

Figure 6(B): Utilizable Water Resources

Table 8

Utilization of Water for Different Purposes in the Year 1996 and 2030 A.D.

(Water in million cubic meters)

Purpose of utilization	*Year 1996*	*Per-centage to total utilization*	*Per-centage to total availability*	*Year 2030*	*Per-centage to total utilization*	*Per-centage to total availability*
1	2	3	4	5	6	7
Drinking	3553.56	9	2.5	7212	7	5
Irrigation						
(A) Surface	24085.24	61	17.3	69.28	67	49
(B) Ground	7107.12	18	5.1	20608	20	15
Total(A+B)	31192.36	79	22.4	89634	87	64
Industry	4738.08	12	3.4		6	5
Total	39484	100.0	28.3	103028	100.00	74
Total availability	139227		100.00	139227		100.00

Source: Government of Maharashtra, *Water and Irrigation Commission*, Vol. 1, July 1999, p. 795.

Demand for water in future period would be always increasing due to increase in population. It is also seen from this table that in the year 2030 A.D., availability of water in the state is 1,39,227 million cubic meters. Out of this, utilization of water for different purposes is found to be 13,028 million cubic meters (74 per cent of available water). Thus, utilization for irrigation purpose and for other purposes were found to be 64 per cent and 10 per cent respectively in this year. Therefore, above facts indicate that utilized water for different purposes in the year 2030 A.D. would be considerably higher than utilized water in the year 1996.

The Ultimate Irrigation Potential in Maharashtra

The study about ultimate irrigation potential of the state has been briefly high lighted in Section A of this chapter. But some different opinions are found in further studies about ultimate irrigation potential of state. Thus in this section an attempt is made to discuss those opinions in respect of state is ultimate irrigation potential. Following are the different opinions about the ultimate irrigation potential in Maharashtra given by various study groups.

1. According to First Maharashtra Irrigation Commission (1962), overall ultimate irrigation potential of the state was thought to be 6.1 mha., out of which 5.2 mha. to be from the surface water resources and 0.9 mha. to be from ground water resources[15].
2. According to Central Water Commission (1972), the total area irrigable from surface flow would be 5.0 mha. and from ground water in the state is estimated at 1.5 mha.. The overall irrigation potential in the state is estimated to be 6.5 mha[16].
3. Second Irrigation Commission of Maharashtra state was recently established in 1995 and this Commission submitted its report to Maharashtra Government in July 1999. This Commission has estimated the ultimate irrigation potential of the state to be 9.7 mha., out of which 4.1 mha. to be from the ground water resources

(based on fifth water land valuation) and 5.6 mha. to be from the surface water resources.

Considering the availability of water resources and land in various basins, this commission was expected that, increase in ground water land, addition of water on account of water shed development, modern irrigation technology and improvement in water management distribution on land, the ultimate irrigation potential of the state would increase up to 12.6 mha. It means due to all above factors there is possible increase in surface water resources from 5.6 mha. to 8.5 mha.. Thus the ultimate irrigation potential of the state would be 12.6 mha. of which 8.5 mha. (67.46 per cent of total potential) and 4.1 mha. (32.54 per cent) would be from surface and ground water resources respectively.

Plan-wise Outlay on Irrigation Projects and Potential Created in Maharashtra

Before the formation of Maharashtra state (1960), the position of irrigation in the state was very poor. After the First Five Year Plan 1951-56, Government of Maharashtra tried to develop many irrigation schemes in the state and efforts are being made to develop irrigation facilities through large, medium and minor irrigation projects. Prior to inception of five year plans, the irrigation facilities to an area of only 2.74 lakh ha. was available i.e. 2.52 lakh ha. from major and medium and 0.22 lakh ha. from minor projects and an amount of Rs. 16.60 crores only was spent for this purpose. However, irrigation development programmes got real boost on inception of the five year plans, particularly from second plan onwards.

The planwise outlay on major, medium and minor projects and created irrigation potential in Maharashtra has been shown in the Table 9. It is seen from this table that in each plan period, provision for irrigation development was around 15 to 25 per cent of the total plan outlay. Up to the end of Eighth Five Year Plan (1992 to 1997), total investment of Rs. 10,756.86 crores i.e. 22 per cent of the state's plan outlay was made on irrigation development, out of which 88.48 per cent was spent on major and medium projects and remaining 11.52 per cent on minor

Table 9
Plan-wise Outlay on Irrigation Development in Maharashtra State

(i) Outlay in Rs. Crores
(ii) Area in lakh ha.

Plan period	*Minor*	*Major or medium*	*Total*	*Total plan expenditure in all sectors*	*Percentage expenditure in irrigation to total*	*Cumulative irrigation potential created*	*Irrigation potential in plan period*
1	*2*	*3*	*4*	*5*	*6*	*7*	*8*
Pre-plan (Before 1951)	NA	NA	16.60	-	-	2.74	2.74
I (1951-56)	2.52	5.59	8.11	154.71	5.24	3.14	0.40
II (1956-61)	2.74	31.20	33.94	226.30	15.00	3.98	0.84
III (1961-66)	6.77	58.22	64.99	434.73	15.00	5.70	1.72
Annual Plans (1966-69)	12.87	46.92	59.79	386.00	15.54	7.18	1.48
IV (1969-74)	47.80	185.27	233.07	1004.51	23.20	11.02	3.84
V (1974-78)	51.40	374.11	425.51	2660.00	16.00	15.70	4.68
Annual plans (1978-80)	25.62	307.53	333.15	1185.08	28.10	17.21	1.50
VI (1980-85)	164.65	1138.66	1303.31	6549.39	20.00	22.70	5.50
VII (1985-90)	241.24	2772.47	3013.71	11219.64	26.86	26.31	3.61
Annual plans (1990-92)	65.78	995.51	1061.29	5550.00	19.12	27.17	0.86
VIII (1992-97)	607.21	3602.68	4209.99	18472.00	22.70	32.21	5.04
Total (1951-97)	1238.70	9518.16	10756.86	47842.36	22.48		

N.A. = Not available

Sources: (i) Report of High Power Committee, Irrigation Department, Government of Maharashtra, November 1981, p. 86.
(ii) Performance Budget, Irrigation Department, Vol. 1, Government of Maharashtra, Vol. I, (1995-96 and 1996-97).
(iii) Second Irrigation Commission, Government of Maharashtra, Vol. I, July 1999, p. 614.

irrigation projects. It means less amount has been spent on minor projects as compared to major and medium projects. It has increased the irrigation potential from 3.14 lakh ha. to 32.21 lakh ha. during 1951-52 to 1996-97. It means there has been near about 10 times increase in irrigation potential during the four and half decades.

Share of Expenditure in Major and Medium, Minor Projects During 1951 to 1997

Share of expenditure in major, medium and minor irrigation project in Maharashtra during last 46 years (i.e. 1951-52 to 1996-97) has been shown in Figure 7. It is seen from this figure that out of the total expenditure incurred in the irrigation sector in the period (1951-52 to 1996-97), major and medium sector accounted for 88.48 per cent and remaining sector viz. minor irrigation schemes, accounting for 11.52 per cent.

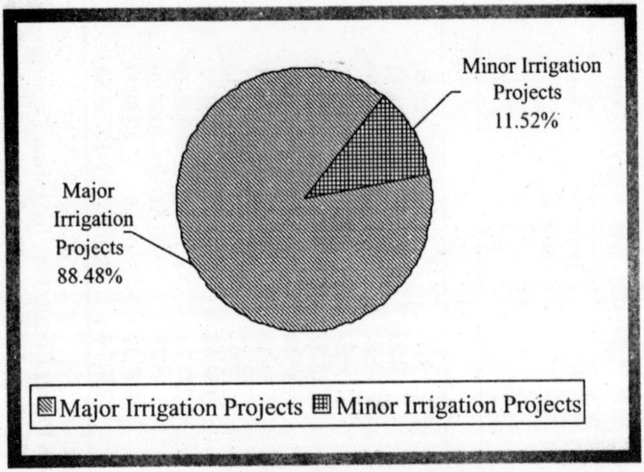

Figure 7 : Share of Expenditure in Major and Medium, Minor Projects During 1951 to 1997

Regionwise Present Status of Irrigation Projects

For smooth functioning entire irrigation system of Maharashtra has been divided into six regions, viz. Amravati, Konkan, Marathwada, Pune, Nagpur and North Maharashtra.

Regionwise present status of irrigation projects completed, on going and proposed by the end of the year 1997-98 in Maharashtra state is shown in the Table 10. It is seen from this table that at present 50 major, 182 medium and 2,880 minor irrigation projects (1,169 minor state level and 1,711 minor local) are already completed by the end of the year 1997-98. There are 49 major, 128 medium and 856 minor projects (469 minor state level and 387 minor local level) are presently under construction and very soon few of them will be providing

Table 10
Region-wise Present Status of Irrigation Projects Completed, On-going and Future in Maharashtra

	Major irrigation			*Medium irrigation projects*		
Region	*Completed*	*Ongoing*	*Proposed*	*Completed*	*Ongoing*	*Proposed*
1	*2*	*3*	*4*	*5*	*6*	*7*
Amravati	6	7	2	31	22	3
Konkan	3	4	3	3	6	18
Marathwada	4	8	-	63	32	1
Pune	14	16	7	21	26	11
Nagpur	9	6	11	34	11	24
North Maharashtra	14	8	3	30	31	6
Maharashtra State	50	49	26	182	128	63

	Minor irrigation projects								
	Completed			*On going*			*Proposed*		
Region	*State level*	*Local level*	*Total*	*State level*	*Local level*	*Total*	*State level*	*Local level*	*Total*
	8	*9*	*10*	*11*	*12*	*13*	*14*	*15*	*16*
Amravati	144	301	445	63	39	102	186	124	310
Konkan	66	111	177	30	64	94	59	229	288
Marathwada	372	478	850	105	88	193	100	419	519
Pune	332	105	437	119	11	130	435	290	725
Nagpur	156	634	790	46	159	205	183	49	232
North Maharashtra	99	82	181	106	26	132	199	121	320
Maharashtra State	1169	1711	2880	469	387	856	1162	1232	2394

Source : Model – Maharashtra Irrigation Development – Present Position in 1996, Working Committee of Second Maharashtra State Irrigation Commission, Aurangabad, p. 145.

irrigation facilities in their command areas. Further, there is a scope for 26 major, 63 medium and 2,394 minor irrigation projects (1,162 minor state level and 1,232 local minor level) to be undertaken in future.

Since Government of Maharashtra has established various Irrigation Development Corporations in different regions of the state i.e. Krishna Valley Development Corporation, Vidarbha Irrigation Development Corporation, Konkan Irrigation Development Corporation, Tapi Irrigation Development Corporation and Godavari Marathwada Irrigation Development Corporation, a number of major, medium and minor irrigation projects have been taken by the state Government through these corporations. Thus, the total irrigation potential created in the state by the end of January 1999 through all the irrigation projects was 35.6 lakh hectares (provisional)[17].

It is seen from the above Graphs [6(A), 6(B) and 6(C)] that the total 99 major, 310 medium and 6,130 minor irrigation projects were undertaken out of which 50 major (50 per cent), 182 medium (58.70 per cent) and 2,880 minor irrigation projects (46.98 per cent) are already completed by the end of the year 1998. Similarly, 49 major, 128 medium and 856 minor projects are presently under construction, and remaining 26 major, 63 medium and 2,394 minor irrigation projects to be undertaken in future.

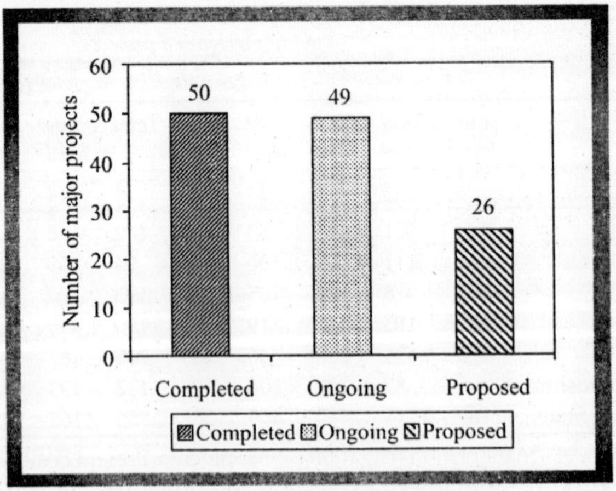

Graph 6(A) : Major Projects up to 1998

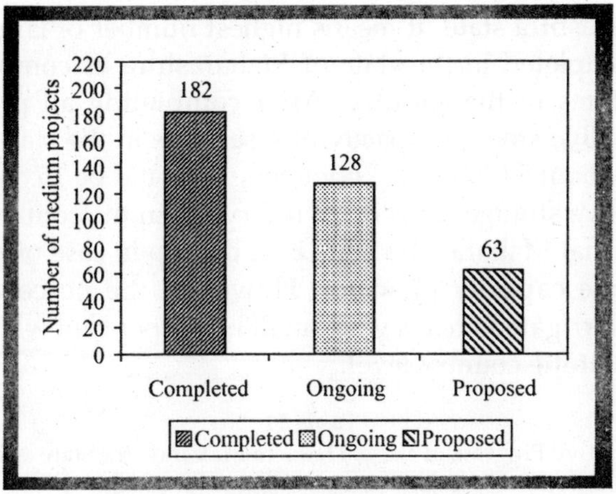

Graph 6(B) : Medium Projects up to 1998

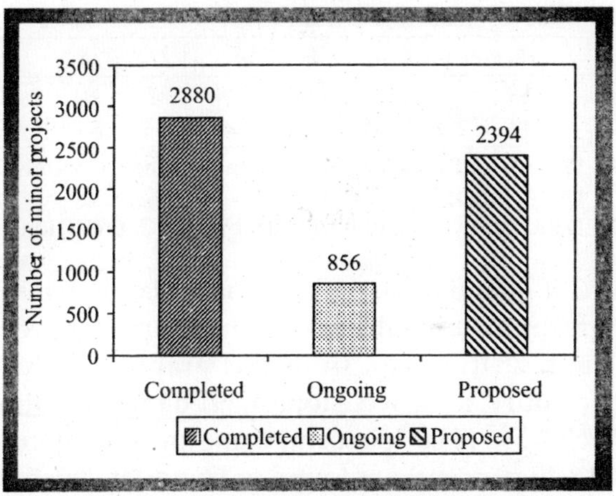

Graph 6(C) : Minor Irrigation Projects up to 1998

Development of Large Dams in Maharashtra

From the 19th century, quantitative progress of large dams of the state and whole country has been shown in the Table 11. It is seen from this table that the total of 3,596 large dams were completed and 695 are under construction in the country during the period 1900 and onwards, out of which 1,229 (34.18 per cent of total completed large dams) were found to be only in Maharashtra state. It means highest number of large dams were completed in the state of Maharashtra as compared to other states in the country. After completing all proposed projects, live storage capacity of reservoirs in the state would be near about 54.19 cubic kilometers. It would be 15.8 per cent of total live storage capacity of reservoirs in the country[18]. We can say that Maharashtra state is at the top in case of creation of storage capacity of water. However, the percentage of cropped irrigated area is very small i.e. 15 per cent which is 35 per cent at the country level.

Table 11
Quantitative Progress of Large Dams in Maharashtra State and India

	No. of dams completed during the period								
State/ India	*Up to 1900*	*1901 to 1950*	*1951 to 1960*	*1961 to 1970*	*1971 to 1980*	*1981 to 1989*	*1990 and onwards*	*Under-taken*	*Total*
1	2	3	4	5	6	7	8	9	10
Maharashtra	16	35	25	146	589	324	94	300	1529
India	42	251	234	461	1190	1066	352	695	4291

Source: 1. Water and Related Statistics Central Water Commission, New Delhi, July, 1995, p. 50.
2. Dam Safety Directorate, Central Water Commission.

Picture of quantitative progress of the large dams in India and Maharashtra during the twentieth century has been shown in the Graph 7. It is seen from this graph that during the twentieth century, there were total 4,291 dams undertaken and out of which 3,596 (83.80 per cent) dams are already completed and 695 (16.20 per cent) are found to be under construction in India. In case of Maharashtra, 1,529 dams have been undertaken and out of which 1,296 (84.76 per cent) are already completed and 300 (15.24 per cent) are found to be under construction during the same period. This shows that the Maharashtra state is well ahead (33.90 per cent) in completion of large dams as compared to other states in India.

Development of Irrigation Potential and Utilization

The planwise irrigation potential created and utilisation from major, medium and minor projects is shown in Table 12. It is

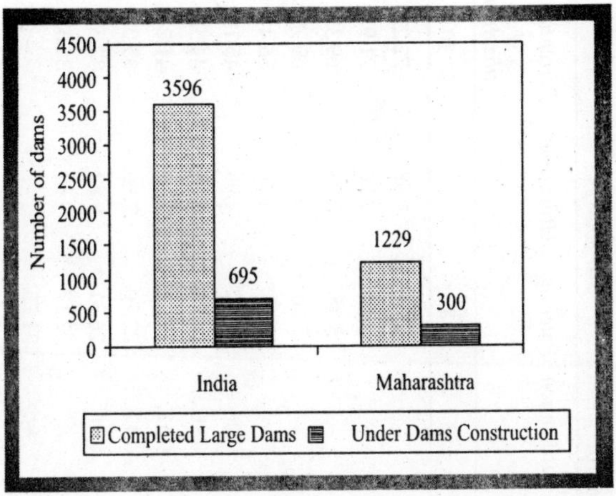

Graph 7 : Progress of Large and Small Dams in India and Maharashtra during 20th Century

seen from this table that prior to the inception of five year plans, irrigation facilities were created on an area of only 2.74 lakh ha (i.e. 2.52 lakh ha. from major and medium projects and 0.22 lakh ha. from minor projects) and its utilization was 72.27 per cent of total created potential. It means position of irrigation development in Maharashtra before the plan period was very poor. However, the Government of Maharashtra has given more priorities to irrigation development from beginning of the planning, particularly from the second plan onwards. It is seen from this table that irrigation potential created from all sources in the first five year plan (1951-56) was 3.14 lakh ha. Out of this, 2.75 lakh ha. (87.58 per cent) was from major and medium projects and remaining 0.39 lakh ha. (i.e. 12.42 per cent) from minor projects. During 1951-52 to 2001-2002, irrigation potential created rose from 3.14 lakh ha. to 38.12 lakh hectares. It means there has been near about 13 times increase in irrigation potential created during last 50 years in the state. At the end of the ninth plan of 1997 to 2002, irrigation potential created was 38.12 lakh ha. out of which, 28.82 lakh ha. was created from major and medium projects and 9.30 lakh ha. from minor irrigation projects. During the period from 1951-52 to 2001-2002, irrigation potential from

Table 12
Plan-wise Irrigation Potential Created and Utilization in Maharashtra (Cumulative)

(Area in lakh ha.)

	Major/medium		*Minor state*		*Minor lift*		*All Sources*		
Plan period	*Potential*	*Utilization*	*Potential*	*Utilization*	*Potential*	*Utilization*	*Potential*	*Utilization*	*Percentage of utilization*
1	*2*	*3*	*4*	*5*	*6*	*7*	*8*	*9*	*10*
Pre-plan (Before 1951)	2.52	1.88	0.22	0.10	–	–	2.74	1.98	72.27
I plan (1951-56)	2.75	2.04	0.39	0.22	–	–	3.14	2.26	71.97
II plan (1956-61)	3.23	2.34	0.75	0.4	–	–	3.98	2.76	69.35
III plan (1961-66)	4.51	3.20	1.19	0.55	–	–	5.70	3.75	65.79
Annual Plans (1966-69)	5.71	3.23	1.47	0.82	–	–	7.18	4.05	56.41
IV plan (1969-74)	8.37	4.10	2.45	0.82	0.20	0.06	11.02	4.98	45.19
V plan (1974-78)	11.24	5.73	3.38	1.13	1.08	0.10	15.70	6.96	44.33
Annual plans (1978-80)	12.32	5.77	3.81	1.30	1.08	0.12	17.21	7.19	41.24
VI plan (1980-85)	16.80	6.56	4.78	1.23	1.12	0.17	22.70	7.96	35.07
VII plan (1985-90)	19.44	8.18	5.75	1.46	1.12	0.18	26.31	9.82	37.32
Annual plan (1990-92)	19.95	8.12	6.10	1.48	1.12	–	27.17	9.60	35.33
Eighth plan (1992-97) (Target)	24.41	–	7.34	–	–	–	31.75	–	–

Contd...

(Area in lakh ha.)

Plan period	Major/medium		Minor state		Minor lift		All Sources		
	Potential	Utilization	Potential	Utilization	Potential	Utilization	Potential	Utilization	Percentage of utilization
1	2	3	4	5	6	7	8	9	10
Annual plan (1992-93)	20.41	9.64	6.37	1.36	1.12	–	27.07	11.00	39.32
Annual plan (1993-94)	12.47	10.32	7.15	1.60	–	–	29.62	11.92	40.24
Annual plan (1994-95)	23.10	–	7.41	–	–	–	30.51	–	–
Annual plan (1995-96)	–	–	–	–	–	–	–	–	–
Annual plan (1996-97)	–	–	–	–	–	–	–	–	–
Ninth plan(1997-2002)	28.82	-	9.30	-	-	-	49.90	-	-

N.B. : Potential Created from Minor Irrigation Including the Lift Irrigation Schemes.

Sources: 1. *Model :* Maharashtra Irrigation Development – Present Position, working committee of Second Maharashtra Irrigation Commission, Aurangabad 1996, p. 145.

2 Second Maharashtra Irrigation Commission, Government of Maharashtra, Vol. 1,1999, p. 614.

3. Jadhav Y. R. Maharashtra water wealth & Regional Imbalances Development, 20 Dec. 2007. p. 139

major and medium projects rose from 2.75 lakh ha to 38.12 lakh ha. It means irrigation potential from major and medium projects has increased by twelve times during last 50 years. In case of minor irrigation projects, potential rose from 0.39 lakh ha. to 9.30 lakh ha. and the increase was around 20 times in the same period. Thus, during last 46 years, more irrigation facility was created from minor projects as compared to major and medium projects in the Maharashtra state.

According to Second Irrigation Commission (1995), ultimate irrigation potential of the state would be 126 lakh ha. Only of an area of 33 lakh ha. (26.19 per cent) has been already created irrigation potential in the state in the year 1997 and remaining irrigation potential of an area of 93 lakh ha. (73.81 per cent) should be created in future period of 33 years.

The percentage of utilized irrigation potential from all projects has also been shown in table 12 In case of Maharashtra, the position of utilization of potential created is very poor. It is seen from this table that during the period 1951 to 1966, the percentage of utilized irrigation potential was 65 to 70 per cent but after this period it has been continuously decreased. At the end of the annual plans (1990-92), it was only 35 per cent of created potential. At the end of annual plan of 1993-94, the percentage of utilized irrigation potential was found to be 40 per cent.

It is seen from Tables 6 and 12 that percentage of utilized irrigation potential in Maharashtra is very low as compared to India.

In fact utilization is as important as creation of irrigation potential. The gap between potential created and its utilization in Maharashtra is shown in Graph 8. It is seen from this graph that the gap between irrigation potential created and potential utilized has became progressively larger in successive plans. After the third plan (1961-66), this gap becomes wider. And at the end of annual plan of 1993-94, this percentage of utilized potential has become 40 per cent.

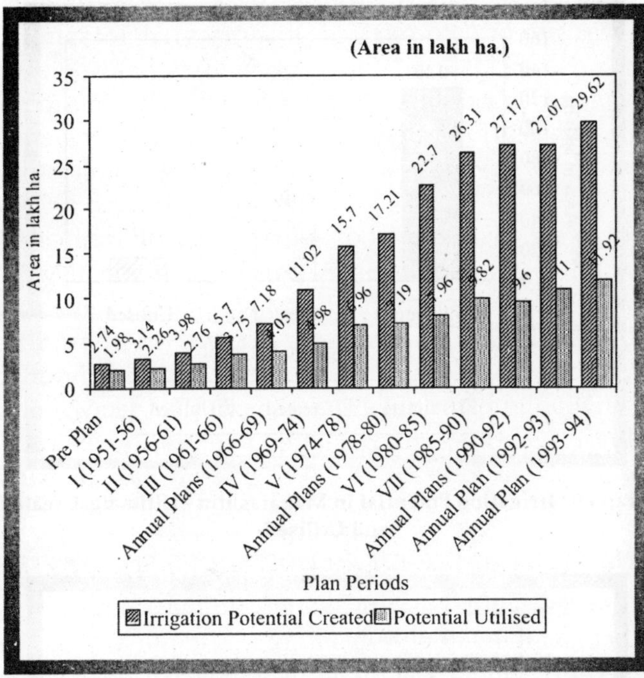

Graph 8 : Development of Irrigation Potential and Utilization in Maharashtra (Cumulative)

Irrigation Potential in Maharashtra - Ultimate, Created and Utilized

State's ultimate irrigation potential, created potential and its utilization in case of major medium and minor projects up to the period 1997 are presented in Graph 9. It is seen from this graph that the ultimate irrigation potential has been recently estimated for state to an area of 126 lakh ha. Out of this 40 lakh ha. is potential created from all irrigation projects and only 10 lakh ha. (31.25 per cent of created potential) is potential utilized by the end of 2007.

Growth of Irrigation in Maharashtra (1960-61 to 1999-2000):

The data about gross irrigated area and gross cropped area in Maharashtra during 1960-61 to 1999-2000 is shown in the Graph 10.

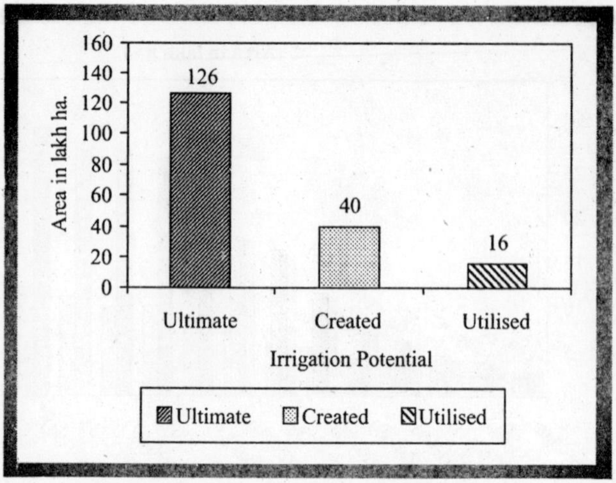

Graph 9 : Irrigation Potential in Maharashtra - Ultimate, Created and Utilised

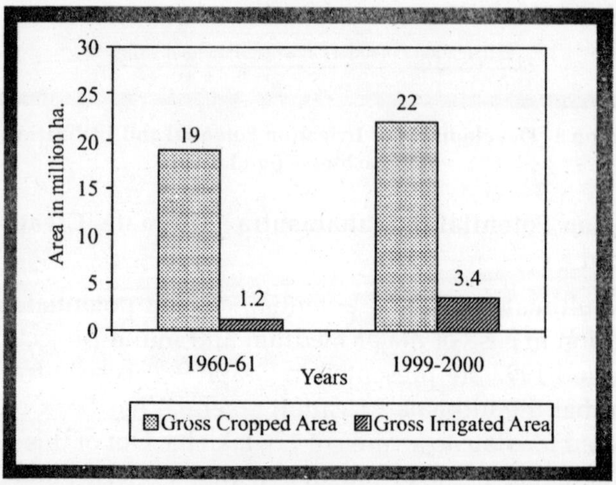

Graph 10 : Growth of Irrigation in Maharashtra State During 1960-61 to 1999-2000

It is seen from this graph that just about an equivalent of 1.2 million ha. of irrigation benefits in the year 1960-61, the corresponding benefits near about tripled by the year 1999-2000 to reach 3.4 million ha. in Maharashtra. As compared to just about 6 per cent of the cropped area under irrigation in the period 1960-61, the irrigation level in state has since increased to 15.41 per cent in the year 1999-2000 though there has been an increase of nearly 20 per cent in the cropped area.

Thus, the quantitative aspects of irrigation facilities created in the state appears more depressing when viewed against the total available irrigation potential of the state from all sources. Out of the total potential estimated to irrigate a net area of 89 lakh hectares only 30.51 lakh hectares or 34.28 per cent has been created up to 1994-95 and only 40 per cent has been utilized. This inadequacy of irrigation in Maharashtra appears less striking once we compare it with the level of irrigation development in India. In 1995-96, the percentage of gross irrigated area to gross cropped area was 15.41 per cent in Maharashtra state, which was less than the corresponding all India average of 38.00 per cent.

Notes and References

1. Igor Shiklomanov, "World Fresh Water Resources" in Paper H.(Leick ed.) Water in Crisis : A Guide to the Worlds Fresh Water, 1993.
2. Water Resources Day 1996: Theme Paper, *Journal of Indian Water Resource Society*, Vol. 2, No. 2, April 1996, p. 2.
3. Water and Related Statistics, Central Water Commission, Ministry of Water Resources, July 1998, p. 2.
4. Water Resources Development in India (1947-1997), Ministry of Water Resources, New Delhi, 1998.
5. Water and Related Statistics, Central Water Commission, Ministry of Water Resources, 1998, pp. 2-4.
6. Seventh Five Year Plan (1985-90), Planning Commission, Government of India.
7. B. N. Navalawala, Indian Perspective in Water Resources Planning, Seminar on Irrigation Water Management, New Delhi, 1992, pp. 18-38.
8. *Bhagirath,* Vol. XXXXVI, April-June 1999, Central Water Commission and Ministry of Water Resources, New Delhi, pp. 78-82.

9. Ray S. K., Green Revolution, How Greens, Facts For You, Annual Number, 1982-83.
10. Arunachalam, B., 'Maharashtra', published by Mahendrakumar A. Sheth for A. K. Sheth and Co., Princess Street, Bombay 1967, p. 3.
11. Economic Survey of Maharashtra, 1999-2000, Directorate of Economics and Statistics, Planning Department, Government of Maharashtra, Mumbai, p. T31.
12. Report of the Irrigation Commission, 1972, Vol. II, Ministry of Irrigation and Power, New Delhi, p. 237.
13. Report of the Fact Finding Committee on Regional Imbalance, Government of Maharashtra, 1984, p. 84.
14. Report of Irrigation Commission, 1972, Vol. II, Ministry of Irrigation and Power, New Delhi, p. 233.
15. Report of First Irrigation Commission, Government of Maharashtra, 1962, pp. 33-35.
16. Central Water Commission, 1972, Vol. II, Government of India, p. 231.
17. Economic Survey of Maharashtra, 1999-2000, Directorate of Economics and Statistics, Planning Department, Government of Maharashtra, Mumbai.
18. Central Water Commission, 1996, Government of India, Statement No. 18, p.17.

Chapter 3

Review of Literature

The impact of irrigation is studied by several social scientists in the past in different parts of India. The studies are of different nature (cross - sectional and longitudinal) and at different levels, at macro level or at micro level i.e. at village level. The ultimate aim of these studies is to bring out the impact of irrigation on various factors or aspects of development at the household or village level. The factors generally touched upon are farm economy, general economic conditions, i.e. change in crop pattern, agricultural productivity or crop yield, cropping intensity, employment, etc. In some cases the social factors are also analyzed.

Irrigation has far-reaching influence on agricultural productivity is well established in the literature. Irrigation has the potential to increase yields, facilitate, the adoption of high yielding varieties and high value crops contribute to agricultural stability, raise cropping intensity, and give a boost to labour absorption in agriculture. There is ample evidence to substantiate these positive influences of irrigation. However, estimating the precise magnitude of impact of irrigation is problematic. Part of the difficulty is that irrigation affects crop yield both directly and also through its influence on the scope for using other inputs especially fertilizers and their efficiency. It is very difficult to accurately assess the ceteris paribus impact of irrigation. What differences in land productivity that one may find between irrigated and unirrigated farming should be treated as the overall impact of irrigation, because there is strong complementarity between irrigation and other inputs such as fertilizers. For instance, several attempts can be found in literature wherein the pure irrigation effect is estimated employing the decompositive methods. The underlying process in such methods involves a decomposition or breaking up of total output into various components and associating these components of total output with various factors of production such as irrigation, fertilizers, etc. There are also other problems which crop up when attempts are made to estimate the impact of irrigation and these pertain to the basic methodology employed in such studies. When the data employed to estimate the impact of irrigation pertains to two time periods, one before and the other after introduction of a particular type of irrigation. The impact of irrigation on income and employment can be reasonably assessed provided, we take due note of other changes that are totally unrelated to irrigation. To do so is a difficult proposition. The reported increase in income of sample farmers to be duly adjusted downwards if there is price inflation in the intervening period. Also, if weather conditions prevailing before and after irrigation situations are not comparable, the results in respect of impact of irrigation on many aspects of farm economy may get destorted[1]. Because of these difficulties, impact studies based on pre- and post- irrigation are not as numerous as those based on with and without irrigation approach.

There are again two approaches, which are used when irrigation impact is judged based on with and without irrigation method. In the first approach two samples of farmers are considered, one with irrigation of a particular category and the other without access to the irrigation of a particular category i.e. the control sample. This approach when followed saves the trouble involved in the time consuming exercise of adjusting the input-output data for price changes. It also eliminates the effects of all other developments that may have taken place since the commencement of irrigation. Yet the approach may yield considerably distorted result about the impact of irrigation on farm economy if the 'control' sample differs from the main sample in respect of soil and topography, farm size and management ability. The other approach based on with and without irrigation method seeks to eliminate the differences due to management ability by comparing the unirrigated area of main sample as 'control' for irrigated area.

In this chapter, an attempt is made to review the empirical work carried out on the aspects of the impact of irrigation by the several social scientists in the past in difference parts of India. Although, it is not possible to comment on all studies in details, a brief account of their findings is given in the forthcoming paragraphs.

Gadgil's (1948)[2] pioneering study evaluating economic effects of irrigation with regard to the Godavari and Pravara canal throws light on many direct and indirect benefits of irrigation. It analyses the beneficial impact of irrigation in relation to dry areas which are deprived of this facility. The study concludes that provision of irrigation facility to the farmers has enabled them to have a superior cropping pattern, higher per acre productivity and larger gross farm income. Besides, indirect benefits have accrued to the people who are involved in processing and transporting of the enhanced agricultural production of the irrigated area. The volume of the trade has increased on account of increased agricultural production and it has encouraged railway traffic, road traffic, trading establishments, etc. Agricultural operations of irrigated area, being labour intensive, have increased the demand for hired labour which, in turn, has raised the wages. This has improved the economic conditions of agricultural labourers. Thus the study concludes that the construction and maintenance of a project has far-reaching effects on the economic life of the community living within its region and also to the same extent on the neighbouring community of the region.

In 1958, the Planning Commission, Government of India, constituted a study group under the chairmanship of D.R. Gadgil of the Gokhale Institute of Economics and Politics, Pune, to measure the direct (i.e. primary) and to the extent possible, the indirect (i.e. secondary) benefits arising from the selected schemes like Sarola canal (Uttar Pradesh), Tribeni canal (Bihar), Damodhar Canal (West Bengal), Cauvery Mettur Project (Tamil Nadu), Nizamsagar Project (Andhra Pradesh) and Ganga Canal (Rajasthan). The study of these different projects was assigned to different economists. For example, the study of Damodhar canal was assigned to Basu Mukherjee[3], Tribeni Canal was assigned to Prof. Diwakar Jha[4] etc. These studies are ex-post assessment of benefits of the irrigation provided by different projects. With the help of primary data, these economists have concluded that irrigation leads to intensive use of land, shift from food to commercial crops, increase of cropping intensity, promotion for the use of modern and traditional inputs, increase of per acre gross production and income, etc.

First Maharashtra State Irrigation Commission (1960) was appointed under the chairmanship of Shri Barve by the Government of Maharashtra to study the overall irrigation development in the state. Barve commission submitted its report in the year (1962)[5] to the Government of Maharashtra and made a comprehensive study of the irrigation potential in the state and hoped that it is possible to create irrigation potential in the state for an area of 52.61 lakh hectares (i.e. 30 per cent of the present cultivable area) from the all surface irrigation sources. The total utilizable surface water resources of 75 per cent dependability were assessed by this commission at about 200 TMC in the state. Therefore Commission assessed that the total ultimate irrigation potential of the state would be 6.1 mha. and out of which 5.2 mha. to be from surface water and remaining 0.9 mha. to be from ground water resources.

Desai and Thingalaya (1965)[6] have studied the yield variability of rice in some selected rice growing districts in the country. Using the national average yield rate of rice as the norms, the inter-district yield variation are analysed and an attempt was made to assess that irrigation is one of the important factors that may be taken to be influencing yield variation.

Rice in India is grown under diverse soil and climatic conditions. Of the 311 rice growing districts in India, the first

177 districts (ranked in descending order according to their percentage share in the total rice production in the country) account for 93.21 per cent of the total rice production, having among them 92.35 per cent of the total area under rice in the country. Among these 177 districts the first 40 districts were selected for this study. Though an element of arbitrariness is inherent in the selection of the above number of districts for the purpose of study, the importance of these 40 districts is the fact that the share of these 40 districts in the total area under the rice cultivation was 43.46 per cent while their contribution to the total rice production was as much as 51.0 per cent. The national average yield rate based on the average of the three year period 1955-56 to 1957-58, works out to be 761 lbs. for the 311 districts. Among the 40 selected districts, the range of yields were narrower with the yield in Sambalpur district in Orissa being the lowest of 467 lbs. An index of yield variability was constructed for the 40 districts by expressing the yield rate of each district as a percentage of national average yield rate. It was observed that this index is above 100 for as many as 27 districts. Of the factor inputs determining the yield rate of rice, availability of irrigation facility was chosen for detailed analysis as a factor determining the yield rate. This choice was made primarily on the grounds of the ready availability of the data pertaining to the area under rice and the area under rice irrigated for all the districts.

The relationship between the percentage of area under irrigated rice and the yield rates in different districts was brought out using 9 sample regression analysis. Thus, it was pointed out that 42 per cent of the variations in the yields are explained by the extent of availability of irrigation facilities. The conclusion that emerges was that yield rates can be stabilized and increased to a considerable extent with provision of irrigation facilities in areas depending entirely on rainfall for crop production.

Kahlon, Miglani and Singh (1971)[7] have attempted to examine a comparative analysis of cropping pattern, cost-benefit relations in crop production on dry and irrigated lands in Ferozepur district (Punjab). The multi-stage stratified random sampling technique with villages as the primary and operational holdings as the ultimate units of study was used for selecting the sample for this investigation. The district was divided into three zones based on agro-climatic conditions. The first zone comprised Moga tahsil, the second zone consisted of Ferozepur and Zira tahsils and Jallalabad block of Fazilka tahsil while the third zone was constituted by Muktasar and Fazilka tahsils excluding Jallalabad block of Fazilka tahsil. Dry farming was predominant in third zone which was purposively selected for this investigation. The total sample of 70 operational holdings was selected under the "Farm management project", from seven randomly selected villages in these two tahsils (Muktasar and Fazilka) was adopted for this study. From this sample, a sub-sample of 41 operational holdings practicing dry farming along with irrigated farming was selected. The remaining 29 holdings which followed irrigated farming exclusively were ignored. As in the project under reference selected holdings were classified into five size groups as below 6 hectares, 6 to 9 hectares, 9 to 14 hectares, 14 to 24 hectares and 24 hectares and above. The cross sectional data on cropping pattern, yield, cost and return for the year 1969-70 were collected from the selected holdings with help of specially constructed pre-tested schedules using the survey method.

It was concluded from this study that crops such as American cotton, desi cotton and Mexican wheat were more important in the irrigated area whereas gura, bajra desi, gram and barley plus gram were more important in the unirrigated area. American cotton was the most important crop on irrigated area during kharif season. This crop covered the largest percentage of the total irrigated area (45.11 per cent). The other major kharif crops in order of importance were fodder, cotton desi, gura, bajra desi, sugarcane, maize hybrid and paddy. The percentage irrigated area under these crops was 17.45, 14.87, 8.66, 5.00, 3.98, 0.94, and 0.76 respectively.

Gura was the most important crop in the unirrigated area during the kharif season, which occupied 40.14 per cent of the total unirrigated area. The other dry farming kharif crops were fodder, bajra desi, pulses and cotton desi. The percentage of rain-fed area under these crops was 27.86, 17.80, 11.50 and 2.88 respectively.

During the rabi season, irrigated crops such as Mexican wheat, wheat desi, and fodder were sown on 53.96, 9.84, 6.70 and 8.21 per cent of the total irrigated area respectively. Crop mixtures such as wheat plus gram and barley plus gram were more important on dry lands as compared with the irrigated ones. The percentage of unirrigated area under wheat plus gram, barley plus gram, gram and oilseeds worked out to 33.96, 23.49, 21.61, 13.31 and 2.23 respectively.

The cropping intensity, cost of cultivation, yields per hectare and gross income per hectare of major crops were more in the irrigated area as compared to that in the unirrigated area. However, the per hectare returns to fixed farm resources from gura, bajra desi and gram were more in the unirrigated area but crop mixtures such as wheat plus gram and barley plus gram gave more returns in the irrigated area.

Moorti (1976)[8] has attempted to study the impact of different sources of irrigation on input output relationship, cropping pattern and the farm practices in Aligarh district of Uttar Pradesh. The basic source of data for this study was drawn from a comprehensive survey of 141 farms undertaken in Aligarh district during 1966-67. This was supplemented by brief surveys for practical information during 1968-69 and 1972-73. Out of the 12 community development blocks in the district three blocks were purposively selected. Keeping in view the transport facilities for survey work, four clusters of villages each representing concentration of one source of irrigation were selected. Ten per cent of the farms from each category under the different systems of irrigation were randomly selected for the study.

In all, 141 farms were finally selected as follows: 36 farms irrigating entirely from state tube wells, 50 farms from private tube wells, 41 farms from Persian wheels and 14 farms from Charsa. The Cobb-Douglas model was chosen for estimating the production function. For studying the impact of different sources of irrigation on cropping pattern, yields and farm practices tabular analysis was done. The variables were used on a per hectare basis to estimate the possibility of land variable being highly correlated with the independent variables. Tests of significance were carried out to ascertain whether the regression coefficients were significantly different from zero.

The following conclusions were emerged from this study:

(1) Maize desi showed a high response to water, its elasticity coefficient being 0.2574 relative to bajra desi whose elasticity was 0.0810. Among rabi crops, the highest elasticity coefficient was recorded in case of peas (0.7948). The production elasticity associated with water variable for Mexican wheat (0.32) was found to be about three times greater in magnitude than that of desi wheat (0.11). The individual elasticities of production associated with water variable for all the crops were less than unity indicating diminishing returns to water resources.

(2) It was found that crops grown on private tubewell irrigated farms have invariably higher yields in all crops than farms irrigated by other sources. The crop yields on farms irrigated by private tubewells were consistently more than 25 per cent higher even for same variety than farms with other sources of irrigation. The crop yields on farms irrigated by Persian wheels were consistently higher than the yields on farms using state tubewells, thereby indicating that the farmers using state tubewells did not get adequate water at the proper time.

(3) The volume of water delivered to crops was substantially higher for the private tubewell farms than for farms irrigating from all other resources.

(4) Farmers irrigating from the private tubewells invariably used higher doses of nitrogen on almost all crops compared with other sources of irrigation, evidently because of timely availability and adequate supply of water.

Patil and others (1978)[9] have attempted to conduct a socio-economic survey in the command area of Girna Irrigation project in Jalgaon district (Maharashtra state). They pointed out that the project has provided economic and social benefits to the farmers of the command area. Economic benefits received in the form of modern cropping pattern, increased use of inputs have helped to increase per hectare productivity and the income to beneficiaries. Therefore, the standard of living of beneficiaries has improved due to irrigation facility.

Pandey's (1979)[10] study on impact of irrigation on rural development in the command area of Kivi-Badua Chandan in the state of Bihar was based on the data collected from field and he had selected villages from the dry and wet areas for the comparison. In all 6 villages - 3 each from wet and dry categories were selected. The households within the villages were selected on the basis of purposive random sampling. Out of the total 2033 households in the 6 villages, a sample of 610 households was selected. These villages were studied with reference to the variables like communication, population, occupation, irrigation, markets, cooperative societies, self/ leased cultivation crop pattern, income, and indebtedness. The study indicated that the overall performance of the irrigated villages was far superior to that of unirrigated villages.

In their study of Bellary district in Karnataka, Mishra and Vivekananda (1979)[11] classified the sample villages under Tungabhadra dam into dry-cum-wet, perennial and wet depending on the availability of water for irrigation. They had selected ten villages from three talukas on the whole. They collected information (household level) from 92 farmers and 9 landless labourers and observed an inverse relationship between the size of the holding and the area irrigated. The pattern of crop cultivation (i.e. cropping) has undergone some basic changes after the introduction of canal irrigation in the villages. Such changes are formed in terms of both the allocation of area under crops and cultivation of new and HYV crops. In wet and perennial villages, the cultivation of kharif paddy and double cropping of paddy and sugarcane accounts for a significant proportion of the irrigated area. Moreover, the farming of HYV and improved variety of paddy in wet and perennial villages and the farming of HYV sugarcane are new practices. The induced effects of quick yielding changed in the field of production refer to higher crop yield per acre in the sample villages, than what they were prior to canal irrigation, despite high cost per acre, the farm business income per acre was positive in irrigated lands. So also the net income per acre. The introduction of canal irrigation has positively effected the employment of labour per person and per acre. The annual employment per person was increased significantly in all the villages, including landless labour.

Meti (1977)[12] was attempted to make an ex-post assessment of the benefits of irrigation of Tungabhadra project in Karnataka. His study was mainly based on "before and after" approach in which he tried to assess the benefits of irrigation by comparing the differences in production, income, savings and investments, asset formation, consumption pattern, social attitudes and values etc. in the area prior to the construction of the canal and in the year of investigation. The analysis also takes into consideration of the controlled area and relates the changes in the project area. He concluded that there are positive changes in production, income, savings and investment, asset formation, consumption pattern, social attitudes, etc.

Patil and others (1950)[13] conducted a study in the Ghod area of Maharashtra about the socio-economic conditions of the farmers in the command area. A sample of 400 holdings, 40 in each cluster were randomly selected. In Karjat taluka 2 clusters, in Shrigonda taluka 5 clusters, from Shirur taluka 3 clusters were selected. Data was collected on land use pattern, crop pattern, agricultural implements, and cropwise labour input, the analysis was presented per farm, and per hectare on adoption of improved agricultural practices like improved seeds, cultivation practices, seed treatment, use of fertilizers and green manure. At each stage, irrigated v/s unirrigated ways of cultivation were compared. The yield rates were compared at two points of time (1969-70 and 1975-76) – before the onset of irrigation and after. The result indicated that post-irrigation was better off over pre-irrigation in all aspects. Consumption of foodgrains (cereals, pulses), protective items like milk, oil, vegetables, spices, meat, fish, egg, fruit beverage per family, per adult unit was observed to have improved in the irrigated area with time.

Patel (1981)[14] has analysed the impact of irrigation on employment at farm level in the command areas of 24 medium irrigation projects in different parts of Gujarat during the period 1976-77 to 1979-80. The study revealed that one hectare of a rainfed farm converted into an irrigated farm would generate about 52 mandays of work in Gujarat.

There were 24 different areas, 12 each were situated in the erstwhile Saurashtra state and in Gujarat respectively. At present, well was the only source of irrigation available to these areas. The analysis was based on the data collected from 100 farm households from each project area under study. Spatially, 40 talukas out of the total of 184 talukas in the state were covered in the bench-mark study. Finally, in all 2400 farm households were studied for the purpose. The selected households were distributed equally among each of the four selected villages for the majority of the areas and among each of the five or six selected villages for the remaining project areas. The sample was designed to include different size groups of land holdings so that it may not be biased towards a particular operational size of land holding. The sample farm households were classified as marginal, small, medium and big farm holding groups. To study the impact of irrigation on employment the selected farmers were divided into two groups. The farmers of the first group were named as the users of irrigation and those of the second group were named as the non-users of the irrigation. The users farming was furth divided into irrigated farming and rainfed farming. The employment impact of irrigation was analysed on the basis of information obtained from the irrigated and rainfed farming of the users of irrigation.

The study estimated additional employment opportunities consequent to irrigation separately for the Saurashtra and Gujarat regions. The result of the regression analysis indicated that one hectare of rainfed farm converted into an irrigated farm would generate about 48 mandays of work in the Saurashtra region and about 52 mandays of work in Gujarat region. To conclude the impact of irrigation on employment at the farm level was very much.

Selvarajan and Subramanian (1981)[15] have attempted to study the economic impact of resource use optimization and water augmentation in farms of Parambikulam Aliyar Project Region (Tamil Nadu). The list of villages and sample farmers selected for the bench-march survey (BMS) provided the sample frame for this study. In the BMS a total of 360 respondents uniformly spread over 12 villages in four talukas of the study region, all selected by random sampling. The data for present study were collected from the selected respondents during the month of December 1975 and January 1976 through personal interviews with the help of pre-tested schedules. The data collected covered the agricultural years 1973-74 and 1974-75. The profit maximization model of linear programming (L.P.) technique was used to find out the normative solutions. The methodology adopted in this study differed from the quoted studies in the sense that they had compared dry and irrigated farms to evaluate the impact of irrigation while in this study, it was evaluated by introducing a well in the selected farm. The economic worthiness of the well was evaluated through the internal rate of return (IRR) method.

The impact of resource use optimization and water augmentation was sought to be evaluated in terms of cropping pattern, cropping intensity, human and bullock labour utilization, farm business income, family labour income, labour earnings per manday and gross and net income. Discussions on impacts of resource use optimization and water augmentation have been confined mostly to the project years, though references have been made about the effect of the well in the non project years on several occasions.

(i) The cropping pattern, existing and as suggested by the different optimum plans was showed in this study. A comparison of existing plan and optimum plan revealed that resource use optimization while suggesting the growing of improved varieties of some currently grown crops on the farm, also introduced new crops. It was observed that optimization favoured growing more number of crops as compared to the existing plan, thereby suggesting trends towards diversification.

(ii) The cropping intensity of existing plan was 169 per cent and by optimal resources use it was increased to 195 per cent.

(iii) Resource use optimization increased the total bullock pair days employed by 18 pair days (an increase of about 17 per cent) and water augmentation by 17 pair days (13.08 per cent) in the project areas and by 12 pair days (9.68 per cent) in the non-project years.

(iv) The mandays utilized at present was 1183 and by resource use optimization, it was increased by 189 mandays (21.87 per cent) in the project years and 241 mandays (18.47 per cent) in the non-project years.

(v) Resource use optimization has increased the gross income by 25.97 per cent, net income by 33.11 per cent, family labour income by 76.91 per cent and farm business income by 45.13 per cent.

The effect of water augmentation was to increase the gross income by 20.56 per cent, net income by 22.67 per cent family labour income by 23.81 per cent and farm business income by 22.90 per cent. The labour earning per manday had increased from Rs. 14.32 to Rs. 19.21 by resource use optimization and from Rs. 19.21 to Rs. 19.44 by water augmentation.

(vi) The study concluded that investment on well was found to be sound either when the farmer uses his own capital or borrows it from the lending institutions. Besides, increasing the farm income, it had also helped to stabilize the farm income.

Alexander (1982)[16] made an attempt to analyse a comparative framework of both irrigated and non-irrigated parts of Ganganagar district in Rajasthan state. He had collected primary data from 900 respondents from various tahsils, of which 600 respondents were from irrigated area and remaining

300 respondents were from uncommand area. The author observed that economically irrigation facilitated intensification of agricultural activity through large use of labour, fertilizers, insecticides and other inputs and enabled the farmers to use improved tools and machines, led to the increase in the amount of per acre production and productivity and gross income, enhanced amount of savings also. In the social front, it has resulted in changes in religious beliefs. Further, there was also sharp difference in the incidence of sickness and mortality rates in the two. He held that irrigation has paved the way for modernization of values and their specialization. Thus, the study not only covered the economic benefits of irrigation but also the social aspects that affect people in the command area.

Satpathy (1984)[17] has attempted to study the irrigation development and its favourable impact on farm economy in Orissa state. Satpathy in his study has elaborately examined the Pervasive character of impact of irrigation both at macro as well as micro levels and collected secondary data for the period 1970-71 to 1980-81. He conducted a micro level field survey in a homogeneous region of Cuttack Sadar I block. His study was based on with and without principle. The sampling technique adopted for a field investigation was based on two stages stratified random sampling with operational holding as the ultimate unit of samples. At the first stage, eight villages were selected for the study with proportional allocation, the number of irrigated and unirrigated villages came to six and two respectively. At the second stage, each village was divided into three strata of size groups I, II and III. From each stratum, 15 per cent sample households were selected at random. Thus total households selected from irrigated and unirrigated villages were 152 and 53 respectively. His study indicated that irrigation possesses significant "area effect, crop pattern effect, employment and yield effect in the state of Orissa. From the study of the evaluation of the impact of the irrigation on farm economy, the following conclusions were drawn:

The index of cropping intensity was higher in irrigated area (157.25 per cent) than in unirrigated area (128.81 per cent). Further, in the irrigated area the cropping intensity in respect of each of the size groups of holdings was found higher than corresponding groups from unirrigated area. The irrigated area exhibited a more diversified cropping pattern in the summer of rabi season as compared to their unirrigated counterparts. The output-input analysis revealed that on the whole input costs for farm business income or cost A_2 was higher for irrigated than that of unirrigated farms. The three measures of farm profit, such as farm business income, return to family labour and management and net income for all size class in irrigated areas were higher than that of unirrigated areas. Provision of irrigation has also enhanced labour employment in the study area. On the whole, a hectare of irrigated farm increased the labour use by 55.80 mandays per annum or increased the employment opportunities by 40.34 per cent as compared to unirrigated area.

Jha (1984)[18] has attempted to study the various aspects of irrigation management. He has discussed the role of irrigation in economic development of an agrarian economy, with particular reference to Bihar state. He had discussed the various irrigation systems and methods of water use in agriculture. This study also presented a review of existing irrigation policy. A study of nature and extent of flood and flood control measure has also been made. In prescribing a national irrigation policy it was tried to consider various view points on irrigation systems in Bihar and to maintain balance in the treatment of the problems. In this study, the term 'irrigation' was used in its agricultural and socio-economic aspects. The agricultural aspect refers to the use of irrigation water and various agricultural practices, cropping pattern and methods of application. The socio economic aspect refers to the satisfaction of the social needs and desires which is essential for any community enterprise.

Azad and others (1984)[19], have studied the economic appraisal of a tubewell irrigation project in Kanpur district, Uttar Pradesh during the year 1982-83. The study was based on an intensive enquiry of 20 farmers owning tubewells. Data for the pre- and post-project periods were collected by survey method. There was a major shift in cropping pattern. The area under low remunerative crops was replaced by high-yielding varieties and other high pay-off cash crops in the post irrigation period. The input cost, value of output and net profit per hectare in almost all the crops were significantly higher in the post project period as compared to the pre-project period. The higher input cost per hectare in the post-project period was due to more use of production oriented cash inputs like manure, fertilizers, HYV, plant projection measures etc. The simple rate of return under the post-project period came to 152.30 per cent. This reveals a very high profitability of the initial investment of the tube well project in the study area. The cost benefit ratio came to 1:2.09. The project not only boosted the productivity of the various crops per unit of land but also increased the labour employment on the farms significantly during the post-project period as compared to the pre project period. Thus, study concluded that the installation of a tubewell project on an eight hectare farm is technically feasible and economically viable.

Sidhu and others (1984)[20], have attempted to make an economic appraisal of various sources of irrigation in Punjab during the year 1982-83. The study was based on the data collected from the farmers of Amritsar, Ludhiana, Patiala districts of Punjab. Sixty farmers were selected from each district by adopting a three-stage random sampling procedure using block as the first stage unit, village as the second stage unit, and farm households as the final unit of the study. The field data were collected for rabi season of the crop year 1982-83.

Some important conclusions emerged from this study are given below. The study indicated the positive relationship between the degree of water supply flexibility and reliability (represented by the sources of irrigation) and use of fertilizers, irrigation and other variable inputs. Owing to the higher use of inputs which was the result of increase in the degree of water supply flexibility and reliability, the yields and economic returns were also higher at flexible source of irrigation. The performance of the farmers having diesel plus electric alternative was much better in all respects compared with all other categories. Indications are available that they operated at higher production frontier as a result of assured irrigation contrasting diesel and electric sources, the latter was found superior to the farmer, electric farms fared better than even diesel plus canal alternative.

Giri and Malik (1984)[21], have attempted to study some economic aspects of public source of irrigation as compared with the private source of irrigation in district Nadia, West Bengal. Field data of the command areas served by two deep tubewells and three shallow tube-wells were collected separately for each individual by survey method. The deep tube-wells and shallow tube-wells were purposively selected in a homogeneous tract of the district of Nadia in West Bengal. The data collected refer to 1983-84 crop season. Of the two deep tube-wells, one was situated in Simhat mouza of Haringhat a block and another one was in Digha mouza of the same block. All the three shallow tube wells were situated in Chandamari mouza of Chakdah block in Nadia district. This study has concluded that the cropping intensity of the deep tube-well was much higher for all the size groups as compared to the other. This study had also concluded that the farmers owing land within the shallow tube-well command area was found less incentive. There was tendency for the ownership holdings and/or operational holdings to get concentrated in the hands of few beneficiaries obviously the shallow tube-well owner must be one of such individuals.

Few suggestions were put forward to harness the irrigation potentiality of the various sources of irrigation. Effective functioning of the beneficiary committee was imperative for better water use, water management and land use pattern. Private sources of irrigation should not be discouraged on the plea of its tendency to create inequality in land distribution. Because these sources have other merits in that the intensity of cultivation is higher than what is observed in public use of irrigation.

Jawahar Thakur and Praduman Kumar (1984)[22] have attempted a comparative study of economic efficiency of different irrigation systems in western Uttar Pradesh. This study was an attempt to examine certain issues with the specific objectives (i) to examine the effect of sources of irrigation on cropping intensity, cropping pattern, use of inputs, yields and income, (ii) to measure the returns to water management under different sources of irrigation.

These objectives were evaluated with primary cross-section data of Meerut district, which had the highest percentage of the total net cultivated area under irrigation in western Uttar Pradesh. From Meerut district, Rajapura development block having the highest percentage (90 per cent) of the area under tube-well irrigation and Jani Khurd block having the highest percentage (63 per cent) of the area under canal irrigation were selected as the sample blocks. Three villages from the tube-well irrigation block and one village from the canal irrigated block were selected at random. All the farmers were classified into three categories (I) private tube-well (PTW), (ii) state tube well (STW) and (iii) canal irrigated farms based on their major source of irrigation. A sample of 40 farms was drawn at random from each category. Input-output data for the agricultural year 1980-81 were collected by survey method.

Output growth as a result of efficient irrigation system takes place in two stages. First, more output was made possible from the existing resources. Second, an adjustment component of water management was evident in movement along production function. A decomposition model that captures the effects of both stages is developed. The first stage will measure the contribution of better water management and the second stage will measure the contribution of changes in the levels of inputs.

The study has pointed out that the problems of irregularity and inadequacy of water supply, over irrigation and consequent drainage losses make water management imperative. Better water management leads to higher yield, increased agricultural output and higher income via additional cropping intensity, a shift to more profitable cropping pattern and higher use of farm inputs.

The intensity of cropping was maximum for PTW (172 per cent) and minimum under STW (166 per cent). Wheat crop was the predominant in the cropping pattern for all the irrigation systems. Sugarcane, a cash crop in the region, occupied the second place and then maize and paddy were the important crops in all the regions. PTW farms had 4 more diversified cropping pattern cultivating potato (5.7 per cent) and oilseed (2.7 per cent) to maximize their returns. The area under intensive irrigated crops (wheat, sugarcane, paddy and potato) was maximum (79 per cent) on PTW farms followed by canal irrigated farms (68 per cent) and minimum under STW farms (58 per cent). Assured and more dependable water supply under PTW has helped the farmers to grow intensive irrigated crops on a larger area as compared to other sources of irrigation.

Per hectare use of inputs was substantially higher on PTW farms as compared to canal irrigated and STW farms. The net income per hectare under PTW farms was three times that of STW and two times that of canal irrigated farms. The better water management under PTW had increased the use of inputs for all crops, and which has resulted in higher yields as compared to the situations under STW and canal irrigated farms. Better water management in terms of assured, timely and adequate water supply under PTW farms accounted for about 40 per cent more output for sugarcane and 45 per cent more output for wheat as compared to the relatively inefficiently managed STW. The contribution of water management on PTW farms as compared to canal farms in terms of output growth was 11 per cent for sugarcane and 29 per cent for wheat.

Substantial positive contribution of better water management to the crop output growth demonstrates the importance of PTW over canal and STW irrigated farms in increasing the yield and income to the farmers. PTW irrigation system was a low cost venture compared to the benefits derived from it. The horizontal expansion of irrigation especially through PTW will enhance agricultural production and farmers income at a rapid rate.

Sisodia (1978)[23] in his study attempted to evaluate the impact of Chambal Command Area Development project on cropping pattern, cropping intensity, and yield levels of principal crops. It also studied the structure of input use, farm income and benefit-cost ratio of the project. All these aspects have been related to the pre-project conditions (before land development). In order to evaluate the economic feasibility of irrigation and land development, the data was collected from the terminal report of "Soil and Water Use Management Pilot Project Chambal Command Area" as started in an area of 1000 acres in different parts of command area with a total cost of Rs. 11.11 lakhs for the period from 1972-73 to 1975-76. In these scheme seven subprojects, named Karati-Bharati, Hadwasi, Sunehra, Sabalgarh, Hingona Khurd and Suzarma II in Morena district and Gurikha in Bhind district were taken up. The number of schemes studied in the project area was six, benefiting 226 cultivators with a gross command area of 433.73 hectares and cultivable command area of 337.48 hectares. The average excavation cost worked out to be 18 paise per cu.ft. The total number of holdings for which input-output data were analysed was 226.

The study had concluded that the intensity of cropping and irrigated area in the projects area increased significantly after land development as compared to situation before land development. In cropping pattern, area under paddy which increased from 6.92 per cent in 1972-73 to 24.63 per cent in 1975-76. The second notable effect of land development was the emerging importance of kharif crops. In the post land development period (1975-76), kharif crops accounted for 40 per cent of the total cropped area, as against only about 28 per cent before land development. Due to improvement in the irrigation system and land development, the area under wheat crop also increased from about 34 per cent of the cropped area to about 39 per cent in 1975-76. The area under low value crops had declined considerably due to the availability of irrigation water in the project areas.

It was observed that the gross returns, farm business income and net income per acre were higher in the post-development conditions as compared to the pre-development conditions.

An investment of one rupee of annual cost resulted in the benefit of Rs. 1.34, Rs. 2.44 and Rs. 1.41 in 1973-74, 1974-75 and

1975-76 respectively, indicated a high degree of feasibility for the cultivators. This study also showed the increase in production and value of production per rupee of investment cost. The development alternative costing Rs. 127.19 per acre per year was expected to increase the production of grain and oilseeds by an average of about 2.36 kilograms per rupee of investment. The increase in gross value of the production was about 3.47 per rupee of investment.

Suryawanshi and Kapse (1985)[24] have studied the impact of Ghod Irrigation project on employment of female in agriculture in Pune and Ahmednagar districts of Maharashtra state. This study was undertaken to examine the scope for increasing employment opportunities due to irrigation over a period of time. The specific objectives of this study were (i) to examine the changes in female labour employment after the introduction of irrigation, (ii) to study the per farm and per hectare labour utilization and participation of female labour over a period of time.

Ghod irrigation project was selected for the study. The above objectives have been studied and the results were compared between two points of time i.e. prior to the introduction of irrigation (Period I : 1968-69), and when the benefits were received to farmers under the Command Area Development Authority (CADA) (period II : 1975-76). The irrigation project benefited in all 38 villages of Pune and Ahmednagar districts of Maharashtra. In all 400 farm families were selected randomly and data were collected by survey method with the help of specially designed schedule. The available working days of female per year were considered by excluding the four hours i.e. one third of a day for household chores from the total potential days. The study was related to only the crop production activity of the farm.

It was found that after the introduction of irrigation facilities in period II, the cropping pattern was changed and shifted in favour of cash and labour intensive crops. In period II cash crops like groundnut and sugarcane were introduced, which gave more employment both to the male and female workers. In general, due to irrigation, for all the crops labour employment increased more than two-fold. This trend was higher in case of female than the male labourers. It was also found that per farm total male and female labour utilization increased from period I to period II. The utilization of male labour on per farm basis was increased from 90 days to 169 days i.e. 88 per cent, whereas in case of females, it increased from 70 days to 178 days i.e. more than two and half fold. In case of family female labour, self farm employment was also almost twice in period II. It was worth noting that in period II, hired labour employment both for males and females was very high i.e. about seven-fold as compared to period I. This study concluded that due to the introduction of irrigation, high labour intensity crops were introduced in the area, which accelerated the labour employment in general and the employment of female labour in particular. Lastly, it was found in the study of employment opportunities for female labour employment in crop production had increased from 57 days to 99 days i.e. by about 74 per cent compared to traditional farming.

Dongade and others (1986)[25] have conducted a socio-economic survey in Khadakwasala Command Area, Maharashtra, which was proposed to take up "farmers" attitude survey in the schemes area of "Maharashtra Water Utilization Project". This study was conducted during the agricultural year 1984-85 and a sample of 100 farmers was selected from five sub-divisions on area proportionate basis. Further, the selection of the farmers from each of the selected villages was done randomly. The selected farmers were categorized into three different size groups of holdings as small (below 2 hectares), medium (2 to 4 hectares) and large (above 4 hectares). Of the total 100 farmers, 43 belonged to small, 33 medium and 23 large categories of holdings. The data were collected by the survey method.

The average cropping pattern in the area showed that the cereals occupied the predominant position (70 per cent). This proportion of cereals in the cropping pattern decreased with the increase in the size of holding, the important cereals were jowar (54 per cent), wheat (8 per cent), bajra (6 per cent) etc. Among the oilseeds, groundnut was an important crop that occupied about 9 per cent of the total cropped area, cash crops occupied 17 per cent of the total area. The important cash crops were sugarcane (13 per cent), vegetables and fruit crops (about 2 per cent each). The cropping intensity at the overall level was 116. It was the highest in small size groups of holdings (122) followed by the large size class (121) and medium size class (104). In general, the intensity of cropping in the area was low and study concluded that there was need to increase the cropping intensity by adopting multiple cropping and by taking some crops during kharif season. The majority of farmers in area have used improved variety seed in various crops. The most important input contributing towards high productivity of crops was fertilizers. The high yielding varieties respond well to higher doses of fertilizers. It was found that per hectare yield of irrigated crops was higher than that of per hectare yield of unirrigated crops in study area.

Vasudeva Rao (1987)[26] has attempted to study how irrigation holds the key for agricultural development and consequently rural development. His study was based on both micro level as well as macro level analysis of the impact of irrigation on agricultural development. This study was an attempt made to understand and assess at micro level (cultivator households) the impact of irrigation under a command area canal system, in Karnataka state, as against the macro background of national level. At macro level, Nargund taluka was compared (over time and extent of benefit derived) with the neighbouring dry taluka Ron. The secondary information was collected on important variables that can be quantified like changes in literacy, population, employment, land use, crop pattern, agricultural implements, social infrastructure etc. This study was conducted in villages under the command area of Malaprabha irrigation project in Dharwar district of Karnataka. Both these two villages were similar in all respects except irrigation facility. For micro level analysis, he selected a sample of size 209 cultivators from irrigated area and 98 cultivators from dry villages. The data was collected for the single agricultural year, July 1980 – June 1981. This study indicated that in irrigated area the family labour participation has come down, with an increase in the land holding size, whereas in dry area, for almost all land holding sizes the work participation by sex and age was uniform. The literates were observed to be more in irrigated village, per acre return in irrigated village have given cotton the top rank, followed by wheat, maize and jowar, as nobody grows jowar on commercial proposition. Money (working capital) invested per acre was observed to be increasing with farm size. The overall ratio of returns to investment was 1.20 in irrigated villages, while it was 0.21 in dry villages. Gross and net revenue (per acre) were found to be increasing with the land holding size. The percentage of profits were different in two villages: 16 per cent (irrigated village) and 12 percentage (dry village). He found that the household income in irrigated village (Rs. 3,790) was higher than that in dry village (Rs. 2052). More households were above poverty line in irrigated village than in dry village. His study concludes that the irrigation has played role of successfully transforming poor villages to prosperity.

Gurjar Rama Kumar (1987)[27] has studied the irrigation impact on land use pattern, cropping pattern, cropping intensity and modernization of agriculture in the Indira Gandhi Canal command area.. This study was based on the time series data for the period 1971-72 to 1980-81. Study found that there was continuous increase in double cropped area because of the introduction of irrigation facility. In case of cereals, regarding crop preference declining trend was observed. Farmers have switched over to pulses, cash crops and fodder crops. There was 24.35 per cent increase in index of cropping intensity during the study period. In this study he found high crop diversification. But in case of assured irrigated area he found change from high to moderate crop diversification. In the study of crop ranking bajra was the first ranking crop prior to the introduction of irrigation. After irrigation he found gram, jowar, wheat, cotton and oilseeds replaced bajra. His study revealed positive impact of irrigation on per unit crop yields in terms of physical and monetary units.

Dhawan (1987)[28] has attempted to compare instability of irrigated farming during the period 1970-71 to 1983-84 with corresponding instability in rainfed farming in 11 states of India.

The author has first prepared estimates of aggregate output / yield of irrigated segment for each of the eleven states of Indian union. Likewise, similar time-series estimates were prepared for the rainfed segment. Cropwise field estimates were from the GCES source and crop aggregation was done in terms of foodgrain energy equivalents (FEFS). The study is divided into two sections, section 1 deals with the question of relative amplitude of fluctuation around the trend. On the other hand, section II presents the results of output dip analysis during protected droughts that occurred during 1970-83. He found that irrigation reduces farm output instability in nine out of eleven states. For all the eleven states taken together, the coefficient of variation of detrended output was 5.4 per cent for the irrigated segment as against 11.4 per cent for the unirrigated segment. He also found that the stability gain in yield due to irrigation was much more than the corresponding stability gain in crop area. It was in the two high rainfall states of Bihar and Madhya Pradesh that irrigation fails to show any moderating influence on agricultural instability.

Dhawan (1988)[29] has attempted to assess the impact of irrigation on farm economy in high rainfall areas of Kal Irrigation project in district Raigad (Maharashtra). The focus of this study was on the impact of the Kal irrigation project on the crop economy of the Konkan area. The main parameters of this economy under evaluation are aggregate crop output, national income generation, income from crop enterprise and labour employment. While doing so, the impact has been measured per crop hectare area of the sample house-holds actually brought under irrigation during 1884-85. In this the author has departed from S.G. Borude and Shobha R. Pawar's analysis in their study "Socio-economic survey in the command area of Kal Irrigation project", as they evaluate the impact per house hold as well as on per capita basis. To that extent, the results presented in this study are of a supplementary nature to their work.

The Kal project is one among the few attempts to harness for irrigation purpose the huge waters of the West-coast rivers of the Konkan Malabar region. The measurement of the irrigation impact was used comparison between farmers with irrigation and those without it. Two categories of villages were selected, one benefiting from the project and the other not benefiting. The sample of benefited villages in the study was 14, the unbenefited villages were chosen from the peripheral region around the Kal project. The 20 village households were chosen randomly from each of the selected villages. Thus, main sample comprises 280 households while the control sample consists of 200 households. In all 480 households were obtained for this study in the year 1984-85.

The study found that the pattern of kharif and rabi seasons cropping in command villages was superior to that in the non-command villages. It was also found that each hectare of canal irrigated area augmented crop output by about 2.7 tones of rice during the survey year 1984-85 and it was over and above about 1.9 tons of rice output under rainfed conditions. The foodgrains production augmenting role of the Kal project was quite impressive. For the entire project, the additional production per year amounts to over 12000 tons of rice valued at nearly 29 million. While the intensity of cropping rose from nearly 100 to 188 per cent, paddy yield rose by 30 per cent.

It was also found that each canal irrigated hectare added to farm business income to the tune of Rs. 4000. As the Kal water was supplied to the farmers at a low price of Rs. 180 per crop hectare, the returns to the irrigation were extremely high from farmers own angle – the each private benefit-cost ratio was almost 10. From the viewpoint of national income concept, each crop hectare under Kal project generated income of order of Rs. 5600 of which nearly Rs. 1100 occurred to farm labour class. As for the farm income gains, about 80 per cent of them accrued to small and marginal farmers. It was also seen that in the wake of a tremendous rise in intensity of cropping, labour employment rose substantially. For each canal irrigated hectare, it worked out to an additional on farm job opportunity for a single person for about 300 days in a year.

Sharma and Crutinho (1988)[30] have assessed the growth of irrigation and its impact on crop land use and crop productivity in Karnataka during the period from 1961-62 to 1976-77. The study indicated that the bulk of the created irrigation potential has been used by farmers for raising a few intensively irrigated crops and has not led to multiple cropping in any significant measure. Shift in favour of high productivity irrigated crops like paddy, maize, wheat and sugarcane are common in all irrigated tracts in the state. Low yield crops like jowar, pulses and oilseeds have lost heavily. Productivity of paddy, wheat, maize and sugarcane has gone up due to increased irrigation facility.

Kullur (1988)[31] has attempted to study the impact of irrigation facilities provided by the left bank canal of Tungabhadra project (Karnataka) on different size groups of farmers in relation to cropping pattern, cropping intensity and productivity as against the controlled areas which are deprived of irrigation facility. The data was collected from 240 respondents (120 from the project command area and 120 from the controlled area) belonging to four tahsils of the Raichur district. He found that irrigation has brought several changes in the cropping pattern of command areas. Commercial crops occupy a substantial portion of the total cultivated area. Irrigation has enhanced per acre gross amount of income of farmers by enabling them to grow commercial crops. Command area has become sugarcane and hybrid cotton growing belts. Irrigation had led to the double and multiple cropping in these areas. Irrigation has enhanced cropping intensity of the project area considerably high, it was 199.35 per cent as against 116.46 per cent in the controlled area. Irrigation has enabled the respondents of project area to adopt new technology and it has facilitated the modernization process of the agricultural sector. Per acre production and gross productivity have increased due to irrigation and use of modern inputs. The double and multiple cropping has increased employment opportunities and improved economic conditions of agricultural labour.

Dhawan (1988)[32] has studied various issues relating to the impact of irrigation on productivity, stability and equity with reference to Indian farm economy. His study was based on secondary sources of data that are compiled and published by government agencies at centre and state level. For this study, data was collected from 11 states for the period 1970-71 to 1983-84. He found that in high rainfall states, the protective as well as the stabilizing role of irrigation fails to emerge and better performance of irrigation in low and medium rainfall states was vitally linked with the superior quality of irrigation. He concluded that investments in irrigation in high rainfall regions are bound to yield low returns in the shape of gains in production and stability. His study reveals that the total output expansion in crop output corresponding to an addition of one gross irrigated hectare amounted to nearly 19 quintals in foodgrain energy equivalents (FEES units) during mid-eighties. This is very substantial addition to output under rainfed condition, country's crop output per hectare was 8 quintals in FEEs units. Gain in output stability was observed in nine out of the eleven states though the extent of gain varies from state to state. The irrigation has lowered the coefficient of variation from 11.4 to 5.4 per cent in the case of output of all crops, from 11.4 to 6.4 per cent in the case of foodgrains output, from 9.3 to 4.3 per cent in respect of over all crop yield and from 2.9 to 1.9 per cent in respect of crop acreage. Evidently, stability gain in yield was much more than the corresponding stability gain in acres. His study revealed that on farm benefits from a unit of irrigated area need not rise with the size of farm holding, small farmers can gain as much benefits per hectare from irrigation as do large farmers. This result is traceable to some sort of equity having been attained by farmers in the use of chemical fertilizers which are a major source of increasing crop yield in modern agriculture.

Sharma and others (1988-89)[33] have attempted to study the resources use variability on irrigated and unirrigated farms in Mandi district of Himachal Pradesh. Specifically, the study was undertaken with following objectives : (I) To work out the variations in the input use for irrigated and unirrigated farms of the selected area under existing and optimal farm plans, (ii) to measure the income changes due to variations in input use for irrigated and unirrigated farms of the selected area under existing and optimal farm plans. Sundernagar block of Mandi district was purposively chosen for this study because of its sufficient underground water resources in valley areas. The study was confined to nine villages out of 18 irrigated villages (having more than 25 per cent area under irrigation) which were selected randomly. The farmers in the selected villages were grouped into categories (I) irrigated farms[3] 50 per cent area under irrigation) and (ii) unirrigated farms (< 50 per cent area under irrigation). Each category was further sub-divided into small farms and large farms by cumulative square root frequency method. Finally, 60 farmers were randomly selected from each category using proportional allocated method. Thus 17 small irrigated farms, 10 large irrigated farms, 21 small unirrigated farms and 12 large unirrigated farms were selected for detailed analysis. The linear programming model was used in this study.

It is evident from this study that proportion of HYVs on irrigated farms was higher compared to unirrigated farms and with increase in farm size, the proportion increased. The study indicated that the fertiliser use per hectare was found to be higher in irrigated farms than that in unirrigated farms. Further it is per hectare farm income was higher in case of small and large farms in irrigated area than the corresponding farms of unirrigated area. There was 61.58 per cent and 16.87 per cent increase in farm income on small and large irrigated farms respectively. The corresponding figures for small and large unirrigated farms were 48.33 per cent and 18.80 per cent respectively.

Pawar (1989)[34] has studied the irrigation impact on agricultural land use in upper Krishna basin of Maharashtra with emphasis on geographical analysis. He made an attempt to highlight physical and demographic setting of region in his study. He assessed the impact of irrigation on landuse, cropping pattern, cropping intensity and crop diversification. For macrolevel study, he used secondary data, collected from the government and private agencies and for micro-level he used his own collected data. He observed that the spatial variation in the environmental and demographic setting have led to the regional imbalances in the development of irrigation facility.

He found that lift irrigation was predominant particularly on river banks of central and southern parts of the region, sharing about 45.62 per cent of total irrigated area. It was followed by dominance of well irrigation (37.40 per cent) in the east, canal irrigation in the north-central and local source of irrigation in north-west. He observed that the use of mechanical and biochemical inputs has increased in irrigated tracts. He found positive influence of irrigation on land use pattern. He observed slight decrease in area under forest. The fallow land and other uncultivated land have recorded decrease whereas net area sown has increased due to irrigation facility. Regarding cropping pattern, he observed that jowar and bajra crops were the dominant in eastern dry part, rice and fodder cultivation prevailed in western heavy rainfall zone. In the central zone, among the irrigated crops sugarcane was the single dominant crop sharing about one-half of the total irrigated area of the region, other irrigated crops were rice, wheat, gram. In view of the overall changes there was shift from foodgrains to sugarcane and from inferior cereals to superior one. He also observed significant increase in intensity of cropping in the central river valley area where adequate irrigation facility was available. The analysis of the differential levels of agricultural development clearly indicates relatively high level of agricultural development in irrigated area.

Ramakrishna and Deshpande (1990)[35] have attempted to study the "irrigation impact on employment and income" in Krishna Raja Sagar (KRS) command area in Mysore and Mandya districts of Karnataka. For the household survey they had selected 56 villages falling in the command area and having good irrigation facilities. In order to juxtapose the irrigated situation as against that of rainfed situation, they selected six villages – not falling in the command area of KRS or any other irrigation project but having similar agro-climatic situation as that of the selected 56 villages. The total number of households selected were 1525 over the command area, of which 1383 were from irrigated villages and 142 belong to rainfed villages representing 'with project' and 'without project', respectively.

It was found that total labour absorption (both male and female) for all crops among the sample households was higher (i.e. 2 lakh male) and 1.1 lakh (female) in irrigated villages than that of labour used in the dry villages (i.e. 0.12 lakh of males and 0.06 lakh of females). Total hired mandays for cultivation of all crops was found to be 165 and 77 in irrigated and rainfed conditions, respectively. In the irrigated condition the hired labour input has an inverse relationship with the size of ownership holding but in the rainfed conditions no such relationship was observed. Proportion of hired labour input under irrigation was about 71 per cent of the total labourers as against 59 per cent in rainfed conditions was observed. Lastly in their analysis of the impact on employment, it was noted that the human labour input increased in the range of 10 to 252 mandays per hectare depending upon the choice of the alternative crop. If any new area is brought under irrigation this range extends from 82 to 368 mandays. The impact of irrigation on productivity of different crops is commendable. It was observed that the productivity of the crops has increased by 2 to 4 times as compared to rainfed conditions. The value of production per hectare in irrigated and rainfed conditions helps us to analyze generation of income due to irrigation. It was noted that irrigation generates income in the range of Rs. 1203 to Rs. 21,497 per hectare per crop, depending upon the change in cropping system components. But if new area is brought under irrigation the income generation would be in the range of Rs. 1200 to Rs. 9,100. This was an important aspect of irrigation impact.

Renuka (1990)[36] has studied rural development through irrigation, a study in Kadam project of Andhra Pradesh. The sampling design of the study was multistage random sampling, canal was the first stage of unit, selection of villages was the second stage of unit and respondents was the last stage unit. The study covered the randomly selected localized villages of Kadam project. A non-localised village, which was adjacent to the selected localized villages, was covered under study to make a comparative study. The source for selecting the respondents was village official records and names of those respondents who were categorized as marginal farmers, small farmers and big farmers were taken after consulting the mandal officials and project officers. The sample respondents representing all the size groups of holding were selected using random sampling methods. Fifty respondents were selected from each village covering various categories of farmers and thus altogether the survey covered a total number of 200 respondents. The primary and secondary data were collected by interview method by canvassing schedules designed for the survey. In this study in case of land utilisation pattern, it is observed that, 68 per cent of total land in the study areas was cultivated. In the localized areas, land utilization was positively associated with level of irrigation. Gross cropped area for the wet land in all the study areas was ranging between 62 acres and 65 acres of land irrespective of their levels of development. Whereas cropping intensity was found to be more in non-localised area – 154.8 acres (where well and tanks are the main source of irrigation). Regarding cropping pattern, it was found that paddy, maize, pulses and jowar were the major crops grown in larger areas, whereas the commercial crops were grown in lesser areas when compared to that of food crops. Thus, the study has revealed that land utilization, cropping intensity and cropping pattern in wet, irrigated dry and unirrigated land differ from village to village and farm size. The study also revealed that gross farm income from all the selected crops was increasing as the level of irrigation increases.

Acharya, Lodha and Solanki (1990)[37] have attempted to study irrigation impact on cropping pattern, land use pattern and yields of crops in the command area of Guda irrigation project located in Bundi district of Rajasthan. This study was based on the primary data collected from 150 farmers coming under the two minors of the left and right bank canals of Guda project. Some secondary data was also collected from the offices of the irrigation department. The study found that cultivated area has increased by 20.6 per cent and the cropping intensity has increased from 70 per cent to 151 per cent during period of 26 years (1956-59 to 1984-85). The cropping pattern was found to be shifted in favour of wheat, sugarcane, barley, gram and jowar. The yields of all crops were found to have increased manifold.

Mishra (1990)[38] attempted to study how irrigation water can be utilized more effectively so that the cultivators can add to the productivity and pay full cost of irrigation by way of revenue in the Orissa state. He used both primary and secondary data for analysis. A sample survey was undertaken in four different regions predominantly irrigated districts of the Orissa state. He found that water rates were quite low in Orissa as compared to the cost incurred. He observed that the cropping pattern was changed for the benefit of farming due to expansion of irrigation facilities in Orissa. Area under commercial crops and HYV has increased in the irrigated area. The cropping intensity was also increased from 121 per cent to 145 per cent during the period 1970 to 1984.

Sharma and others (1990)[39] have studied cropping pattern, cropping intensity, cost-benefit analysis and income in relation of irrigated and unirrigated farms. This study was based on primary data collected from the households of irrigated and unirrigated villages of Shriganganagar district of Rajasthan. The study found that the overall cropping intensity in irrigated zone was 126 per cent as against 98 per cent in unirrigated zone. It was found in irrigated zone that commercial crops like cotton, mustard and wheat occupy remarkable part of cropped area, whereas traditional crops like jowar, bajra, and gram cover bulk of the cropped area in unirrigated zone. It was observed that irrigation leads to mechanization, modernization and replacement of human labour. Hired labour found to have replaced family labour in irrigated zone. It was also found that the rate of change in income due to unit change in cropped area was more than four times in irrigated zone as compared to unirrigated zone.

Dhawan (1991)[40] has studied irrigation impact on intensity of cropping. The all-India changes in intensity of cropping and irrigation were reviewed and results of regression analysis based on time series data for the period 1950-87 were presented. Cross-section of data for 14 states were analyzed through regression methods for the seven points of time, namely,

1953-57, 1958-62, 1963-67, 1968-72, 1973-77, 1978-82 and 1983-87. The basic framework for assessing the relationship between intensity of cropping and irrigation, the study has used the multiple regression technique. The study was observed that the evidence was in favour of the hypothesis that the impact of irrigation on intensity of cropping remains more or less the same over time, somewhere between 0.39 and 0.46. It was observed from the statewise impact of irrigation on cropping intensity that the impact has turned out to be below the all India level which was in the range of 0.46 - 0.66, in Gujarat, Haryana and Tamil Nadu. In four states of Uttar Pradesh, Punjab, Rajasthan and Madhya Pradesh the impact was at an average level. Only Maharashtra and Karnataka both in the Deccan plateau, show above all India impact of irrigation.

Raghuvanshi and others (1991)[41] have studied the socio-economic impact of irrigation management on employment and farm income. This study was based on primary data collected from 57 farmers of 9 villages under Debathau distributory of Salawa command in Meerut district of Uttar Pradesh. The study found that the level of education of farmers influences the adoption of irrigation management technology and income. It was also found that income level goes hand in hand with farmers technical knowledge of irrigation water management technology. A farmer with more knowledge of irrigation management technology is more likely to use optimum dose of water and takes interest in scientific management. The study also reveals that the employment on irrigated farmers was much higher than on unirrigated farms.

Ashturkar and Satpute (1992)[42-43] have conducted socio-economic surveys in the command area of upper Penganga project and Purna project in districts of Nanded and Parbhani of Maharashtra. In Purna project, total samples of 988 were selected for study. The sample was drawn from 32 villages of the command area of Purna irrigation project out of which a sample of 828 cultivators and 160 landless labourers was selected randomly for the study. The selection of cultivators was drawn on probability proportion of numbers of cultivators in different size groups of holdings. The data were collected for both studies by survey method. The information was collected during the year 1987-88. They studied different socio-economic factors of beneficiaries of command areas of these two projects. In upper Penganga command area they found that average employment days per working male, female and children showed that male labourers got more employment (233 days) followed by female (226 days) and children (63 days) per year. In Purna command area, they found that average employment days in case of male labourers was 223 days, followed by female (209 days) and children (55 days) per year. In case of cropping pattern, it was found that cash crops were the main group of crops occupied 43.40 per cent of the gross cropped area. The cereals and pulses had the share to the extent of 40.12 per cent and 1.17 per cent in the gross cropped area, whereas 15.09 per cent of the gross cropped area was allotted to the oilseed crops.

Dhawan (1993)[44] used time-series data in his study of trends and new te4ndencies in Indian irrigated agriculture. It was found that the impact of irrigation expansion on intensity of cropping is bound to appear higher if conventional measure of irrigation ratio is used. Further, his study also found that the impact of irrigation on intensity of cropping remains more or less same overtime, somewhere between 0.39 and 0.46. In the conventional measure of intensity of cropping, his multiple regression analysis reveals definite evidence of the close relation between irrigation development and the rise in intensity of cropping at all India level.

The regression analysis across 14 states for the pooled data for the period 1983-84 to 1987-88 shows value of cropping intensity was 0.46 percentage points. But time series analysis for the period 1950-51 to 1987-88 reveals somewhat higher impact value of irrigation namely 0.65 percentage points. The overall yield level of the irrigated segment has risen at a rate of about 2 per cent per annum in the case of Punjab, Haryana, Gujarat and Madhya Pradesh – it exceeds 3 per cent in Andhra Pradesh. Moreover, irrigation reduces yield instability, which is a gain both for farmer and the economy at large. By and large, whatever was true for all crops taken together also holds good for foodgrains group, mainly because of those group's predominant share in the irrigated as well as unirrigated segment of state agriculture. Further, this study also found that the relationship between irrigation and foodgrain production was nearly of one to one correspondence at the all India level. The estimated elasticity of foodgrains with respect to irrigation was about 1.03, signifying a proportionate relationship between foodgrains production and irrigation expansion.

Jai Prakash and Padam Chand Jain (1993)[45] in their study have attempted to examine the impact of irrigation and farm size on the investment and utilization of farm resources, the levels of input used and output produced in Etah district of Uttar Pradesh. This study was based on primary data. They had selected 30 villages from all the tahsils (6 village per tahsil) in this district. They have selected total 205 farmers which consists of 113 farmers from the irrigated villages and 92 farmers from the non-irrigated villages. Thus 40 small farmers, 42 medium farmers and 31 large farmers were selected from irrigated villages and 35 small farmers, 36 medium farmers and 21 large farmers were selected from non-irrigated villages. These selections were made through the technique of random sampling. The study was based on primary data for the year 1990-91.

The study concluded that irrigation has always shown a positive impact with the gross output as elasticities of output with respect to irrigative measures were positive and significant in almost all the cases. The irrigated farmers were having marginal benefit than the unirrigated farmers in almost all the cases.

Vaidyanathan and others (1994)[46] have studied to assess irrigation impact on productivity of land at national level and state level. They used the multiple regression technique to assess the irrigation impact. The estimates of the value of production per hectare of irrigated and unirrigated areas were based on official data on land use, irrigation, crop patterns and yield productivity was measured in terms of market value of output per unit area. The basic source of data for this study was estimates of the area and production of principal crops in

India published annually by the Directorate of Economics and Statistics, Ministry of Agriculture. Government of India.

The study concluded that the productivity of irrigated area shows a significant rising trend in a majority of states covered (eight out of thirteen) while only four showed a significant trend in rainfed areas. The differential between irrigated and rainfed yields have been rising in all the states and thus, in a large majority of states, but not all, irrigated yields was more stable than unirrigated yields.

All above studies relating to irrigation impacts are in respect of change in cropping pattern, land use pattern, cropping intensity, crop productivity, crop yield, employment and farm income etc. In the analysis of the beneficial impacts of irrigation most of the studies reveal that provision of irrigation facility to the farmers has enabled them to have a superior cropping pattern, better land use pattern, higher cropping intensity, higher per hectare productivity, more employment facility and larger gross farm income than the farmers in unirrigated area. All the results of above studies reveal favourable impact of irrigation on farm economy and ultimately on life of the rural people.

The beneficial impacts of irrigation have been studied by different researchers for various parts of India. Most of the studies are of different nature viz. micro- or macro-levels, and at different levels viz. cross-sectional and longitudinal levels. The ultimate aim of these studies was to find out the impact of irrigation on various aspects of development either at the household level or village level. All the aspects are generally touched upon are farm economy, general economic conditions, and rural development, etc.

Thus, it was also necessary to study the irrigation impact on agriculture in low arid region. Therefore the district like Osmanabad is purposively selected for the present study.

Notes and References

1. Dhawan B.D., Irrigation in India's Agricultural Development, Sage Publications India Pvt. Ltd., New Delhi, 1988, p. 64.
2. Gadgil D.R., Economic Effects of Irrigation, Report of Survey of the Direct and Indirect Benefits of Godavari and Pravara Canals,

Gokhale Institute of Politics and Economics, Pune, 1948, pp. 1-135.

3. Basu S.K. and Mukherjee, Evaluation of Damodhar Canal (1959-60), Asia Publishing House, Bombay, 1963, pp. 1-138.
4. Diwakar Jha, Evaluation of Benefits of Irrigation Tribeni Canal Report, Orient Longman, Bombay, 1967, pp. 1-205.
5. First Maharashtra State Irrigation Commission, Government of Maharashtra, 1962.
6. Bashir A Desai and Thingalaya N.K., Irrigation factor and Yield Variability in Rice Growing Districts in *India, Indian Journal of Agricultural Economics,* Vol. XX, No. 3, July-September, 1965, pp. 63,64.
7. Kahlon A.S., Miglani S.S. and Hanwant Sing, A Comparative Analysis of Dry and Irrigated Farming in Ferozepur District, Punjab, *Indian Journal of Agricultural Economics,* Vol. XXVI, No. 4, 1971, pp. 318, 226.
8. Moorti T.V., Impact of Different Sources of Irrigation on Input-Output Relationship, Cropping Pattern and Farm Practices, Seminar Series XIII, Role of Irrigation in the Development of India's Agricultural, Indian Society of Agricultural Economics, Bombay, 1976, pp. 99-103.
9. Patil R.G., Suryawanshi S.D. and Kapse P.M., Socio-Economic Survey of Girna Irrigation Project in Jalgaon District (Maharashtra), Mahatma Phule Krishi Vidyapeeth, Rahuri (Maharashtra), 1978.
10. Pandey M.P., The Impact of Irrigation on Rural Development : A Case Study, Concept Publishing Company, New Delhi, 1979, pp. 191.
11. Mishra G.P. and Vivekananda M., Impact of Canal Irrigation in Rural Areas: A Case Study of Bellary District, in M.V. Nadkarni (edited), Impact of Irrigation Studies of Canal, Well and Tank Irrigation in Karnataka, Himalaya Publishing Company, Bombay, part III, 1979, pp. 1-114.
12. Meti T.K., Tungabhadra Irrigation, Strategy and Accelerator of Development, Vol. 1, Karnataka University, Dharwad, 1977.
13. Patil P.G., Suryawanshi S.D. and Kapase P.M., An Investigation into Socio-Economic Conditions in Ghod Irrigation Project Area

(Maharashtra), Mahatma Phule Krishi Vidyapeeth, Rahuri, 1980, pp. 15-107.

14. Patel A.S., Irrigation – Its Employment Impact in the Command Areas of Medium Irrigation Projects in Gujarat, *Indian Journal of Agricultural Economics,* Vol. XXXVI, No. 4, 1981.

15. Selvarajan and Subramanian, Economic Impacts of Resource use optimization and Water Augmentation in Farms of Parambikulam Aliyar Project, Region, *Indian Journal of Agricultural Economics,* Vol. XXXVI, No. 1, January-March 1981, pp. 89-100.

16. Alexandar A.C., Agricultural Development and Social Transformation, *Journal of Rural Development,* Vol. No.1. January 1982, pp. 1-71.

17. Satpathy T., Irrigation and Economic Development, Ashish Publishing House, New Delhi, 1984, pp. 148-170.

18. Jha U.M., "Irrigation and Agricultural Development", Deep and Deep Publishing, New Delhi, 1984, pp. 135-214.

19. Azad M.P., Singh R.I., Yadav R.N. and Singh C.P., Economic Efficiency of Tubewell Irrigation in Kanpur District, Uttar Pradesh (A Case Study), *Indian Journal of Agricultural Economics,* Vol. XXXIX, No. 3, July-September, 1984, pp. 552.

20. Sidhu D.S., Ramesh Chand and Kaul J.K., An Economic Analysis of Various Sources of Irrigation in Punjab, *Indian Journal of Agricultural Economics,* Vol. XXXIX, No. 3, July-September, 1984, pp. 506-511.

21. Giri A.K. and Malik, Some Economic Aspects of Public Source of Irrigation – A Comparison with Private Source of Irrigation, *Indian Journal of Agricultural Economics,* Vol. XXXIX, No. 3, July-September, 1984, pp. 512-520.

22. Jawahar Thakur and Praduman Kumar, Comparative Study of Economic Efficiency of Different Irrigation Systems in Western Uttar Pradesh, *Indian Journal of Agricultural Economics,* Vol. XXXIX, No. 3, July-September, 1984, pp. 521-527.

23. Sisodia J.S., An Economic Analysis of Farm Development Programme – A Case Study of Chambal Command Area Development Project, Madhya Pradesh, *Indian Journal of Agricultural Economics,* Vol. XXXIX, No. 1, January-March, 1978, pp. 93-99.

24. Suryawanshi S.D. and Kapse P.M., Impact of Ghod Irrigation Project on Employment of Female Agricultural Labour, *Indian Journal of Agricultural Economics,* Vol. 40, No. 3, July-September, 1985, pp. 240-244.
25. Dhongade M.P., Suryawanshi S.D. and Deshmukh P.D., Farmers attitude Survey in Khadakwasala Command Area (Maharashtra), Mahatma Phule Agricultural University, Rahuri, 1986, pp. 1-63.
26. Vasudeva Rao, Rural Development Through Irrigation, Ashish Publishing House, New Delhi, 1987, pp. 27-133.
27. Gurjar Ram Kumar, Irrigation for Agricultural Modernization, Scientific Publishers, Jodhpur, 1987.
28. Dhawan B.D., How Stables is Indian Irrigated Agriculture, *Economic and Political Weekly,* Vol. XXII, No. 39, 26 September, 1987, p. A93.
29. Dhawan B.D., Impact of Irrigation on Farm Economy in High Rainfall Areas. The Kal Project, *Economic and Political Weekly,* Vol. XXIII, No. 52-53, December 24-31, 1988, pp. A-173 – A-180.
30. Sharma T.C. and Crutinho, Growth of Irrigation and Its Impact on Crop Land use and Crop Productivity in Karnataka in Shinde S.D. (Edited), Reading in Irrigated Farming, 1988, pp. 181-198.
31. Kullur M.S., Irrigation and Economic Development, Chugh Publications, Allahabad, 1988.
32. Dhawan B.D., Irrigation in India's Agricultural Development – Productivity, Stability and Equity, Sage Publishers, New Delhi, 1988, pp. 26-29.
33. Sharma R.K., Moorti T.V. and Sharma A.K., Resources Use Variability on Irrigated and Unirrigated Farms in Mandi District of Himachal Pradesh, *Indian Journal of Agricultural Economics,* Vol. 69, , 1988-89, pp. 40-48.
34. Pawar C.T., Impact of Irrigation – A Regional Perspective, Himalaya Publishing House, Bombay, 1989.
35. Ramakrishna K. S. and Deshpande R. S., Irrigation Impact on Employment and Income, *Agricultural Situation in India,* Vol. XLIV, No. 10, 10 January, 1990, pp. 797-802.
36. Renuka C., Irrigation and Rural Development, A Study in Kadam Project of Andhra Pradesh, Ph.D. Thesis, Kakatiya University, Warangal (A.P.), September, 1990, pp. 6-244.

37. Acharya S. S., Lodha N. R. and Solanki A.S., In Water Management Problems and Prospects in Command Areas, Edited by Jaspalsing and Others, Himanshu Publications, Udaipur, 1990, p. 113.

38. Mishra K.M., Irrigation and Economic Development, Ashish Publishing House, New Delhi, 1990.

39. Sharma P.M., Bhati R.S. and Shekhawat R.S., Some Magnitudes and Directions of Irrigational Effects on Farm Economy of Shriganganagar District, Rajasthan, in 'Water Management – Problems and Prospects in Command Areas', Edited by Jaspalsing, Himanshu Publications, Udaipur, 1990, p. 169.

40. Dhawan B.D., Role of Irrigation in Raising Intensity of Cropping, *Journal of Indian School of Political Economy,* Vol. III, No. 4, October-December, 1991, pp. 632-671.

41. Raghuvanshi C.S., Madhuresh Chandra and Gupta, Socio-Economic Impact of Irrigation Management on Employment and Farm Income : An Empirical Study, *Water Management,* Vol. 1, No. 1, July, 1991 p. 37.

42. Ashturkar B.W. and Satpute T.G., Socio-Economic Survey of Upper Penganga Command Areas, Marathwada Agricultural University, Parbhani, 1992.

43. Ashturkar B.V. and Satpute T.G., Evaluation Survey of Purna Command Area, Marathwada Agricultural University, Parbhani, 1992.

44. Dhawan B.D., Trends and New Tendencies in Indian Irrigated Agriculture, Commonwealth Publishers, New Delhi, 1993, pp. 15, 21, 79, 219.

45. Jai Prakash and Padamchand Jain, Role of Irrigation in Stabilising Agricultural Production, Radha Publications, New Delhi, 1993, pp. 151-157.

46. Vaidyanathan A., Asha Krishnakumar, Rajagopal A. and Varatharajan D., Impact of Irrigation on Productivity of Land, *Journal of Indian School of Political Economy,* Vol. VI, No. 4, October-December, 1994, pp. 601-643.

Chapter 4

Impact of Irrigation on Agriculture – A Macro-Level Analysis

Agricultural growth has been made one of the foremost components of development strategy in India. Within the overall strategy of agricultural growth, irrigation has been accepted as major programme for modernizing Indian agriculture. Irrigation has been assigned such a crucial role because this is a single most important factor which can facilitate the further utilization of our scarce farm land resource and can facilitate acceptance of improved technology at the farm level[1].

The necessity of irrigation arises because nearly 70 per cent of the country's gross cropped area depends exclusively on rainfall which is unevenly distributed both in space and time. Thus, irrigation is deemed necessary for maximum production of most of the crops especially in the arid and semi-arid regions and even in areas of high rainfall it is necessary for multiple cropping. According to Indian Council of Agricultural Research, production of irrigated crop is on an average 50-100 per cent higher than that of the unirrigated crop in the same area.

Due to irrigation, India has been in a comfortable position with regard to availability of food-grains over last three decades. The country's granaries are now more than full and there is enough grain stored up to prevent any famine. In all probability, it was the protective motive which triggered off the development of irrigated agriculture in low and medium rainfall regions, whereas the desire to augment crop output through an additional irrigated crop in the dry season arose much later. Any way, the productive motive now dominates the development of irrigation in India. The aim is not only additional cropping during the dry season but also substantial step-up in crop yield through the simultaneous use of irrigation, chemical fertilizers, high yielding varieties of seeds, etc. In this yield raising effort, irrigation acquires primacy because the agro-climate conditions are not suitable to use the chemical fertilizers in rainfed farming.

In the precise context of agricultural production, the direct effects of irrigation can be said to consist of (a) Area or Acreage effect, (b) Crop pattern effect, (c) Per hectare yield effect, and (d) Total output effect. Firstly, irrigation leads to an expansion of gross cropped area by making double and multiple cropping possible. Secondly, it raises yield per unit of area by inducing the use of other complementary yield raising inputs i.e. fertilizers, pesticides, high yielding variety seeds, etc. Thirdly, for given set of output and input prices, irrigation may raise production by enabling farmers to allocate their lands to high yielding and high valued crops. Lastly, irrigation may raise production by highly utilizing the land resources. Investment in irrigation becomes an indirect investment for eradicating much of the rural poverty. Therefore, the development of irrigation is found to be emphasized, with irrigation acting as a Iynchpin in the entire effort directed towards rural development in India.

Certain important studies undertaken on this issue may briefly be summarized. Ghosh has indicated the pervasive character of irrigation impact that operates through interaction of area, yield and crop pattern phenomena[2]. Bhardwaj has shown that irrigation can raise the productivity in three ways, i.e. by making possible multiple cropping, by increasing the yield per unit cost and allowing the production of more lucrative crops[3].

Gadgil concluded that the main direct effect of irrigation is to put the previously cultivated lands to new uses or to make them more productive in former uses or to bring new lands under use for the first time[4]. Mukhopadhyaya illustrated this through the positive and statistically significant co-efficient for interaction between irrigation and fertilizers[5]. Singh *et al.*, as well as Gaikwad and Desai have shown that the provision of irrigation causes higher crop yields per unit of land and generates increased agricultural incomes[6]. Similarly, the number of scholars from various regions of India have all confirmed the productive role of irrigation while highlighting its contribution for higher rates of agricultural growth. Now each of these effects as they operate in Osmanabad district are discussed in the present chapter.

Thus an attempt has been made in the present chapter to assess the impact of irrigation on agriculture in Osmanabad district. In this chapter an attempt has been made to assess the macro level impact of irrigation on agriculture in all talukas of Osmanabad district and district as a whole during 1982-83 to 1995-96. The chapter has been divided into five parts. The first part deals with the impact of irrigation on cultivated area i.e. growth in net, total, and double cropped area. The second part deals with the impact of irrigation on intensity of cropping. In the third part an attempt has been made to study the impact of irrigation on cropping pattern. In the fourth part the impact of irrigation on yield has been dealt with and in the fifth part, an attempt has been made to study the correlation between irrigation and total crop production. The statistical techniques used in this chapter are discussed in introduction.

For assessing the impact of irrigation on crop pattern, eleven main crops, covering large areas and having significant acreage under irrigation have been considered. These are paddy, jowar (kharif), bajra, tur, sugarcane and oilseeds of kharif season, and wheat, jowar (rabi), gram, oilseeds and fruits and vegetables of rabi season.

AREA EFFECT OF IRRIGATION

An impact of irrigation through which it increases the gross cropped area is called its "area effect" or "cultivated area effect".

This phenomenon consists of three components, first increase in net sown area which becomes possible on account of irrigation facilitating reclamation of waste land and extending cultivation to hitherto uncultivated land, second increase in double cropped area which is directly related to the irrigation facilities in any region. Thus double cropping is possible only with the development of irrigation facilities and shows how many times a piece of land is used for crop production. Thus, lastly, it increases gross cropped area, that arises out of an irrigation encouraging the intensive cultivation of currently cultivated land, that is the index of cropping intensity. Both these components through positive interaction lead to absolute increase in gross cropped area and thereby "area effect" or "cultivated area effect".

Net Cropped Area

The first component of "acreage effect" operated in Punjab and in regions served by Rajasthan canals, where the cultivated areas increased significantly on account of reclamation of waste land and progressive decline in fallow land, consequent upon the availability of irrigation water[7]. But in district like Osmanabad of the Maharashtra State this cultivated area does not seem to have increased much long with the extension of irrigation facility. The total geographical area, net cropped area, double cropped area and total cropped area for six talukas in the Osmanabad district and district as a whole during 1982-83 to 1995-96 has been shown in Table 1. And percentage share of net cropped area to total geographical area has been calculated for six talukas in the district and for district as a whole during 1982-83 to 1995-96 and is presented in the Table 2. It is seen from the Tables 1 and 2 that in the study area, the percentage of net cropped area to total geographical area was 74.98 per cent in 1982-83, while in 1995-96 it was 79.16 per cent. Thus, during last fourteen years (1982-83 to 1995-96), there was increase of 4.18 per cent in net cropped area in Osmanabad district. This shows that, there was positive increase in irrigation and net cultivated area of the district. But this is the small increase (4.18 per cent) in net cropped area during the last

Table 1

Taluka-wise Total Geographical Area and Cultivated Cropped Area in Osmanabad District (1982-83 to 1995-96)

(Area in hundred hectares)

Taluka / District	*Year*	*Total geogra-phical area*	*Net cropped area*	*Area cropped more than once*	*Total cropped area*	*Net irrigated area*
Osmanabad	1982-83	1326	1036	43	1079	188
Kallam		1227	948	30	978	78
Omerga		1465	1286	44	1330	73
Tuljapur		1524	800	40	840	185
Paranda		1055	894	51	945	103
Bhoom		887	648	21	669	40
District		7484	5612	229	5841	667
Osmanabad	1986-87	1326	1093	69	1162	194
Kallam		1227	895	80	975	124
Omerga		1465	1234	269	1503	120
Tuljapur		1524	931	206	1137	228
Paranda		1055	926	169	1095	110
Bhoom		887	617	62	679	86
District		7484	5696	855	6551	862
Osmanabad	1990-91	1326	1094	143	1237	216
Kallam		1227	979	146	1125	148
Omerga		1465	1208	333	1541	176
Tuljapur		1524	1073	407	1480	356
Paranda		1055	963	291	1254	120
Bhoom		887	665	99	764	120
District		7484	5982	1419	7401	1136
Osmanabad	1995-96	1326	1115	122	1237	177
Kallam		1227	727	255	982	116
Omerga		1465	1269	235	1504	122
Tuljapur		1524	1164	312	1476	317
Paranda		1055	950	298	1248	189
Bhoom		887	700	255	955	79
District		7484	5925	1477	7402	1000
Percentage change during 1982-83 to 1995-96		5.28	544.98	26.72	49.92	

Source: Socio-Economic Review and District Statistical Abstract of Osmanabad District, Directorate of Economics and Statistics, Government of Maharashtra, 1985-86, 1989-90, 1990-91 and 1998-99.

fourteen years. This shows that the scope for bringing new lands under plough is limited and there has been deterioration in the already existing sown area.

It is also seen from the Table 1 that, in 1982-83 the irrigated area in Osmanabad district was 66,700 hectares and the net cultivated area was 5,61,200 hectares. But in 1995-96 while irrigated area went up to 1,00,000 hectares i.e. it was increased by 49.92 per cent, the cultivated area went up to 5,92,500 hectares, i.e. nearby increase of 5.28 per cent. Thus the growth of irrigation in Osmanabad district has, therefore, little impact on the first component of area effect.

A perusal of Table 2 shows, that during the last fourteen years (1982-83 to 1995-96) there was a gradual increase in net cultivated area. During last fourteen years, the percentage share of net cropped area to total geographical area in the district has registered an increase of 4.18 per cent. The talukas of Tuljapur (23.89 per cent), Bhoom (5.87 per cent) Osmanabad (5.97 per cent) and Paranda (5.32 per cent) have registered higher percentage increase in net cultivated area than the

Table 2
Percentage Share of Net Cropped Area to Total Geographical Area in Osmanabad District (1982-83 to 1995-96)

(Area in hundred hectares)

Taluka	*1982-83*	*1986-87*	*1990-91*	*1995-96*	*Change in Percentage (1982-83 to 1995-96)*
Osmanabad	78.12	82.42	82.50	84.09	(5.97)
Kallam	77.26	72.94	79.79	59.25	(-18.01)
Omerga	87.78	84.23	82.46	86.62	(-1.16)
Tuljapur	52.49	61.08	70.41	76.38	(23.89)
Paranda	84.73	87.77	91.28	90.05	(5.32)
Bhoom	73.05	69.56	74.97	78.92	(5.87)
District	74.98	76.11	79.93	79.16	(4.18)

N.B. : Figures in the brackets show change in percentage share of Net Cropped Area to Total Geographical Area during (1982-83 to 1995-96)

Source: Estimated from the Data Collected from Socio-Economic Review and District Statistical Abstract of Osmanabad District, Directorate of Economics and Statistics, Government of Maharashtra, 1985-86, 1989-90, 1990-91 and 1998-99.

district as a whole, and talukas of Kallam (-18.01) and Omerga (-1.16) have registered decrease in net cultivated area.

This increase may be due to the land reclamation going on especially in the talukas of Tuljapur, Paranda, Osmanabad and Bhoom and due to increase in irrigation facilities. The decrease in net cultivated area in Kallam taluka may be due to construction of a major project (Manjra irrigation project) on Manjra river. Any way, a perusal of tables 4.1 and 4.2 shows that, during the last fourteen years, the growth of irrigation in Osmanabad district and its four talukas have positive impact on net cropped area.

Gross Cropped Area

More important than this increase in cultivated area, is the second component of "area effect", that is, increase in gross cropped area resulting from the higher crop intensity. The provision of irrigation facilities and other inputs provides an opportunity to use the available land resource more intensively. With the development of irrigation, gross cropped area has also increased in the study area. Percentage share of gross cropped area to total geographical area (from 1982-83 to 1995-96) has been calculated for Osmanabad district and for its talukas and is presented in Table 3. It is seen from the Table 3 that, during the last fourteen years (1982-83 to 1995-96), the percentage share of gross cropped area to total geographical area has increased from 78.04 per cent to 98.89 per cent in the study area. Thus, the growth of irrigation in the study area has, therefore, positive impact on the gross cropped area. This shows that there was an intensive use of land in this district.

A perusal of Table 3 shows that, during last fourteen years, the percentage share of gross cropped area to total geographical area in the study area has registered an increase of 20.85 per cent. Tuljapur (41.73 per cent), Bhoom (32.35 per cent), Paranda (28.72 per cent), Omerga (12.49 per cent), Osmanabad (11.98 per cent) and Kallam (0.33 per cent) talukas have recorded marginal increase in gross cropped area. Thus, this shows that all talukas in Osmanabad district and district as a whole have recorded positive change in the percentage share of gross cropped area during the last fourteen years.

Table 3
Percentage Share of Gross Cropped Area to Total Geographical Area in Osmanabad District (1982-83 to 1995-96)

(Area in hundred hectares)

Taluka	*1982-83*	*1986-87*	*1990-91*	*1995-96*	*Change in Percentage (1982-83 to 1995-96)*
Osmanabad	81.37	87.69	93.29	93.29	(11.92)
Kallam	79.70	79.46	91.69	80.03	(0.33)
Omerga	90.10	102.59	105.19	102.59	(12.49)
Tuljapur	55.12	74.61	97.11	96.85	(41.73)
Paranda	89.57	103.79	118.86	118.29	(28.72)
Bhoom	75.42	76.55	86.13	107.77	(32.35)
District	78.04	87.53	98.89	98.89	(20.85)

N.B.: Figures in the brackets show change in percentage share of Gross Cropped Area to Total Geographical Area during (1982-83 to 1995-96)

Source: Estimated from the Data Collected from Socio-Economic Review and District Statistical Abstract of Osmanabad District, Directorate of Economics and Statistics, Government of Maharashtra, 1985-86, 1989-90, 1990-91 and1998-99.

Among the talukas in the district, Tuljapur (41.73 per cent), Bhoom (32.35 per cent) and Paranda (28.72 per cent) talukas have recorded higher increase in gross cropped area than the district average (20.85 per cent). And rest of the talukas, namely, Omerga (12.49 per cent), Osmanabad (11.98 per cent) and Kallam (0.33 per cent) have recorded lower increase in gross cropped area than the district average. Thus, the growth of irrigation in talukas of Osmanabad district and district as a whole has, therefore, positive impact on gross cropped area.

A perusal of Table 3 shows that the percentage of gross cropped area to geographical area in the study region was about 78.04 per cent during 1982-83. This shows that, there were also more utilized land resources in the district. The four talukas, namely, Omerga (90.10), Paranda (89.57), Osmanabad (81.37) and Kallam (79.70) recorded higher percentage share of gross cropped area than that the district average in 1982-83, while the talukas of Bhoom (75.42) and Tuljapur (55.12) had low percentage of gross cultivated area. While in 1995-96, the percentage of gross cropped area to geographical area in the study area was about 98.89 per cent. This shows that there was intensive use of land in the district. Three talukas, namely, Paranda (118.29), Bhoom (107.77) and Omerga (102.59) have recorded higher percentage than the district average in 1995-96, and three talukas, namely, Kallam (80.03), Osmanabad (93.29), and Tuljapur (96.85) had low percentage of gross cultivated area than the district average.

Thus during last fourteen years, there was 20.85 per cent increase in percentage of gross cultivated area to geographical area in the district and the district recorded positive changes in gross cropped area. And the talukas, namely, Tuljapur (41.73), Bhoom (32.35), Paranda (28.75), Omerga (12.49), Osmanabad (11.98) and Kallam (0.33) have experienced increase in percentage share of gross cropped area to geographical area. The district Osmanabad and almost all talukas of this district have recorded positive changes in gross cropped area during the period under study.

Double Cropped Area

Area under double cropping shows that how many times a piece of land is used for the crop production or how intensively the agriculture land is being utilized. Double cropping is possible only with the development of irrigation facilities. Percentage share of double-cropped area to net-cropped area (from 1982-83 to 1995-96) was calculated for Osmanabad district and for its talukas and is presented in Table 4.

It is seen from the table 4.1, that during last fourteen years, there was increase of 49.92 per cent in net irrigated area and 500 per cent increase in double cropped area in the district. Thus, the growth of irrigation in the district has, therefore, more impact on second component of area effect. At the same time it is also seen from the Table 4 that percentage of double cropped area to net cropped area has increased by 20.85 per cent during last fourteen years. Thus this fact also shows that the growth of irrigation in the district has positive impact on the double cropped area and there was an intensive use of land in the district.

A perusal of Table 4 shows that the percentage share of double cropped area to net cropped area in the district was 4.08 per cent in the period 1982-83, and in the talukas of Paranda (5.70 per cent), Tuljapur (5.00 per cent), Osmanabad (4.15 per cent), it was higher than that of district's average. And remaining talukas, namely, Omerga (3.42 per cent), Bhoom (3.24 per cent) and Kallam (3.16 per cent) have the lower percentage than the district average of 4.08 per cent. While by the 1995-96, the percentage share of double cropped area to net cropped area was 24.93 per cent in the Osmanabad district. The talukas, namely, Bhoom (36.43), Kallam (35.07), Paranda (31.37), Tuljapur (26.80) have higher percentage share of double cropped area than the district average. While Osmanabad (10.94) and Omerga (18.52) talukas have recorded lower percentage share of double cropped area to net cropped area than the district average of 24.93 per cent.

Table 4
Percentage share of Double Cropped Area to Net Cropped Area in Osmanabad District (1982-83 to 1995-96)

(Area in hundred hectares)

Tahsil/Year	*1982-83*	*1986-87*	*1990-91*	*1995-96*	*Change in Percentage (1982-83 to 1995-96)*
Osmanabad	4.15	6.31	13.07	10.94	(6.79)
Kallam	3.16	8.94	14.91	35.07	(31.91)
Omerga	3.42	21.80	27.57	18.52	(15.10)
Tuljapur	5.00	22.13	37.93	26.80	(21.80)
Paranda	5.70	18.23	30.22	31.37	(25.67)
Bhoom	3.24	10.05	14.89	36.43	(33.19)
District	4.08	15.01	23.72	24.93	(20.85)

N.B.: Figures in the brackets show the change in percentage share of Double Cropped Area to Net Cropped Area during (1982-83 to 1995-96)

Source: Estimated from the Data Collected from Socio-Economic Review and District Statistical Abstract of Osmanabad District, Directorate of Economics and Statistics, Government of Maharashtra, 1985-86, 1989-90, 1990-91 and 1998-99.

Thus, during the last fourteen years, (1982-83 to 1995-96) there was 20.85 per cent increase in the percentage share of double cropped area to net cropped area in the study area. And during the same period the talukas, namely, Bhoom (33.19), Kallam (31.91), Paranda (25.67) and Tuljapur (21.80) recorded higher increase in the percentage share of double cropped area to net cropped area than the district average of 20.85 per cent. The remaining talukas viz. Osmanabad (6.79), Omerga (15.10) recorded lower percentage share than that of district average. This shows that, all the talukas in the Osmanabad district and the district as a whole recorded positive change in the percentage share of double cropped area during last fourteen years. Double cropping is possible only with the development of irrigation facilities especially under the semi-arid conditions of this district. It has been observed that there was continuous increase in double cropped area in all talukas and the district as a whole during last fourteen years. Thus, this shows that, the growth of irrigation in Osmanabad district and in almost all its talukas during period under study have positive impact on cultivated area.

CROPPING INTENSITY INDEX

Intensity of cropping is considered as an indicator of the degree of intensity to which land is used for agricultural purpose. It is the ratio between the gross cropped area and the net cultivated area usually expressed in percentage terms. How many crops a cultivator can produce in a year on his land or in other words to what extent a cultivator will practice double cropping. Intensity of cropping will depend on several factors, such as availability of irrigation water, use of manures and the nature of crops which he decides to grow. As regards the irrigation water and manure, it may be argued that improvement in their use induce intensity of cropping. As regards the nature of crops, it may be pointed out that there are crops which can be combined and can be grown on the same plot of land one after the other in different seasons during the same agricultural year. There are certain crops like sugarcane, which are of long duration crops, do not permit another crop in the same year[8].

The fact is that irrigation alone does not constitute the sole factor determining the intensity of cropping.

Intensity of cropping is a single indicator of the extent of multiple cropping on land under plough, that is the number of crops being raised in a sequence. If a piece of land is cultivated once in a year, the index number would be 100 per cent and twice or thrice it would be more than 100 per cent. Most important is that increase in cultivated area, is the second component of "area effect", that is, increase in gross cropped area resulting from higher crop intensity. The net cropped area, gross cropped area, area cropped more than once and net irrigated area (during 1982-83 to 1995-96) for the district Osmanabad and its talukas has been shown in Table 1. The intensity of cropping for the six talukas in the district and district as a whole has been calculated for the period of fourteen years (1982-83 to 1995-96) and is presented in Table 5 and in Graph 1. It is seen from this table and graph that throughout the period under study i.e. from 1982-83 to 1995-96, the intensity of cropping during 1982-83 was only 104.08 per cent and it rose to 124.93 per cent in 1995-96. Thus, there was 20.85 percentage

Table 5

Intensity of Cropping in Osmanabad District (1982-83 to 1995-96)

Taluka	*1982-83*	*1986-87*	*1990-91*	*1995-96*	*Change in Percentage (1982-83 to 1995-96)*
Osmanabad	104.15	106.31	113.07	110.94	(6.79)
Kallam	103.16	108.94	114.91	135.07	(31.91)
Omerga	103.42	121.80	127.57	118.52	(15.10)
Tuljapur	105.00	122.13	137.93	126.80	(21.80)
Paranda	105.70	118.25	130.22	131.37	(25.67)
Bhoom	103.24	110.05	114.89	136.43	(33.19)
District	104.08	115.05	123.72	124.93	(20.85)

N.B. : Figures in the brackets show the change in intensity of cropping during 1982-83 to 1995-96.

Source: Estimated on the basis of Data Collected from Socio-Economic Review and District Statistical Abstract of Osmanabad District, Directorate of Economics and Statistics, Government of Maharashtra, 1985-86, 1989-90, 1990-91 and 1998-99.

points increase in the intensity of cropping during the last fourteen years. From 1982-83 onwards there has been gradual increase in the intensity of cropping.

In 1982-83, highest intensity of cropping was recorded in the Paranda taluka (105.70 per cent). Tuljapur (105.70) and Osmanabad talukas (104.15) have also recorded higher percentage of cropping intensity than the district average. In these talukas irrigation facilities were highly developed. The talukas, which recorded low percentage of cropping intensity than the district average, are Kallam (103.16), Bhoom (103.24), and Omerga (103.42).

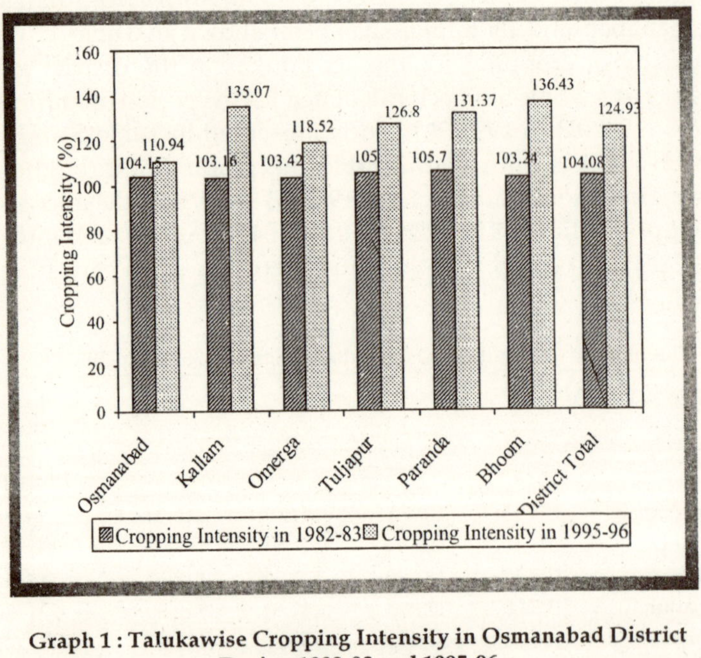

Graph 1 : Talukawise Cropping Intensity in Osmanabad District During 1982-83 and 1995-96

In the year 1995-96, Bhoom taluka (136.43) recorded the highest percentage of cropping intensity followed by Kallam (135.07), Paranda (131.37) and Tuljapur (126.80) talukas. They also recorded higher percentage of cropping intensity than the district average of 124.93 percent. Thus, these figures show that, the intensity of cropping is higher in those talukas where irrigation facilities are highly developed. To some extent cropping intensity is also dependent on the cropping pattern. If a substantial proportion of the cultivated area is under long standing crops like sugarcane the intensity will be low. But the farmers in the study area find growing of sugarcane more remunerative than raising consequently two or three crops. The talukas, which recorded less percentage of cropping intensity than the district average (124.93 per cent), are Osmanabad (110.94 per cent) and Omerga (118.52 per cent).

A perusal of Table 5 and Graph 1 shows that during last fourteen years, there was 20.85 per cent increase in district's intensity of cropping. It is also observed that almost all the talukas have recorded a gradual increase in cropping intensity during the last fourteen years. The talukas of Bhoom (33.19 per cent), Kallam (31.19 per cent), Paranda (25.67 per cent), Tuljapur (21.80 per cent), Omerga (15.10 per cent), and Osmanabad (6.79 per cent) have recorded increase in cropping intensity. Thus the growth of irrigation in Osmanabad district and its all talukas during last fourteen years have positive impact on cropping intensity.

From the Table 5, it is observed that the talukas could be grouped into two categories, those having more increase in intensity and those having less increase in intensity than the district average increase. During last fourteen years, it is observed that, four talukas, namely, Bhoom (33.19 per cent), Kallam (31.19 per cent), Paranda (25.67 per cent) and Tuljapur (21.80 per cent) have recorded higher increase in intensity of cropping than the district average of 20.85 per cent. Two talukas, namely, Osmanabad (6.79 per cent) and Omerga (15.10 per cent) have registered an increase less than the district average.

A perusal of Table 15 showing the intensity of irrigation and Table 5 showing the intensity of cropping reveals that there is a high correlation between both the aspects. These figures show that intensity of cropping is a function of irrigation because generally intensity of cultivation is higher with the higher intensity of irrigation and that it is lower with lower irrigation. In 1982, the intensity of irrigation was low consequently the intensity of cropping was also low. But by 1995-96, there was increase in intensity of irrigation in the district and talukas of the district. Consequently there was also increase in cropping intensity. Thus, intensity of irrigation is comparable with intensity of cropping. Intensity of cropping is invariably higher than the intensity of irrigation. This is so because double cropping is practiced not only on irrigated but also on unirrigated lands.

Thus, from this, it might be reasonable to contend that "area effect" of irrigation as it operates in context of enhancing the effectiveness of this crop intensity rise has been positive in Osmanabad district.

IMPACT OF IRRIGATION ON CROPPING PATTERN

The third aspect of irrigation impact on agriculture in the Osmanabad district is the changing crop pattern as evidenced in the district in recent years. Cropping pattern simply means the proportion of area under different crops at a point of time, whereas change in cropping pattern refers to change in proportion of area under different crops at two different points of time. Of course, all changes in cropping pattern can not be said to be irrigation induced. Some shifts in crop pattern do not take place on account of economic and institutional factors, such as urbanization, changes in food habits of the people, input requirements of crops, relative price movements of the agricultural products, state policy on subsidies and change in technology. Thus, the cropping pattern of any area is generally controlled by physical, socio-economic and technological factors. But it is often seen that irrigation is the most important factor that determines to such changes in the crop patterns and makes possible the production of more remunerative crops. For example, as Bhardwaj has pointed out that while on irrigated holdings in Punjab only 50 per cent of the cropped area was devoted to food crops, on unirrigated holdings on the other hand, 73 to 94 per cent of the cropped area went to food crops. Similarly in Tamilnadu, the irrigated holdings concentrate on paddy, a relatively more valuable crop, while the unirrigated holdings mainly produce dry grains like

'Oumbu' and 'Cholam'[9]. While classifying the effects of irrigation, Prof. D. R. Gadgil identified the change in cropping pattern as one of the direct effects of irrigation. The introduction of irrigation brings alterations in area allocations among crops. The availability of irrigation water enhances double cropped area. Farmers take more than one crop on the same piece of land and hence the crop rotation undergoes a change. Further, the proportion of area under rabi and hot weather (summer) crops also increases due to irrigation facility. Due to introduction of irrigation, the shift is observed from "low water requiring crops" to "high water requiring crops". Before introduction of irrigation, rainfed crops dominated cropping pattern. With the changes and availability of water crops like sugarcane, oilseeds, fruits etc., which require more water per unit of land, were encouraged. The availability of water changes the cost structure because of the change in the inputs. This increases the need for earning higher profits and hence proportion of area under non-foodgrains, which gives more profit, profit increase thereby alters crop pattern. As such, it may broadly be stated that, it is the irrigation expansion that plays the dominant role in the context of crop pattern changes.

There are two important agricultural seasons. The main kharif season crops sown in Osmanabad district are paddy, jowar (hybrid), bajra, tur and oilseeds (kharif), while jowar, wheat, gram, oilseeds, fruits and vegetables are sown during the rabi season. Sugarcane is annual crop, which is considered in kharif season for this study. The cropwise cultivated area and the percentage share of cropwise cultivated area in kharif and rabi seasons to gross cultivated area has been calculated for the district as a whole and for its talukas for a period of fourteen years (from 1982-83 to 1995-96) and is presented in Table 6. Similarly the percentage change in cropwise area to gross cropped area over period of fourteen years has been shown in Table 7.

Crop Pattern Effect of Irrigation : Kharif Season

Kharif crops are those crops which are grown during the monsoon period which is the wet season of the country.

Agriculture year begins in June in India. The introduction of kharif season irrigation in the study area has helped the farmers to switch over from low yielding dry crops to high yielding wet crops like paddy, sugarcane and oilseeds. Paddy is ideally suited for continuous availability of water in the field throughout its growing period. It is field-to-field irrigation system which has helped the farmers to give preference to paddy cultivation. Sugarcane cultivation with the help of perennial source of irrigation is bound to produce high output impact when introduced in low and medium rainfall areas. Kharif oilseeds are partly dependent on irrigation and which is very helpful for growing oilseeds in low rainfall time of study area. Therefore, oilseeds cultivation with the help of seasonal irrigation is also bound to have high output impact when introduced in low rainfall area of this district. A perusal of Table 6 shows that, in 1982-83, the district's cropped area under kharif season was 2,29,887 hectares and in 1995-96 it was 3,32,2186 hectares. Thus, during 1982-83 to 1995-96, there has been 44.50 per cent increase in kharif cultivated area in the district.

A perusal of Tables 6 and 7 shows that, the percentage share of area under kharif crops to the gross cropped area in the district during 1982-83 was about 39.36 per cent. In 1982, kharif jowar (16.39 per cent) occupied the highest cropped area in kharif season. Thus, kharif jowar (16.39 per cent) was the most important crop of kharif season followed by tur (9.56 per cent), oilseeds (7.63 per cent), sugarcane (2.44 per cent), paddy (2.88 per cent) and bajra (0.96 per cent). While in 1995-96, the percentage share of land under kharif crops to gross cropped area in the district was about 45.02 per cent. During last fourteen years (i.e. 1982-83 to 1995-96), percentage share of kharif cultivated area to gross cropped area in the district has increased by 5.66 per cent. In 1995-96, oilseeds occupied (15.57 per cent) highest cropped area under kharif season as it was the most favoured crop in the district followed by kharif jowar (12.83 per cent), tur (10.61 per cent), sugarcane (2.30 per cent), paddy (2.19 per cent) and bajra (1.52 per cent). There was marginal increase in the cultivated area under oilseeds (7.94 per cent), tur (1.05 per cent) and bajra (0.56 per cent), and

Table 6

Cropwise Cultivated Area and the Percentage Share of Area Under Different Crops to Gross Cropped Area in Osmanabad District (1982-83 to 1995-96)

(Area in hectares)

			Kharif Crops							Rabi Crops					
Talukas	*Year*	*Gross Cropped Area*	*Paddy*	*Jowar*	*Bajra*	*Tur*	*Sugar-Cane*	*Oil-seeds*	*Total Kharif*	*Jowar*	*Wheat*	*Gram*	*Oil-seeds*	*Fruits& Veg.*	*Total Rabi*
Osmanabad	1982-83	107838	2400	23297	330	9817	2032	4681	42557	30215	7785	8590	9253	305	56148
		(100.00)	(2.23)	(21.60)	(0.31)	(9.10)	(1.88)	(4.34)	(39.46)	(28.02)	(7.22)	(7.97)	(8.58)	(0.28)	(52.07)
	1986-87	116185	2310	28461	N.G.	9710	2175	11975	54631	32791	1990	8310	10863	339	54293
		(100.00)	(1.99)	(24.50)		(8.36)	(1.87)	(10.31)	(47.02)	(28.22)	(1.71)	(7.15)	(9.35)	(0.29)	(46.73)
	1990-91	123593	2510	28531	N.G.	11631	4658	14193	61523	26641	6621	8510	14894	694	57360
		(100.00)	(2.02)	(23.08)		(9.41)	(3.77)	(11.48)	(49.78)	(21.56)	(5.36)	(6.89)	(12.05)	(0.56)	(46.41)
	1995-96	123646	1490	24900	449	9613	5100	12623	54193	41250	3755	8009	12189	285	65488
		(100.00)	(1.21)	(20.14)	(0.36)	(7.79)	(4.12)	(10.21)	(43.83)	(33.36)	(3.04)	(6.48)	(9.86)	(0.23)	(52.96)
Kallam	1982-83	97769	1717	28369	290	9613	3775	9521	53285	12580	7604	5358	6360	350	32252
		(100.00)	(1.76)	(29.02)	(0.30)	(9.83)	(3.86)	(9.74)	(54.50)	(12.87)	(7.78)	(5.48)	(6.51)	(0.36)	(32.99)
	1986-87	97456	1030	25925	899	270	1250	2655	32029	10000	3600	6300	8677	N.G.	28577
		(100.00)	(1.06)	(26.60)	(0.92)	(0.28)	(1.28)	(2.72)	(32.87)	(10.26)	(3.69)	(6.46)	(8.90)		(29.32)
	1990-91	112516	1772	26267	13543	11300	8000	12836	73718	13543	4143	9893	15515	161	43255
		(100.00)	(1.57)	(23.34)	(12.04)	(10.04)	(7.11)	(11.41)	(65.52)	(12.04)	(3.68)	(8.79)	(13.79)	(0.14)	(38.44)
	1995-96	96078	1482	20692	3682	9361	2060	17587	54864	12776	1255	3293	11459	N.G.	28783
		(100.00)	(1.54)	(21.54)	(3.83)	(9.74)	(2.14)	(18.30)	(57.10)	(13.30)	(1.31)	(3.43)	(11.93)		(29.96)

Contd...

(Area in hectares)

Talukas	Year	Gross Cropped Area	Kharif Crops: Paddy	Jowar	Bajra	Tur	Sugar-Cane	Oil-seeds	Total Kharif	Rabi Crops: Jowar	Wheat	Gram	Oil-seeds	Fruits& Veg.	Total Rabi
Omerga	1982-83	133005	2124	28091	2103	13929	1678	17942	65867	28210	4595	6700	3822	1226	44553
		(100.00)	(1.60)	(21.12)	(1.58)	(10.47)	(1.26)	(13.49)	(49.52)	(21.21)	(3.45)	(5.04)	(2.87)	(0.92)	(33.50)
	1986-87	150299	2150	35268	2110	12540	1756	24208	78032	28410	4620	5950	5068	1206	45254
		(100.00)	(1.43)	(23.47)	(1.40)	(8.34)	(1.17)	(16.11)	(51.92)	(18.90)	(3.07)	(3.96)	(3.37)	(0.80)	(30.11)
	1990-91	154067	4010	24150	1000	22420	2275	27477	81332	21405	3639	9950	17308	1033	53335
		(100.00)	(2.60)	(15.67)	(0.65)	(14.55)	(1.48)	(17.83)	(52.79)	(13.89)	(2.36)	(6.46)	(11.23)	(0.67)	(34.62)
	1995-96	150342	5620	19905	3040	18460	3075	32139	82239	28310	4820	8490	13960	459	56039
		(100.00)	(3.74)	(13.24)	(2.02)	(12.28)	(2.05)	(21.38)	(54.70)	(18.83)	(3.21)	(5.65)	(9.29)	(0.31)	(37.27)
Tuljapur	1982-83	84007	6063	11569	2316	11240	5984	6513	43685	12664	4033	5974	2445	712	25828
		(100.00)	(7.22)	(13.77)	(2.76)	(13.38)	(7.12)	(7.75)	(52.00)	(15.07)	(4.80)	(7.11)	(2.91)	(0.85)	(30.75)
	1986-87	113699	4135	6200	1051	12391	2112	16150	42039	27075	1472	4509	18344	7099	58499
		(100.00)	(3.64)	(5.45)	(0.92)	(10.90)	(1.86)	(14.20)	(36.97)	(23.81)	(1.29)	(3.97)	(16.13)	(6.24)	(51.45)
	1990-91	147998	5944	16694	3158	20450	6983	17454	70683	27298	4423	4722	18751	6653	61847
		(100.00)	(4.02)	(11.28)	(2.13)	(13.82)	(4.72)	(11.79)	(47.76)	(18.44)	(2.99)	(3.19)	(12.67)	(4.50)	(41.79)
	1995-96	147540	6836	17819	136	18980	4175	27835	75781	27810	9413	4616	18730	7344	67913
		(100.00)	(4.63)	(12.08)	(0.09)	(12.86)	(2.83)	(18.87)	(51.36)	(18.85)	(6.38)	(3.13)	(12.69)	(4.98)	(46.03)
Paranda	1982-83	94538	540	450	260	7220	570	2390	11430	54670	4510	3320	12240	185	74925
		(100.00)	(0.57)	(0.48)	(0.28)	(7.64)	(0.60)	(2.53)	(12.09)	(57.83)	(4.77)	(3.51)	(12.95)	(0.20)	(79.25)
	1986-87	109484	588	N.G.	1433	8173	1540	12736	24470	54808	3175	7565	18094	330	83972
		(100.00)	(0.54)		(1.31)	(7.47)	(1.41)	(11.63)	(22.35)	(50.06)	(2.90)	(6.91)	(16.53)	(0.30)	(76.70)
	1990-91	125369	467	708	1839	8164	2200	13056	26434	76729	3003	3974	12345	688	96739
		(100.00)	(0.37)	(0.56)	(1.47)	(6.51)	(1.75)	(10.41)	(21.08)	(61.20)	(2.40)	(3.17)	(9.85)	(0.55)	(77.16)
	1995-96	124800	N.G.	N.G.	298	10241	1184	11610	23333	77959	5011	8139	9562	329	101000
		(100.00)			(0.24)	(8.21)	(0.95)	(9.30)	(18.70)	(62.47)	(4.02)	(6.52)	(7.66)	(0.26)	(80.93)

Contd...

(Area in hectares)

			Kharif Crops							Rabi Crops					
Talukas	*Year*	*Gross Cropped Area*	*Paddy*	*Jowar*	*Bajra*	*Tur*	*Sugar-Cane*	*Oil-seeds*	*Total Kharif*	*Jowar*	*Wheat*	*Gram*	*Oil-seeds*	*Fruits& Veg.*	*Total Rabi*
Bhoom	1982-83	66919	1068	3955	290	4022	198	3530	13063	33204	4327	5023	9203	474	52231
		(100.00)	(1.60)	(5.91)	(0.43)	(6.01)	(0.30)	(5.28)	(19.52)	(49.62)	(6.47)	(7.51)	(13.75)	(0.71)	(78.05)
	1986-87	67858	472	11736	1795	6787	479	8171	29440	16867	2997	3106	7767	331	31068
		(100.00)	(0.70)	(17.29)	(2.65)	(10.00)	(0.71)	(12.04)	(43.38)	(24.86)	(4.42)	(4.58)	(11.45)	(0.49)	(45.78)
	1990-91	76332	833	10178	1300	9700	800	15556	38367	14493	3918	3371	10106	277	32165
		(100.00)	(1.09)	(13.33)	(1.70)	(12.71)	(1.05)	(20.38)	(50.26)	(18.99)	(5.13)	(4.42)	(13.24)	(0.36)	(42.14)
	1995-96	95437	766	11333	3607	11617	1357	13096	41776	25366	5424	4169	8567	359	43885
		(100.00)	(0.80)	(11.87)	(3.78)	(12.17)	(1.42)	(13.72)	(43.77)	(26.58)	(5.68)	(4.37)	(8.98)	(0.38)	(45.98)
District	1982-83	584076	13912	95731	5589	55841	14237	44577	229887	171543	32854	34965	43323	3252	285937
(Total)		(100.00)	(2.38)	(16.39)	(0.96)	(9.56)	(2.44)	(7.63)	(39.36)	(29.37)	(5.62)	(5.99)	(7.42)	(0.56)	(48.95)
	1986-87	654981	10685	107590	7288	49871	9312	75895	260641	169951	17854	35740	68813	9305	301663
		(100.00)	(1.63)	(16.43)	(1.11)	(7.61)	(1.42)	(11.59)	(39.79)	(25.94)	(2.73)	(5.45)	(10.51)	(1.42)	(46.06)
	1990-91	739871	15536	106528	20840	83665	24916	100572	352057	180109	25747	40420	88919	9506	344701
		(100.00)	(2.10)	(14.40)	(2.82)	(11.31)	(3.37)	(13.59)	(47.58)	(24.34)	(3.48)	(5.46)	(12.03)	(1.28)	(46.59)
	1995-96	737843	16194	94649	11212	78290	16951	114890	332186	213471	29678	36716	74467	8776	363108
		(100.00)	(2.19)	(12.83)	(1.52)	(10.61)	(2.30)	(15.57)	(45.02)	(28.93)	(4.02)	(4.98)	(10.09)	(1.19)	(49.21)

N.B. :Figures in the brackets indicate the percentage to the Gross Cropped Area.

N.G. :Shows not grown.

*Source:*Estimated on the Basis of Data Collected from Socio-Economic Review and District Statistical Abstract of Osmanabad District, Directorate of Economics and Statistics, Government of Maharashtra, 1985-86, 1989-90, 1990-91 and 1998-99.

Table 7

Percentage Change in Area Under Important Crops in Osmanabad District (1982-83 to 1995-96)

Talukas	*Kharif Crops*							*Rabi Crops*					
	Paddy	*Jowar*	*Bajra*	*Tur*	*Sugar-Cane*	*Oil-seeds*	*Total Kharif*	*Jowar*	*Wheat*	*Gram*	*Oil-seeds*	*Fruits& Veg.*	*Total Rabi*
Osmanabad	-(1.02)	-(1.46)	+(0.05)	-(1.30)	+(2.24)	+(5.87)	+(4.37)	+(5.35)	-(4.18)	-(1.49)	+(1.28)	-(0.05)	+(0.91)
Kallam	-(0.22)	-(7.47)	+(3.53)	-(0.09)	-(1.71)	+(8.56)	+(2.60)	+(0.42)	-(6.47)	-(2.01)	+(5.31)	-(0.36)	-(3.03)
Omerga	+(2.14)	-(7.88)	+(0.44)	+(1.81)	+(0.79)	+(7.89)	+(5.18)	-(2.38)	-(0.24)	+(0.61)	+(6.41)	-(0.62)	+(3.77)
Tuljapur	-(2.59)	-(1.69)	-(2.67)	-(0.52)	-(4.29)	+(11.12)	-(0.64)	+(3.78)	+(1.57)	-(3.98)	+(9.78)	+(4.13)	+(15.28)
Paranda	-(0.57)	-(0.20)	-(0.03)	+(0.57)	+(0.34)	+(6.77)	+(6.60)	+(4.64)	-(0.75)	+(3.01)	-(5.29)	+(0.07)	+(1.67)
Bhoom	-(0.79)	+(5.96)	+(3.35)	+(6.15)	+(1.14)	+(8.45)	+(24.25)	-(23.04)	-(0.79)	-(3.14)	-(4.77)	-(0.33)	-(32.07)
District	-(0.19)	-(3.56)	+(0.56)	+(1.05)	-(0.14)	+(7.94)	+(5.66)	-(0.44)	-(1.60)	-(1.01)	+(2.67)	+(0.63)	+(0.26)

N.B. : Figures in brackets show change in percentage of Area Under Different Crops to the Gross Cropped Area.

Source: Estimated on the Basis of Data Collected from the Socio-Economic Review and District Statistical Abstract of Osmanabad District, Directorate Economics and Statistics, Government of Maharashtra, 1985-86, 1989-90, 1990-91 and 1998-99.

decrease in the area under kharif jowar (-3.56 per cent), paddy (-0.19 per cent) and sugarcane (-0.14 per cent) during last fourteen years in the study district. From this, it is seen that there was very high increase in percentage of area under oilseeds (7.94 per cent), and a very high decrease in percentage of area under kharif jowar i.e (-3.56 per cent) and small decrease in percentage of area under paddy (-0.19 per cent) and sugarcane (-0.14 per cent).

A perusal of Tables 6 and 7 shows that, during the last fourteen years, the percentage share of kharif cultivated area to gross cropped area in the district has increased by 5.66 per cent. There was a gradual increase in the area under kharif crops in the district as a whole during the last fourteen years. This increase was seen in the five talukas, namely, Bhoom (24.25 per cent), Paranda (6.60 per cent), Omerga (5.18 per cent), Osmanabad (4.37 per cent) and Kallam (2.60 per cent), and decrease (-0.64 per cent) in Tuljapur taluka.

During the last fourteen years, there has been a change in cultivated area under different crops and the change in percentage share of kharif crops to gross cropped area in the district. An attempt is made to correlate the irrigation facilities with the spatial distribution of kharif crops in the study area (see Tables 15, 6 and 7).

Paddy

Paddy is an aquatic plant which requires high rainfall or assured irrigation facilities. Paddy occupied 2.19 per cent (1995-96) of the gross cultivated area in Osmanabad district. Cultivated area under paddy has increased by 16 per cent during the last fourteen years. But its percentage share in gross cropped area has registered a decrease of -0.19 per cent. The area under paddy has registered an increase in Omerga taluka by 2.14 per cent, significant increase in paddy cultivation is found in Omerga taluka where the irrigation facilities were developed. The area under paddy has registered a decrease in Tuljapur (-2.59 per cent), Osmanabad (-1.02 per cent), Bhoom (-0.79 per cent), Kallam (-0.22 per cent) and Paranda (-0.20 per cent) talukas. But perusal of Table 15 shows that there was

1.13 per cent increase in paddy irrigated area during the last fourteen years. Almost all the talukas of the district have recorded an increase in paddy irrigated area.

Jowar (Kharif)

Jowar (kharif) can withstand drought to a considerable extent and is grown both as dry as well as an irrigated crop. It is a staple food of this study area and is also used as fodder. But kharif jowar is denoted as an inferior food as compared to rabi jowar. Jowar (kharif) was the important crop during 1982-83 as it occupied 16.39 per cent of the gross cultivated area.

A perusal of table 4.6 shows that, in 1982-83, jowar occupied (16.39 per cent) highest percentage share of gross cropped area in the district. During last fourteen years, there was decrease (-3.56 per cent) in area under kharif jowar. In the whole study area decrease of -7.82 per cent is observed in the jowar irrigated area and -3.56 per cent in jowar cultivated area. During the last fourteen years, the talukas of Omerga (-7.88 per cent), Kallam (-7.47 per cent), Osmanabad (-1.46 per cent), Tuljapur (-1.69 per cent), and Paranda (-0.57 per cent) have recorded decrease in jowar cultivated area. Only Bhoom taluka has recorded the highest (5.96 per cent) increase in area under jowar in the district. Almost all the talukas have registered decrease in jowar irrigated area (see Table 15). With the development of irrigation facilities, the farmers of this region gave preference to the cultivation of oilseeds, sugarcane and other cash crops instead of growing this coarse cereal. Thus due to irrigation facilities this crop has been replaced by other remunerative crops like oilseeds, sugarcane, etc. The increasing impact of irrigation has negatively affected this crop.

Bajra

Bajra was a drought resistant crop requiring less amount of rainfall. From the Table 6, it is observed that during 1982-83, there was only 0.96 per cent of the gross cropped area under bajra in the district. Bajra crop occupied 1.52 per cent of the gross cropped area of the study region in 1995-96. It has registered an increase of 0.56 per cent over a period of fourteen years. The area under bajra has registered increase in the talukas of Bhoom (3.35 per cent), Kallam (3.53 per cent), Omerga (0.44 per cent) and Osmanabad (0.05 per cent) and it has registered decrease in two talukas of Tuljapur (-2.67 per cent) and Paranda (-0.03 per cent). During last fourteen years, a decrease of -7.44 per cent is observed in bajra irrigated area and an increase of 0.56 per cent in bajra cultivated area in the study region.

Tur

Tur was the important pulse crop and it occupied 9.56 per cent of gross cultivated area of the district in 1982-83. During 1995-96, it occupied 10.61 per cent of gross cultivated area of the Osmanabad district. Thus, it has registered an increase of 1.05 percentage points in cultivated area and a decrease of -13.62 per cent in irrigated area in the district during the last fourteen years. Area under tur has registered an increase in three talukas, namely, Bhoom (6.15 per cent), Omerga (1.81 per cent) and Paranda (0.50 per cent). While it has registered decrease in area in Osmanabad (-1.30 per cent), Tuljapur (-0.52 per cent) and Kallam (-0.09 per cent) talukas. But all the talukas in the district have recorded a decrease in tur irrigated area.

Sugarcane

Sugarcane was an important cash crop and it occupied 2.44 per cent (1982-83) of the gross cultivated area of the district under study. Similarly, sugarcane occupied 2.30 per cent of the gross cropped area of the district in 1995-96. But it registered decline in both cultivated area (-0.14 per cent) and in irrigated area (-4.48 per cent) during the last fourteen years. This crop registered a decrease in area in two talukas, namely, Tuljapur (-4.29 per cent) and Kallam (-1.71 per cent). But this crop has registered an increase in area in remaining talukas, namely, Osmanabad (2.24 per cent), Bhoom (1.14 per cent), Omerga (0.79 per cent) and Paranda (0.34 per cent) during the period under study. Two talukas, namely, Osmanabad and Bhoom have recorded an increase in percentage of irrigated area under sugarcane (see Table 15). Tuljapur, Kallam and Paranda talukas have recorded a decrease in percentage of irrigated area under sugarcane.

Oilseeds

Groundnut, sunflower and sesamum are the important oilseed crops grown in kharif season which are mostly dependent on irrigation facilities at the time of rainless period in the study area. It is seen from the Table 6 and 7 that, kharif oilseeds occupied 7.63 per cent (1982-83) of the gross cultivated area of the district. And it was 15.57 per cent of the gross cultivated area in 1995-96. Thus, oilseeds have registered an increase in cultivated area of 7.94 percentage points and 11.00 per cent increase in irrigated area during the last fourteen years. It has registered an increase in area in almost all talukas of the district. Tuljapur taluka has registered the highest increase (11.12 per cent) in area under kharif oilseeds, followed by Kallam (8.56 per cent), Bhoom (8.45 per cent), Omerga (7.89 per cent), Paranda (6.77 per cent) and Osmanabad (5.87 per cent) talukas. There was increase in both irrigated and cultivated area under oilseeds crops during last fourteen years in the study region. This shows that with the development of irrigation facilities in the district, farmers of this region gave more preference to the cultivation of oilseed crops. Thus, increasing irrigation has positive impact on this crop.

Crop Pattern Effect of Irrigation: Rabi Season

The rabi season starts after the harvest of kharif crops in September-October. The rabi crops are fine grained and requires a good amount of irrigation water. Since this is not a rainy season and winter rains are not common, water is obtained mainly from man-made sources of irrigation. The important rabi crops grown in this district viz. jowar, wheat, gram, oilseeds, fruits and vegetables, are considered in this study.

A perusal of Table 6 shows that in 1982-83, crop-wise cultivated area of rabi season of the whole district was 2,85,937 hectares and in 1995-96, it was 3,63,108 hectares. Thus during last fourteen years (from 1982-83 to 1995-96), there was 27 per cent increase in rabi cultivated area. Similarly a perusal of Tables 6 and 7 shows that, the percentage share of rabi cultivated area to gross cropped area in the district was 48.95 per cent in 1982-83 and 49.21 per cent in 1995-96. The percentage share of rabi cropped area to gross cropped area in the district has increased by 1.26 per cent over the period of last fourteen years.

The study region is an exclusively jowar (rabi) growing area. Cultivated area under jowar (rabi) was about 29 per cent in 1982-83, while after a lapse of fourteen years, it registered small decrease of -0.44 per cent. In 1982-83, jowar was the most important crop, occupied 29.37 per cent area of the district followed by oilseeds (7.42 per cent), wheat (5.62 per cent), gram (5.99 per cent) and fruits and vegetables (0.56 per cent). In 1995-96, jowar (28.93 per cent) remained the most important crop followed by oilseeds (10.09 per cent), gram (4.98 per cent), wheat (4.02 per cent), and fruits and vegetables (1.19 per cent). There was marginal decrease in cultivated area under jowar (-0.44 per cent), wheat (-1.60 per cent), gram (-1.01 per cent) and marginal increase in area under oilseeds (2.67 per cent) and fruits and vegetables (0.26 per cent) in the district during last fourteen years in rabi season.

Thus, it is seen from the Tables 6 and 7 that, during the last fourteen years percentage share of rabi cultivated area to gross cultivated area in Osmanabad district has increased by 1.26 per cent. In most of the talukas, the percentage share of area under rabi crops has registered an increase of 15.28 per cent in Tuljapur, 3.77 per cent in Omerga, 1.67 per cent in Paranda and 0.91 per cent in Osmanabad talukas. Rest of the two talukas, namely, Bhoom (-32.07 per cent) and Kallam (-3.03 per cent) have recorded a decrease in rabi cultivated area. Thus it is observed that during the last fourteen years there has been a change in the percentage share of rabi crops. An attempt is made to correlate the irrigation facilities with the spatial distribution (see Tables 15, 6 and 7) of area under rabi crops in the study area.

RABI CROPS

Jowar

Jowar (rabi) is the most important rabi crop and the farmers of this district have specialized in jowar cultivation. Jowar can be grown successfully with the help of irrigation in this area of scanty rainfall. Therefore, it is the extent to which irrigation can be provided to this crop which determines its area extent and yield capacity. Jowar crop requires two waterings for growing. Jowar was the most important crop in 1982-83, which occupied 29.37 per cent of the total cropped area in the study district. In 1995-96, again it occupied 28.93 per cent of the total cropped area of the district. Therefore, jowar is the most important rabi crop in Osmanabad district. It has registered a small decrease of -0.44 per cent. But most of the talukas have recorded increase in area under rabi jowar over the period under study. Osmanabad taluka has recorded the highest (5.35 per cent) increase in area under jowar followed by Paranda (4.64 per cent), Tuljapur (3.78 per cent) and Kallam (0.42 per cent) talukas. Rest of the two talukas, namely, Bhoom (-23.04 per cent) and Omerga (-2.38 per cent) have recorded decrease in area under rabi jowar. Thus, during last fourteen years, area under rabi jowar crop in the district has increased and this increase is attributed to the increase in irrigation facilities and cropping of short duration crops. It is seen from the table 3.15 that, irrigated area under jowar (rabi) has increased by 4.34 per cent during the last fourteen years in the study area.

Wheat

In 1982-83, wheat occupied 5.62 per cent of gross cultivated area of the district, while in 1995-96, wheat covered an area of 4.02 per cent of the gross cropped area of the district. During the last fourteen years, the cultivated area (-1.60 per cent) and the irrigated area (-4.57 per cent) under wheat have decreased. Only Tuljapur taluka has recorded an increase of 1.57 per cent in cropped area and 6.09 per cent in irrigated area and thus recorded a significant increase in wheat crop. Remaining five talukas have recorded a decrease in cropped area and irrigated area under wheat over the period under study. This crop has lost its importance and there was shift in its area to other cash crops like oilseeds.

Gram

Gram is important for both livestock and human being as a nutritive crop which also helps in soil management. It rarely needs supplemental irrigation. A perusal of Tables 6 and 7 shows that, gram covers an area of 5.99 per cent of the gross cropped area of Osmanabad district in 1982-83. It occupies 4.98 per cent of the district's gross cropped area in 1995-96. Thus, after a lapse of fourteen years, percentage share of area under gram to gross cropped area in the district has decreased by -1.01 per cent. Tuljapur taluka (-3.98 per cent) has recorded the highest decrease in area under gram followed by Bhoom (-3.14 per cent), Kallam (-2.01 per cent) and Osmanabad (-1.49 per cent) talukas. But the talukas such as Paranda (3.01 per cent) and Omerga (0.61v) have recorded an increase in area under gram. Over the period of this study, it is seen from the tables 3.15 and 4.7 that there was 7.58 per cent increase in irrigated area and -0.1 per cent decrease in cultivated area of gram in Osmanabad district. Thus, increasing impact of irrigation has negatively affected this crop in the study area.

Oilseeds (Rabi)

Among the total rabi oilseeds grown in this study area, safflower, linseed, sunflower and groundnut are the important oilseed crops which covered 7.42 per cent (1982-83) of the gross cropped area of the district. While in 1995-96, these crops occupied 10.09 per cent of the gross cropped area of the district. Thus, during last fourteen years, there was 2.67 per cent increase in area under rabi oilseeds and 11.22 per cent increase in irrigated area under these crops of the study area. So during last fourteen years, it is observed that, there was an increase of 2.67 per cent in its area. Similar increase was also observed in Tuljapur (9.78 per cent), Omerga (6.41 per cent), Kallam (5.31 per cent) and Osmanabad (1.28 per cent) talukas. Rest of the talukas, namely, Paranda (-5.29 per cent) and Bhoom (-4.77 per cent) have recorded a decline in area under rabi oilseeds. There was 11.22 per cent increase in the irrigated area under this crop in the study area during the last fourteen years. Thus, it is observed that farmers are increasingly shifting from the cultivation of wheat and gram to oilseeds cultivation as they find it more remunerative and high yielding crop. Oilseed crops require less amount of watering as compared to other crops in rabi season. From the point of view of the farmers, the growing of oilseeds is more remunerative than the growing of foodgrains.

During last fourteen years it is observed that, with the development of irrigation facilities, the farmers of this district gave more preference to rabi oilseeds as compared to foodgrain crops. Thus, increasing irrigation has positive impact on oilseed crops.

Fruits and Vegetables

Among the fruits and vegetables grown in Osmanabad district, banana, grapes, mango and onion are the important crops. Fruits like banana and grapes require both more watering and money expenditures. A perusal of Tables 6 and 7 shows that fruits and vegetables have occupied 0.56 per cent of the gross cropped area of the district in 1982-83, while in 1995-96, these crops covered an area of about 1.19 per cent of gross cropped area. Thus, during last fourteen years, the cultivated area under this crop has increased by 1.19 per cent. Similarly, percentage of area under fruits and vegetables to gross cropped area has increased by 0.63 per cent in Osmanabad district. Further irrigated area under these crops has also increased by 1.76 per cent over the period in the district. Two talukas, namely, Tuljapur and Paranda have recorded highest increase in cultivated area and also increase in irrigated area under these crops. The cultivated area under fruits and vegetables in this district has increased and this increase is attributed to the increase in irrigation facilities. Therefore, development of irrigation in the study area has positive impact on fruits and vegetables. Thus, irrigation development was in favour of farmers of Osmanabad district in diversification of crops from the traditional cereal crops to commercial crops. Therefore, growth of irrigation in the district has a positive impact on commercial crops.

IMPACT OF IRRIGATION ON YIELD

Irrigation water alone cannot push the yield of crops. The quantity of produce is a function of several variables and irrigation is only one of them. But irrigation is a catalystic factor and on the availability of which depends the use of other inputs like fertilizers, high yielding varieties of seeds, etc. This change in the character of cultivation under irrigation leads to greater productivity of crops previously cultivated. Such improvements in the per hectare yield are technology induced and irrigation constitutes the major causative factor behind such yield rate enhancement. Studies on the relative contribution of various component elements in the growth of agricultural output by Kalhon and Johl, Minhas and Vaidyanathan and Prabha have established that increase in per hectare yield is attributable to the adoption of new agricultural technology emerging from rapid expansion of irrigation facilities[10].

Dhawan has studied various issues relating to the impact of irrigation on productivity with reference to Indian farm economy. His study reveals that the total output expansion in crop output per irrigated hectare was nearly 19 quintals in food grain energy equivalents (FEEs units) during mid-eighties. Under rainfed condition, country's crop output per hectare was 8 quintals in FEEs units[11]. Sharma has attempted to study the socio-economic impact of major irrigation projects in India. The study was found that average yields of all crops are substantially higher (8 to 500 per cent) in "after" project situation as compared to "before" project situation[12].

We may now examine irrigation impact on yields of important crops in Osmanabad district. The yearwise yields of important crops and the percentage change in yields of important crops in the study area during 1982-83 to 1996-97 have been calculated and are presented in Table 8.

Kharif Crops

It is seen from the Table 8 that, during last fifteen years (1982-83 to 1996-97), there was considerable increase in yields of kharif crops in Osmanabad district.

Among the kharif crops, bajra crop recorded highest increase in yields (101.05 per cent) in the district followed by tur (54.10 per cent), kharif jowar (33.24 per cent), paddy (11.64 per cent), sunflower (2.78 per cent) and there was decrease in

Table 8
Cropwise Yields and Percentage Change in Yields of Main Crops in Osmanabad District (1982-83 1996-97)

(Crop yields in kg/ha, sugarcane yields in dressed cane/ha and fruits yields in tonnes/ha)

Crops	Year-wise yields				Percentage change in yields during 1982-83 to 1996-97
	1982-83	1986-87	1990-91	1996-97	
Kharif Crops					
1. Paddy	627	131	959	700	11.64
2.Jowar (kh.)	1074	209	1022	1431	33.24
3. Bajra	379	192	404	762	101.05
4. Tur	390	117	272	601	54.01
5. Sugarcane	82610	56985	74020	61877	-25.10
6. Groundnut	690	112	567	478	-30.72
7. Sunflower	647	170	576	665	2.78
Rabi Crops					
1. Rabi jowar	433	261	770	893	106.24
2. Wheat	721	387	959	1000	38.70
3. Gram	404	149	509	586	45.05
4. Safflower	655	433	328	587	-10.38
5. Groundnut	1234	1734	800	1476	19.61
6. Sunflower	488	510	581	652	33.61
7. Banana	16.64	—	—	53.81	223.38
8. Grapes	11.40	—	12.60	35.80	214.04
9. Onion	9.42	—	10.00	12.00	27.40

Source : Districtwise Agricultural Statistical Information of Maharashtra, Part II, Commissionerate of Agriculture, Pune, 1986-87, 1995-96 and 1997-98.

yields of sugarcane (–25.10 per cent) and groundnut (–30.72 per cent) during last fifteen years. It shows that any coarse grains have made drastic improvement in their yield. This is mainly due to the fact that, high yielding variety of coarse grains has come a bit later, they are drought resistant. Being a kharif or monsoon crop, they depend considerable on rainwater and they do not require much irrigation water. While sugarcane require plenty of irrigation water and it cannot resist even a slight drought. Consequently, there is hardly any unirrigated sugarcane. Sugarcane cultivation with the help of perennial source of irrigation is bound to give high yields. Similarly, paddy requires a lot of irrigation water but being a kharif crop, there may not be much irrigation from artificial source of water. Rest of the crops like kharif jowar, bajra, sunflower, groundnut depend mainly on rainwater but during the drought period, these crops require irrigation water, which is useful for increase in crop yields.

RABI CROPS

A perusal of Table 8 shows that during the last fifteen years (1982-83 to 1996-97), the percentage increase in yields of rabi crops have been comparatively higher than that of kharif crops. Banana recorded highest increase of 223.38 percentage in yields during last fifteen years, followed by grapes (214.04 per cent), rabi jowar (106.24 per cent), gram (45.05 per cent), wheat (38.70 per cent), sunflower (33.61 per cent), onion (27.40 per cent), groundnut (19.61 per cent), and only safflower recorded decrease or negative change (-10.38 per cent) in its yield during last fifteen years in Osmanabad district. Among the food-grain crops, rabi jowar recorded the highest yield in Osmanabad district. This may due to the availability of irrigation facilities and high yielding varieties of jowar and the farmers preference for giving full inputs to this grain because this is most favourable crop and farmers get more returns from it. There was considerable increase in yields of wheat and gram also. There was also increase in the yields of oilseeds in Osmanabad district. Fruits like banana and grapes recorded highest increase in yields in Osmanabad district. This may be due to the farmers preference for giving full inputs to the fruits as this is highly remunerative crop as compared to other crops. All rabi crops recorded positive changes during last fifteen years in Osmanabad district. Most of the rabi crops depend on irrigation water as compared to kharif crops. Thus, it can be concluded that, during last fifteen years (1982-83 to 1996-97), irrigation has helped for increasing yields of kharif and rabi crops in Osmanabad district.

CROP PRODUCTION EFFECT OF IRRIGATION

It is now understandably an established fact that irrigation is expected to modernise agriculture where it not only brings larger area under cultivation but also stimulates and increases agricultural production also. The interaction effect of irrigation in Osmanabad district, i.e. the expansion of the aggregate volume of agricultural crop output resulting from extension of net area under cultivation, increase in intensity of farming, suitable shifts in crop pattern and higher productivity in crops per unit of land may now be examined. It is well known fact that with the development of irrigation facilities the agricultural production has also increased. Table 9, which seeks to highlight this phenomenon, presents increase in total production of all crops with increase in irrigated area in the district during the period 1984-85 to 1995-96. So it was worthwhile to see the correlation between total irrigated area and total crop production, irrigated area under food-grains and food-grains production and irrigated area under nonfood-grains and nonfood-grains production. Taking year-wise data from 1984-85 to 1995-96 for Osmanabad district, correlation coefficient was computed and is presented in Table 9.

The Table 9 reveals that total crop production, foodgrains production and non-foodgrains production in the district have increased with the increase in irrigated area since 1984-85. While during 1984-85 to 1995-96 the mean of the total production, foodgrains production, non-foodgrains production in the district were 9539, 2423.57 and 7115.43 tons respectively. A perusal of table 4.9 shows that the correlation co-efficient between total irrigated area and total crop production during 1984-85 to 1995-96 in the district was 0.79 and this positive correlation coefficient is found to be significant at 5 per cent level. It has been observed that the district with more irrigation facilities during a period of twelve years recorded high correlation mainly due to irrigation facilities which led to the use of high yielding varieties of seeds and fertilizers and therefore, resulted in high crop production. The result shows a high positive correlation coefficient between total irrigated area and total crop production. This suggests that irrigation is very important ingredient for increasing agricultural production. It is the fact that as irrigation increases the use of other inputs like fertilizers, high yielding varieties of seeds also increases.

The correlation coefficient between irrigated area under foodgrains and foodgrains production (including cereals and pulses) in the district was 0.19 but it is found to be statistically insignificant. This shows that during the last twelve years, irrigation development was in favour of farmers of the district in diversification of crops from the traditional cereal crops to commercial crops. It is seen from the table 4.8 that most of the land of Osmanabad district during the kharif and rabi seasons was under jowar cultivation and after lapse of fourteen years (1982-83 to 1995-96), jowar (rabi) remained the first ranking crop. However, there was decrease in rabi jowar by –0.44 per cent and shift in first ranking crop from jowar (kharif) to oilseeds in kharif season. This shows that there has been diversification of crops from the traditional cereal crops to commercial crops in the district.

The correlation coefficient between irrigated area under non-foodgrains and non-foodgrains production (including oilseeds, sugarcane, fruits and vegetables) in the district recorded positive correlation (0.85) and this coefficient is found to be significant at 1 per cent level. After a lapse of twelve years (1984-85 to 1995-96) (see Tables 8 and 9), there was shift in first ranking crop from jowar (kharif) to oilseeds in kharif season and oilseeds were remained as the second ranking crop in rabi season. Therefore the results show a high positive correlation between irrigated area under non-foodgrains and production of non-foodgrains in the district. This suggests that irrigation has the dominant role in non-foodgrains production. It is the fact that as irrigation increases the use of other inputs like fertilizers, high yielding varieties of seeds also increase. It may, therefore, be concluded that during the last twelve years (1984-85 to 1995-96) because of expansion and intensive utilization of irrigation facilities, the Osmanabad district has made rapid strides in agricultural production. This shows that irrigation development in the Osmanabad district has beneficial production effect.

Table 9
Correlation Between Total Irrigated Area and Total Crop Production, Irrigation Area Under Food-grains and Food-grains Production and Irrigated Area Under Non-food-grains and Non-food-grains Production in Osmanabad District. (1984-85 to 1995-96)

(Area in hectares and production in metric tonnes)

Year	*Total irrigated area*	*Total crop produc-tion*	*Irrigated Area Under Food-grains*	*Food-grains produc-tion*	*Irrigated Area under non food-grains*	*Non food-grains produc-tion*
1984-85	94218	4682	65508	3247	28710	1435
1985-86	95835	3036	69211	1991	26624	1045
1986-87	101978	5325	66457	968	35521	4357
1987-88	121327	9128	74757	3289	46570	5839
1988-89	146576	10781	80323	2333	66253	8448
1989-90	138282	14140	75393	3497	62889	10643
1990-91	152403	19529	82428	3577	69975	15952
1991-92	135397	13033	70497	1526	64900	11507
1992-93	115924	10636	67240	3505	48684	7131
1993-94	112522	11672	67953	3952	44569	7720
1994-95	121278	17326	68932	2724	52346	14602
1995-96	122071	14258	70182	3321	51889	10937
Mean	104129.36	9539.00	61348.64	2423.57	42780.71	7115.43
Standard Deviation	18961.13	5016.83	5473.97	927.98	14499.56	4710.61
R	0.79**		0.19		0.85***	

** Significant at 5 per cent level

*** Significant at 1 per cent level

Sources: Estimated from (1) The data collected from Socio-Economic Review and District Statistical Abstract of Osmanabad District, Directorate of Economics and Statistics, Government of Maharashtra, 1986-87 and 1998-99.

(2) District-wise Agricultural Statistical Information of Maharashtra Part II, Commissionerate of Agriculture, Pune, 1986-87, 1995-96 and 1997-98.

Thus from the macro-level analysis, it can be concluded that extension of irrigation facilities has made positive impact on agriculture in Osmanabad district. The growth of irrigation in the district has positive effect on cultivated area. The impact of irrigation on extension of cultivated area (net, total and double) shows that the scope for bringing new lands under plough is limited. The extension of irrigation facilities had led to the expansion of double and gross cropped area. The cropping intensity in the district has increased from 104.08 per cent in 1982-83 to 124.93 per cent in 1995-96. Thus, growth of irrigation has positive impact on cropping intensity. Irrigation in the district has made favourable shift in cropping pattern from low value crops to high value crops. Similarly, growth of irrigation has positive impact on both crop yields and output in the district. Positive correlation between total irrigated area and total crop production and between irrigated area under non-foodgrains and non-foodgrains production was observed in the study area. Thus, the irrigation development in Osmanabad district has beneficial area effect, intensity effect, crop pattern effect, yield effect and production effect. Thus the impact of irrigation on agriculture in Osmanabad district is favourable.

Notes and References

1. Vyas V.S., Foundation of Indian Agriculture, Ed. by Vadilal Dadli Vora and Company Publishers Private Ltd., Bombay, 1968.
2. Ghosh R.N., Agriculture in Economic Development with special reference to Punjab, Vikas Publications, New Delhi, 1977, p. 63.
3. Bhardwaj Krishna, Production Conditions in Indian Agriculture, A Study Based on Farm Management Survey, Cambridge University Press, 1974, p. 43.
4. Gadgil D.R., Economic Effects of Irrigation, Report of Survey of the Direct and Indirect Benefits of Godavari and Pravara Canals, Pub. No. 17, Gokhale Institute of Economics and Politics, Pune, 1948, p. 22.
5. Mukhopadhyaya S.K., Sources of Variation in Agricultural Productivity, Macmillan Company of India, 1974, p. 64.
6. Singh J.P. *et al.*, New Seeds, Adoption and Yields, Institute of Social and Economic Change, Ahmedabad, 1979, p. 17.

   Gaikwad V.R. and Desai V.M., Development of Incentive Agriculture Lessons from Intensive Agricultural District Programme, Indian Institute of Management, Ahmedabad, p. 12.

7. Ghosh R.N., *op. cit.*, p. 63.
8. Mishra S., A Comparative Study of the Economics of Minor Sources of Irrigation in Uttar Pradesh (A Report), Oxford and I.B.H. Publishing Co., 1968, p. 39.
9. Bhardwaj Krishna, *op. cit.*, p. 48.
10. Kalhon A.S. and Johl S.S., Agricultural Growth Rates in Punjab, Punjab Agricultural University, 1968.

    Minhas B. S. and Vaidyanathan A., Growth of Crop Output in India, 1951-54 to 1958-61, An Analysis by Component Elements. *Journal of the Indian Society of Agricultural Statistics*, Vol. XVII, 1965.

    Prabha Chander, Districtwise Measurement and Decomposition of Agricultural Output in Punjab, *Indian Economics Review*, Vol. VI, 1971.
11. Dhawan B.D., Irrigation in India's Agricultural Development–Productivity, Stability and Equity, Sage Publishers, New Delhi, 1988, p. 26.
12. Sharma S.D., Socio-Economic Impacts of Major Irrigation Projects, Proceedings of Fifty Eighth Annual Research and Development Session, Vol. II, Central Board of Irrigation and Power, Bangalore, 19-22 April, 1993.

CHAPTER 5

IMPACT OF IRRIGATION ON AGRICULTURE – A MICRO-LEVEL ANALYSIS

In the preceding chapter, we have examined the macro level impact of irrigation on agriculture in Osmanabad district during 1982-83 to 1995-96. Thus an attempt has been made in the present chapter to assess the micro-level impact of irrigation on agriculture in the study area. For assessing the impact of irrigation on land use pattern, cropping intensity, cropping pattern, per hectare crop income, costs and returns, and employment creation, a comprehensive field survey of 142 farms in the study region was conducted during the year 1999-2000.

For assessing the impact of irrigation on these aspects, we have adopted 'with' and 'without' approach. In this approach a comparison of "with project situation" as against the "without project situation" is made by way of collecting and analysing data from beneficiaries (i.e. from irrigated area) and non-beneficiaries (i.e. from unirrigated area). Before analysing these aspects, here it is necessary to discuss the structure of the farm economy in the study area.

STRUCTURE OF FARM ECONOMY

The discussion in this section is focussed on the different structural aspects of the farm economy and comparison between irrigated and unirrigated samples with reference to such structure. The total number of sample holdings in each size class, its percentage to total samples, aggregate area operated in each size class and its percentage to the total area and mean size of holdings are presented in Table 1 below.

Table 1
Distribution of Sample Farms by Size Class in Study Region

(Area in hectares)

Size of land holdings (farms)	*No. of holdings*	*Net cultivated area*	*Mean size of holdings*
(a) Irrigated area			
Small (up to 2 ha.)	39	54.06	1.39
	(48.75)	(22.75)	
Medium (2.01 to 4 ha.)	23	123.09	2.63
	(28.75)	(51.80)	
Large(Above 4 ha.)	18	123.09	6.87
	(22.50)	(51.80)	
Overall	80	237.61	2.97
	(100.00)	(100.00)	
(b) Unirrigated area			
Small (up to 2 ha.)	34	44.88	1.32
	(54.84)	(33.58)	
Medium (2.01 to 4 ha.)	16	35.00	2.19
	(25.81)	(26.19)	
Large(Above 4 ha.)	12	53.76	4.48
	(19.35)	(40.23)	
Overall	62	133.64	2.16
	(100.00)	(100.00)	

Note: Figures in brackets indicate the percentage to the total.
Source: Field survey.

This table reveals that in case of irrigated farms, 77.50 per cent of farm households belonging to size class small and medium together control only 48.20 per cent of total net sown area. At the same time, 22.50 per cent of the farm households of size class large control 51.80 per cent of the total net sown area. Similar pattern of land holding also prevails in case of unirrigated farms, where 80.66 per cent of farm households of size class small and medium together control 59.77 per cent of the total net sown area. On the other hand, only 19.35 per cent of farm households of size class large control 40.23 per cent of the total net sown area. The overall mean size of land holdings in the district is 2.97 ha. for irrigated sample farms as against 2.16 ha. for unirrigated sample farms. Similarly, mean size of land holding increases with increase in size of holdings in both irrigated and unirrigated samples farms.

Per Farm and Per Hectare Family Size in Study Area

Total family members, family size (per hectare and per farm) in irrigated and unirrigated area have been shown in Table 2. It is seen from columns 3 and 4 of this table that mean size of family per farm is 4.58 in irrigated and 3.95 in unirrigated area. It increases with increase in the size of holdings in both irrigated as well as unirrigated farms which shows that relatively larger farms have more members to support. But when the size of the family is considered vis-a-vis number of persons per hectare, the opposite trend is noticed. The size of family per hectare is inversely related to the size of holding, indicating that relatively smaller farms had larger members to support as compared to relatively larger farms. This means land-man ratio is unfavourable to the small operators.

Table 2
Total Family Members, Per Farm and Per Hectare Family Size in Irrigated and Unirrigated Area

	Total family members				
Size class of farms	*Male*	*Female*	*Total*	*Family size (per farm)*	*Family size (Per ha.)*
(a) Irrigated area					
Small	83	71	154	3.95	2.85
Medium	51	49	100	4.35	1.65
Large	55	56	111	6.17	0.90
Overall	189	176	365	4.58	1.54
(b) Unirrigated area					
Small	66	58	124	3.65	2.76
Medium	31	25	56	3.50	1.60
Large	35	30	65	5.42	1.21
Overall	132	113	245	3.95	1.83

Source: Field survey.

THE LEVEL OF LITERACY AND ILLITERACY IN SAMPLE FARMS OF STUDY AREA

The level of literacy and illiteracy both in irrigated and unirrigated areas has been presented in Table 3. It is seen from this table that the overall level of literacy (male and female) is 86.85 per cent of the total family members in irrigated area as against 77.58 per cent of total family members in unirrigated area. This shows that overall level of literacy in irrigated area is higher (86.85 per cent) as compared to level of literacy (77.55 per cent) in unirrigated area. It is true for each of the size group of farms in irrigated area when compared with respective size groups in unirrigated area. The level of literacy for the small, medium and large farms is 81.17 per cent, 92.00 per cent and 90.00 per cent respectively in irrigated area as against it is 74.19 per cent, 85.71 per cent and 76.92 per cent for the small, medium

Table 3
The Level of Literacy and Illiteracy in Irrigated and Unirrigated Area

Size group of farms	Literacy			Illiteracy			Total family members
	Male	*Female*	*Total*	*Male*	*Female*	*Total*	
(a) Irrigated area							
Small	76	49	125 (81.17)	11	18	29 (18.33)	154.00 (100.00)
Medium	50	42	92 (92.00)	00	08	08 (8.00)	100 (100.00)
Large	55	45	100 (90.00)	00	11	11 (10.00)	111 (100.00)
Overall	181	136	317 (86.85)	12	36	48 (13.15)	365 (100.00)
(b) Unirrigated area							
Small	51	41	92 (74.19)	15	17	32 (25.81)	124 (100.00)
Medium	29	19	48 (85.71)	3	5	8 (14.29)	56 (100.00)
Large	29	21	50 (76.92)	6	9	15 (23.08)	65 (100.00)
Overall	109	81	190 (77.58)	24	31	55 (22.45)	245 (100.00)

Source: Field survey.

and large farms respectively in unirrigated area. In the study of level of literacy in relation to size groups of the farms, the level of literacy is highest 92.00 per cent for the medium farms in irrigated area followed by 90.00 per cent and 81.17 per cent for the large and small farms respectively. In unirrigated area, the level of literacy is also highest, i.e. 85.71 per cent, for the medium farms and lowest 74.19 per cent in small farms. Thus, there is no significant relation between the level of literacy and the size group of farms both in irrigated and unirrigated area.

But when level of illiteracy in irrigated and unirrigated area is considered opposite trend is noticed. The overall illiteracy is 13.15 per cent in irrigated area as against 22.45 per cent in unirrigated area. This fact shows that illiteracy in irrigated area is lower than that in the unirrigated area. This is true for each size group of farms in irrigated area when compared to respective size group of farms in unirrigated area. In study of level of illiteracy in relation to size group of farms, it is highest 18.33 per cent for the small farms and lowest 8.00 per cent for the medium farms in irrigated area. In unirrigated area, illiteracy is also highest of 25.81 per cent for the small farms and lowest of 14.29 per cent for the medium farms. So there is no significant relation between the illiteracy and the size group of farms both in irrigated and unirrigated areas.

IMPACT OF IRRIGATION ON LAND USE PATTERN

Land use pattern is significantly influenced by irrigation facility. Irrigation permits intensive use of land and thereby increases the gross cropped area. It brings more area under cultivation and it is also possible to cultivate double or multiple crops during a year, which enhances double cropped area.

Land Use Pattern of Sample Farms in Study Area

The land use pattern of irrigated and unirrigated farms have been shown in Tables 4 and 5. In this case, total land is grouped in different major types of uses viz. irrigated and unirrigated land, net area sown, double cropped area and uncultivable area. Uncultivable area includes barren land and land under non-agricultural use. The practice of leasing in or leasing out of

Table 4

Land Use Pattern of Sample Farms in Irrigated Area (1999-2000)

(Area in hectares)

Particulars	*Size groups of farms*			
	Small (up to 2 ha.)	*Medium (2.01-4 ha.)*	*Large (above 4 ha.)*	*Overall*
Irrigated land area				
(a) Canal	10.20 (18.10)	14.60 (20.12)	19.80 (10.99)	44.60 (14.43)
(b) Well	37.70 (66.89)	28.26 (38.95)	67.20 (37.30)	133.16 (43.08)
(c) Lift/other	1.00 (1.77)	9.40 (12.96)	2.20 (1.22)	12.60 (4.08)
Total irrigated area (a+b+c)	48.90 (86.76)	52.26 (72.03)	89.20 (49.51)	190.36 (61.59)
Unirrigated land area	5.16 (9.16)	8.20 (11.31)	33.89 (18.81)	47.25 (15.29)
Total cultivated (1+2) area or net area sown	54.06 (95.92)	60.46 (83.34)	123.09 (68.32)	237.61 (76.88)
Double cropped area	9.24 (17.09)	15.29 (25.29)	12.50 (10.15)	37.03 (15.58)
Uncultivable area	2.30 (4.08)	12.09 (16.66)	57.07 (31.68)	71.46 (23.12)
Total area (3+5)	56.36 (100.00)	72.55 (100.00)	180.16 (100.00)	309.07 (100.00)

Note: (1) Figures in brackets indicate the percentage to the total.
(2) Percentage of double cropped area is considered with respect to respective cultivated area (i.e. net area sown).

Source: Field survey.

land is found to be not popular in both irrigated and unirrigated areas. The total land area of 80 irrigated farms was 309.07 ha. as against 199.69 ha. for the 62 unirrigated farms. In case of irrigated farms, 76.88 per cent of the total area is the cultivated land or net sown area and remaining 23.12 per cent of total area is the uncultivated or barren land. In case of unirrigated sample farms, the proportion of total area brought under net cultivation during the survey year is about 66.92 per cent and remaining 33.08 per cent of total area is uncultivable or barren land. These facts clearly indicate that irrigated sample farms are able to put relatively higher proportion of their total land under cultivation as compared to unirrigated sample farms. Further, the proportion of land under double or multiple cropping to net sown area is 15.58 per cent in irrigated area as against only 3.14 per cent in unirrigated area. Therefore, because of irrigation facilities, the irrigated farmers are more efficient in land utilization than the unirrigated farmers.

Table 5
Land Use Pattern of Sample Farms in Unirrigated Area (1999-2000)

(Area in hectares)

Particulars	*Size groups of farms*			
	Small (up to 2 ha.)	*Medium (2.01-4 ha.)*	*Large (above 4 ha.)*	*Overall*
Cultivated area	44.88	35	53.76	133.64
	(91.07)	(69.43)	(53.76)	(66.92)
Double cropped area	2.60	1.00	0.60	4.20
	(5.79)	(2.85)	(1.12)	(3.14)
Uncultivable area	4.40	15.41	46.24	66.05
	(8.93)	(30.57)	(46.24)	(33.08)
Total area (1+3)	49.28	50.41	100.00	199.69
	(100.00)	(100.00)	(100.00)	(100.00)

Note: (1) Figures in brackets indicate the percentage to total.
(2) Percentage of double cropped area is considered with respect to respective cultivated area (i.e. net area sown).

Source: Field survey.

The farm-size wise land use pattern in irrigated area reveals that the small farmers (land holding up to 2 ha.) are the most efficient in making proper use of land for the crop cultivation during the survey year. The proportion of land area under cultivation to total area is found to be highest 95.92 per cent for small farms in irrigated area. The proportion of land area under cultivation to total area in case of size class of medium and large farms is 83.34 per cent and 68.32 per cent respectively. In case of unirrigated farms, the proportion of land area under cultivation to the total area for the size class of small, medium and large farms were 91.07 per cent, 69.43 per cent and 53.76 per cent respectively. From this, it is seen that each size class of farms in irrigated area are the most efficient in making proper use of land for the crop cultivation than the respective size class of farms in unirrigated area. Further it is also seen that proportion of cultivated area to the total area decreases with the increase in size class of farms in both irrigated as well as unirrigated area. Thus, the small farms in irrigated and unirrigated areas are the most efficient in making best utilization of land resources. In irrigated area, the proportion of double-cropped area to net area sown is found to be highest of 25.29 per cent in case of medium farms, followed by small farms (17.09 per cent) and large farms (10.15 per cent). In unirrigated area, the proportion of double-cropped area to net area sown for size class of small, medium and large farms were 5.79 per cent, 2.85 per cent and 1.12 per cent respectively. This fact clearly indicate that proportion of double-cropped area to net sown area in each size class of farms in irrigated area is higher than that of respective size class of farms in unirrigated area.

Thus, it is revealed from the data presented in the Tables 4 and 5 that in case of all size class farms and for whole region, the proportion of net sown area to the total area and the proportion of double cropped area to the net sown area in irrigated farms are relatively higher as compared with unirrigated farms. These facts clearly indicate that land use pattern in irrigated farms is better than unirrigated farms.

The farm size wise availability of irrigation facilities from different sources viz. canal, wells and lifts in the irrigated area has been shown in Table 4. It is seen from this table that 61.59 per cent of the total area is the irrigated area from different sources of irrigation in case of irrigated farms as against no irrigation facility is available in case of the unirrigated farms. Thus, well was the dominant source of irrigation having 43.08 per cent of land area under irrigation followed by canal (14.43 per cent) and lifts (4.08 per cent).

The farm size wise picture of irrigated land reveals that there is inverse relationship between irrigated area and size class of farms. It is the highest of 86.76 per cent of total area in case of small irrigated farms and then it showed declining trend with increase in size class of farms and found to be the lowest of 49.51 per cent in case of large farms.

Land use pattern in irrigated and unirrigated farms is presented in Figure 1. It is seen from the Figures 1 and 2 that the total land area in irrigated farms is 309.07 hectares and it is 237.61 hectares in case of unirrigated farms. The proportion of cultivated area to total area in irrigated farms is 76.88 per cent as against 66.92 per cent in unirrigated farms. This fact shows that proportionate area under cultivation to total land area is higher in irrigated farms than that in unirrigated farms. Similarly, it is also seen from the Figures 3 and 4 that 237.61 hectares is net sown area in irrigated farms and 133.64 hectares in case of unirrigated farms. The proportion of double cropped area to net sown area is 15.58 per cent in irrigated farms as against only 3.14 per cent in case of unirrigated farms. This shows that double or multiple cropping in irrigated farms is comparatively higher than unirrigated farms.

From all above facts it can be concluded that the availability of irrigation facilities leads to more use of land resources, for the cultivation and double or multiple crops. Further, it can be said that higher the proportion of irrigated area, the greater will be the use of land resources and the area under double

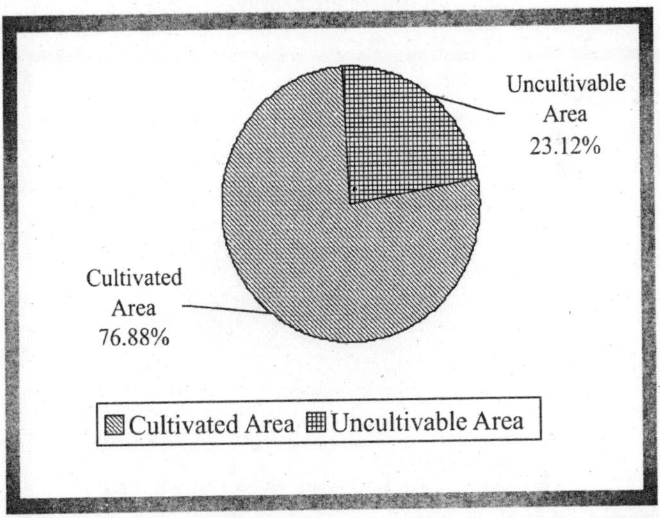

Figure 1 : Proportions of Cultivated and Uncultivable Area to Total Area in Irrigated Farms

cropping and vice-versa. Hence, it proves that land use pattern of the irrigated farms is more useful than that of land use pattern of unirrigated farms.

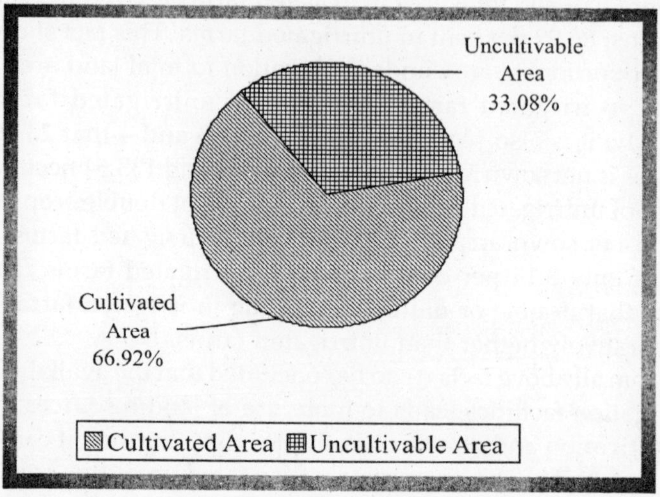

Figure 2 : Proportions of Cultivated and Uncultivable Area to Total Area in Unirrigated Farms

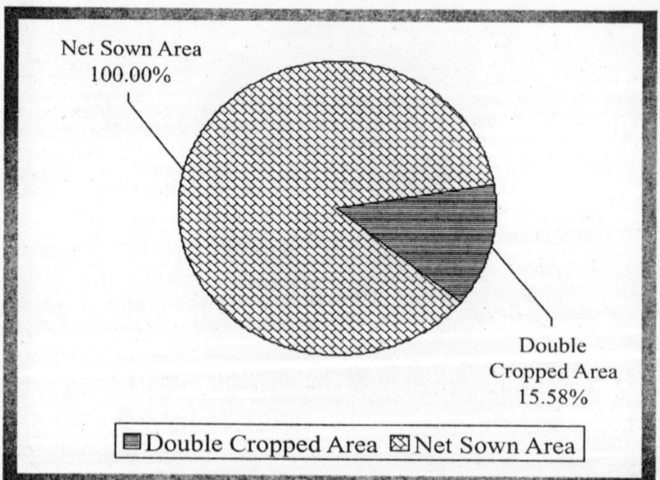

Figure 3 : The Proportion of Double Cropped Area to Net Sown Area in Irrigated Farms

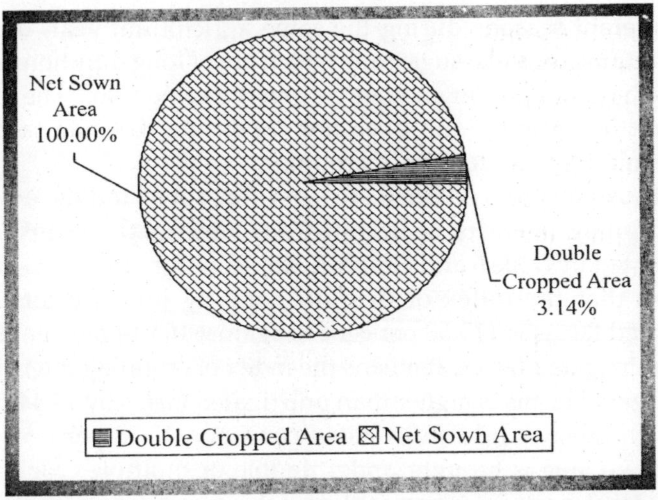

Figure 4 : The Proportion of Double Cropped Area to Net Sown Area in Unirrigated Farms

IMPACT OF IRRIGATION ON CROPPING INTENSITY

Cropping intensity is considered as an indicator of the degree of intensity to which land is used for agricultural purposes. As we stated in chapter V, it is a ratio between the gross cropped area and the net cultivated area usually expressed in percentage terms[1]. It is the indicator which gives an idea regarding the number of times the same piece of land is used for growing number of crops during a particular year. In other words, cropping intensity gives idea about how intensively land is used for crop cultivation.

$$\text{Cropping intensity} = \frac{\text{Gross cropped area}}{\text{Net cropped area}} \times 100$$

The intensity of cropping will depend on several factors, such as availability of irrigation water, use of manures and nature of crops. As regards the irrigation water and manures, it may be argued that improvement in their use induces intensity of cropping. As regards the nature of crops, it may be pointed out that while there are crops which can be combined and can be grown on the same piece of land one after the other in different seasons during the same agricultural year, there are certain crops like sugarcane which are of long duration and as such do not permit another crop in the same year[2]. The fact is that irrigation alone does not constitute the sole factor determining the intensity of cropping.

Thus, the gross cropped area, net area sown and the index of cropping intensity of irrigated and unirrigated farms are presented in Table 6 and Graph 1. It is seen from this table and graph that the index of overall cropping intensity of the irrigated farms is 115.58 per cent as against 103.14 per cent for the unirrigated farms. It means the index of cropping intensity in irrigated farms is higher than unirrigated farms by 12.44 per cent. In other words, in irrigated condition 15.58 per cent of net sown area is brought under double or multiple cropping as against only 3.14 per cent of net sown area is brought under double or multiple cropping in unirrigated farming. This fact indicates that irrigation has contributed to more intensive use of land in irrigated farms and on the other hand, the cultivation of unirrigated farms is mainly based on monsoons which is uncertain and unpredictable. Therefore, the unirrigated farms are unable to raise more than one crop in unirrigated land.

Table 6
Gross Cropped Area (GCA), Net Area Sown (NAS) and Index of Cropping Intensity (ICI) in the Study area

Farm size	*GCA (in ha.)*	*NAS (in ha.)*	*ICI (percentage)*
(a) Irrigated farms			
1. Small	63.30	54.06	117.09
2. Medium	75.75	60.46	125.29
3. Large	135.59	123.09	110.16
Overall	274.64	237.61	115.58
(b) Unirrigated farms			
1. Small	47.48	44.88	105.79
2. Medium	36.00	35.00	102.86
3. Large	54.36	53.76	101.12
Overall	137.84	133.64	103.14

Source: Field survey

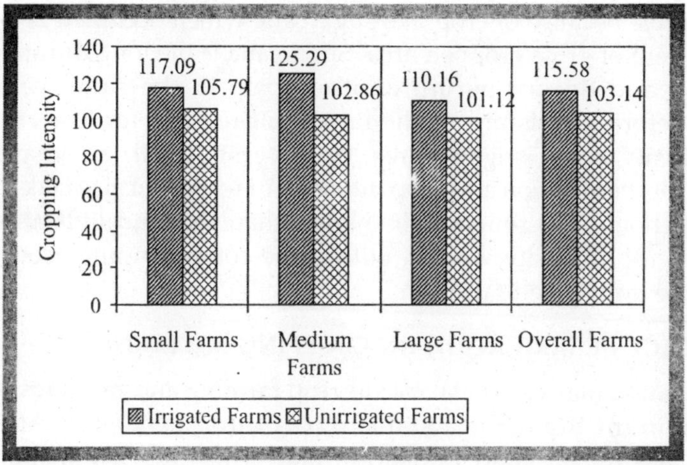

Graph 1: Farm Size-wise Cropping Intensity in the Study Area

The farm size wise data about cropping intensity reveals that the index of cropping intensity is relatively higher for each size group of farms in irrigated area than that of corresponding farms in unirrigated area. In case of irrigated area the cropping intensity index is found to be highest of 125.29 per cent for medium size class of farms and lowest of 110.16 per cent for large farms. In unirrigated area, size class of small farms has the highest crop intensity of 105.79 per cent and size class of large farms has the lowest intensity of 101.12 per cent. Thus, there is inverse relationship between the cropping intensity and the size class of farms in unirrigated area.

Thus, the second component of area effect of irrigation i.e. increase in gross cropped area resulting from enhanced cropping intensity is 20.85 per cent. As such our hypothesis is that provision of irrigation results in increased cropping intensity, which was substantiated in chapter V on the basis of macrolevel data, is further confirmed here by findings of the case study.

Although it was not strictly in conformity with our objective, yet incidentally we investigated into the causes as to why the crop intensity index in the irrigated study area increased only by 115.58 per cent and not more. It may be possible because of crop like sugarcane which occupied 28.82 per cent of gross cropped area. Sugarcane is the long duration crop and do not permit another crop in the same year. Therefore, this is one of the important reasons for low crop intensity in the irrigated area. However, in the irrigated area the land utilisation and crop intensity in respect of size class of land holding is found to be higher than the land utilisation and crop intensity worked out for the corresponding groups of the unirrigated farms.

IMPACT OF IRRIGATION ON CROPPING PATTERN

Irrigation plays a crucial role in crop farming and provides an important input for a stable agricultural economy. After discussing the land utilisation and crop intensity in both irrigated and unirrigated farms, an analysis of the extent of the area under all crops during survey year (1999-2000) is taken up in order to get the information about cropping pattern in irrigated and unirrigated areas.

Cropping pattern simply means the proportion of area under different crops at a point of time, whereas irrigation leads to change in cropping pattern refers to change in proportion of area under different crops at two different points of time. While classifying the effects of irrigation, Prof. Gadgil identified that the change in cropping pattern as one of the direct effect of irrigaiton[3]. The cropping pattern of any area is generally controlled by physical, socio-economic and technological factors. In semi-arid regions, like the study area, where rainfall is comparatively less, availability of irrigation water determines the cropping pattern. There are two main agricultural seasons (kharif and rabi) in the study area. The kharif crops generally depend considerably on natural rain water. The rabi crops are heavy and require more irrigation water. Further perennial crop like sugarcane requires large amount of irrigation water. Irrigation leads to the change in cropping pattern. It brings new varieties of existing crops and entirely new crops under cultivation in the same region. Further, the proportion of area under rabi and commercial crops increases with increase in irrigation water. Due to irrigation, it is observed that farmers are increasingly shifting from the cultivation of low value crops to high value crops.

Cropping Pattern in Sample Farms of Study Area

The data about area under different crops grown by sample farms in irrigated and unirrigated area was collected in the survey for the year 1999-2000. The proportion of area under different crops to gross cropped area for different size class of farms in irrigated and unirrigated area has been presented in Tables 7 and 8. These tables show the farm size wise cropping

Table 7

Cropping Pattern of Irrigated Sample Farms for Kharif and Rabi Seasons (1999 – 2000)

(Area in hectares)

	Size class of farms			
Crops	*Small*	*Medium*	*Large*	*Overall*
Kharif Season				
1. Jowar (Hy.)	5.30 (8.37)	7.30 (9.66)	14.00 (10.33)	26.60 (9.69)
2. Bajra	-	1.00 (1.32)	-	1.00 (0.36)
3. Rice	1.90 (3.00)	1.40 (1.85)	1.20 (0.89)	4.50 (1.64)
4. Tur	7.10 (11.22)	7.80 (10.33)	28.30 (20.86)	43.20 (15.74)
5. Udid	3.60 (5.69)	3.80 (5.03)	3.69 (2.72)	11.09 (4.04)
6. Sunflower	-	1.30 (1.72)	-	1.30 (0.47)
7. Others	1.50 (2.37)	0.40 (0.53)	1.60 (1.18)	3.50 (1.27)
Sub-total (1 to 7)	19.40 (30.65)	23.00 (30.44)	48.79 (35.98)	91.19 (33.23)
Rabi Season				
1. Jowar (Rabi)	7.10 (11.22)	12.60 (16.68)	25.60 (18.88)	45.30 (16.51)
2. Wheat	2.30 (3.63)	3.70 (4.90)	5.90 (4.35)	11.90 (4.34)
3. Gram	0.20 (0.32)	1.20 (1.59)	1.80 (1.33)	3.20 (1.17)
4. Others	-	-	0.20 (0.15)	0.20 (0.07)
Sub-total (1 to 4)	9.60 (15.17)	17.50 (23.16)	33.50 (24.71)	60.60 (22.08)
Summer Season				
1. Groundnut	8.90 (14.06)	11.45 (15.16)	13.20 (9.74)	33.55 (11.22)
Perennial				
1. Sugarcane	23.60 (37.28)	18.10 (23.96)	37.40 (27.58)	79.10 (28.82)
2. Turmeric	1.40 (2.21)	2.70 (3.57)	1.30 (0.96)	5.40(1.79)
Sub-total (1 to2)	25.00 (39.49)	20.80 (27.53)	38.70 (28.54)	84.50 (30.79)
Fruits and Vegetables	0.40 (0.63)	2.80 (3.71)	1.40 (1.03)	4.60 (1.68)
Grand Total	63.30 (100.00)	75.55 (100.00)	135.59(100.00)	274.44(100.00)

Note: Figures in brackets indicate the percentage to total.
Source: Field survey

Table 8
Cropping Pattern of Unirrigated Sample Farms for Kharif and Rabi Seasons (1999-2000)

(Area in hectares)

	Size class of farms			
Crops	*Small*	*Medium*	*Large*	*Overall*
(a) Kharif Season				
1. Jowar (Hy.)	8.73 (18.39)	5.00 (13.89)	14.40 (26.99)	28.13 (20.56)
2. Bajra	0.80 (1.68)	1.00 (2.78)	2.40 (4.50)	4.20 (3.07)
3. Rice	1.60 (3.37)	2.20 (6.11)	1.20 (2.25)	5.00 (3.65)
4. Tur	17.85 (37.59)	9.40 (26.11)	14.56 (27.29)	41.81 (30.55)
5. Udid	1.00 (2.11)	3.60 (10.00)	0.80 (1.50)	5.40 (3.95)
6. Matki	1.40 (2.95)	2.30 (6.39)	2.30 (4.31)	6.00 (4.38)
7. Sunflower	4.60 (9.69)	1.20 (3.33)	5.60 (10.49)	11.40 (8.33)
8. Groundnut	3.40 (7.16)	0.00 (0.00)	0.40 (0.74)	3.80 (2.78)
9. Others	0.80 (1.68)	1.00 (2.78)	2.40 (4.50)	4.20 (3.07)
Sub-total (1 to 9)	40.18 (84.63)	25.70 (71.39)	44.06 (82.57)	109.94 (80.34)
(b) Rabi season				
1. Jowar (Rabi)	7.10 (14.95)	10.30 (28.61)	8.90 (16.68)	26.30 (19.22)
2. Wheat	–	–	0.40 (0.75)	0.40 (0.29)
3. Gram	0.20 (0.42)	–	–	0.20 (0.15)
Sub-total (1 to 3)	7.30 (15.37)	10.30 (28.61)	9.30 (17.43)	26.90 (19.66)
Grand total	47.48 (100.00)	36.00 (100.00)	53.36 (100.00)	136.84 (100.00)

N.B.: Figures in brackets indicate the percentage to total.
Source: Field survey

pattern of irrigated and unirrigated farms. Further, different crops are classified into five categories viz. kharif, rabi, summer season, fruits and vegetables and the perennial crops. It is seen from these tables that the total area under different crops is 274.44 ha in irrigated sample farms, as against 136.84 ha in case of unirrigated farms. It is seen from these tables that, proportion of area under kharif season was 33.23 per cent of gross cropped area in irrigated farms as against 80.34 per cent in case of unirrigated farms. Thus, proportionate area under kharif season crops in unirrigated farms was higher than that in irrigated farms. Similarly, proportion of area under rabi season crops was 22.08 per cent in irrigated farms as against 19.60 per cent in unirrigated farms. This shows that, proportionate area under rabi season crops in irrigated farms was higher than that in unirrigated farms. Further, there was 30.79 per cent area under perennial crops, 12.22 per cent area under summer crops and 1.88 per cent area under fruits and vegetables in the irrigated farms. This is because in rainfed condition kharif crops are depended only on monsoon rainy water. Kharif crops are generally cheap and coarse and the farmers depend considerably on natural rain water. On the contrary, under the irrigated condition, the farmers are observed to be shifting cultivation area from low value crops too high value crops. The groundnut and sugarcane are found to be very popular commercial crops in irrigated area.

Kharif Season Crops

In kharif season, cereals like jowar (Hy.) and pulses like tur, udid were the predominant in both irrigated and unirrigated farms. In irrigated area, tur was most important crop which occupied 15.74 per cent of total cropped area in kharif season followed by jowar (hybrid) (9.69 per cent), udid (4.04 per cent), rice (1.64 per cent), sunflower (0.47 per cent) and bajra (0.36 per cent). On the contrary, in unirrigated farms the highest area in kharif season was found in the case of tur (30.55 per cent) followed by jowar (hybrid) (20.56 per cent), sunflower (8.33 per cent), matki (4.38 per cent), udid (3.95 per cent), rice (3.65 per cent), bajra (3.07 per cent) and groundnut (2.78 per cent). From this it is concluded that the proportionate area under kharif season crops to gross cropped area of unirrigated farms is higher than that of irrigated farms.

Rabi Season Crops

In rabi season, cereals like jowar and wheat were important crops both in irrigated and unirrigated farms. It is revealed from the Tables 7 and 8 that in overall crop pattern, rabi jowar has got top priority in the crop preference from farmers both in irrigated and unirrigated areas of the study region. This is because jowar is the main food crop of this region and it also gives fodder as by-product which is essential for feeding livestock. In case of irrigated farms the proportion of area under jowar (rabi) was 16.51 per cent followed by wheat (4.34 per cent), gram (1.17 per cent) and other crops (0.07 per cent). In unirrigated farms, jowar (rabi) was most favoured crop which covers 19.22 per cent of the gross cropped area followed by wheat (0.29 per cent) and gram (0.15 per cent). Thus, overall picture reveals that proportion of area under rabi crops in irrigated farms (22.08 per cent) was higher than the proportion of area under rabi crops in unirrigated farms (19.66 per cent).

Further, under irrigated condition, it is revealed from the Table 7 that the proportion of area under commercial crops like sugarcane, groundnut and fruits and vegetables was found to be very high in irrigated farms. Sugarcane was the most popular commercial crop in irrigated farming. The proportionate area under sugarcane crop was 28.82 per cent followed by groundnut (12.22 per cent), turmeric (1.97 per cent) and fruits and vegetables (1.68 per cent). In unirrigated area, the proportionate area under commercial crops like sunflower was 8.33 per cent and groundnut 2.78 per cent. From this it is seen that the proportionate area under commercial crops in irrigated farming was higher than the proportionate area under commercial crops in unirrigated farming. This indicates that cropping pattern of irrigated farming was in favour of commercial crops.

Farm size class wise observation has revealed that proportionate area under kharif crops to gross cropped area is the highest of 35.98 per cent for large farms and lowest of 30.44 per cent in case of medium farms in irrigated area. In unirrigated area, the proportionate area under kharif crops is the highest of 84.63 per cent for the small farms and lowest of 71.39 per cent in case of medium farms. Thus, it is observed from the tables 5.7 and 5.8 that proportionate area under kharif crops for each size class of farms in unirrigated area is higher than respective size class of farms in irrigated area. In irrigated area, proportionate area under rabi crops to gross cropped area is the highest of 24.71 per cent for the large farms and the lowest of 15.17 per cent in case of small farms. This fact indicates that the proportion of area under rabi crops increases with the increase in size class of farms in irrigated area. In unirrigated area, the proportionate area under rabi crops is the highest of 28.61 per cent for the medium farms and the lowest of 15.37

per cent for the small farms. There was no significant relation between proportion of area under rabi crops and size class of farms in unirrigated area. Further, it is also revealed by the Table 7 that in irrigated condition, the proportionate area under sugarcane crop to gross cropped area is the highest of 37.28 per cent for the small farms and the lowest of 27.58 per cent for the large size class of farms. Thus, the proportion of area under sugarcane crop decreases with the increase in the size class of farms in irrigated area. This fact indicates that there is inverse relationship between the proportion of area under sugarcane and the size class of farms in irrigated area. These tables also reveal that the proportionate area under commercial crops like sugarcane, groundnut, turmeric and vegetables is higher in irrigated area than the proportionate area under commercial crops (like groundnut and sunflower) in unirrigated area.

Thus, in overall crop pattern, the commercial crops are the dominant in irrigated area whereas in case of unirrigated area, the food grain crops are the dominant. The study has highlighted that the provision of irrigation has led to the process of commercialisation where the farmers prefer to grow high value crops instead of low value crops.

Cropping Pattern According to Crop Groups in the Study Area

The data about proportion of area under total cereals, pulses and cash crops in irrigated and unirrigated areas according to size class of farms has been presented in Table 9 and Figure 5. It is seen from this table and figure that all types of crops are grown in irrigated and unirrigated (rainfed) area except sugarcane, turmeric and vegetables which are grown only in irrigated condition. It is seen from this table and figure that overall gross cropped area is 274.44 ha. in irrigated farms as against 136.84 ha. in unirrigated farms. In irrigated condition, the proportionate area under cash crops to gross cropped area is 45.17 per cent as against only 11.11 per cent in unirrigated area. This fact shows that proportionate area under cash crops is higher in irrigated area as compared to proportionate share of cash crops in unirrigated area. Empirical studies have also proved this point[4]. It means the irrigation has encouraged the farmers to grow cash crops (commercial crops). The proportion of area under cereal crops to gross cropped area is higher (49.80 per cent) in unirrigated area as compared to proportion of area under these crops (33.81 per cent) in irrigated area.

Thus, the irrigation has discouraged the growth of cereal crops. Similarly, the proportion of area under pulses is also higher (39.03 per cent) in unirrigated area as compared to proportion of area under pulses (21.02 per cent) in irrigated area. This fact also indicates that irrigation has not encouraged the growth of pulses. Empirical studies also support this view[5].

From all above facts, it can be said that the irrigation facility leads to increase in the proportion of area under cash crops (commercial crops) like sugarcane, oilseeds and reduction in

Table 9
Area Under Total Cereals, Pulses and Cash Crops in Study Area (1999-2000)

(Area in hectares)

	Size class of farms			
Types of crops	*Small*	*Medium*	*Large*	Overall
(a) Irrigated Area				
Cereals	18.10	26.40	48.30	92.80
	(28.59)	(34.94)	(35.62)	(33.81)
Pulses	10.90	12.80	33.99	57.69
	(17.22)	(16.94)	(25.07)	(21.02)
Cash crops	34.30	36.35	53.30	123.95
	(54.19)	(48.12)	(39.31)	(45.17)
All crops	63.30	75.5	135.59	274.44
	(100.00)	(100.00)	(100.00)	(100.00)
(b) Unirrigated Area				
Cereals	19.03	19.50	29.70	68.23
	(40.08)	(54.17)	(55.66)	(49.86)
Pulses	20.45	15.30	17.66	53.41
	(43.07)	(42.50)	(33.10)	(39.03)
Cash crops	8.00	1.20	6.00	15.20
	(16.85)	(3.33)	(11.24)	(11.11)
All crops	47.48	36.00	53.36	136.84
	(100.00)	(100.00)	(100.00)	(100.00)

Note: Bracketed figures indicate the percentage to total.
Source: Field Survey.

proportion of area under cereals and pulses. From this study it can be concluded that irrigation has altered the area allocation between crops in favour of commercial crops in the study area.

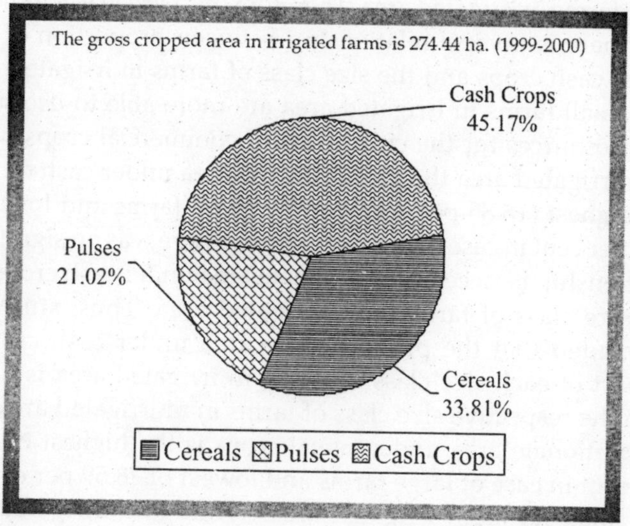

Figure 5 : Proportionate Area Under Different Crops in Irrigated Area

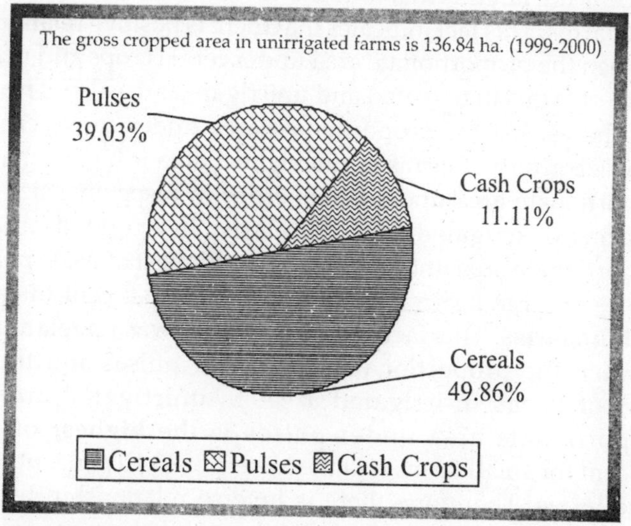

Figure 5A : Proportionate Area Under Different Crops in Unirrigated Area

Across the size of holdings, it is observed that the proportionate area under cash crops is the highest of 54.19 per cent for the small farms and lowest of 39.31 per cent in case of large farms in irrigated area. Therefore this fact clearly indicates that there is inverse relationship between proportion of area under cash crops and the size class of farms in irrigated area. The small farms in irrigated area are more able to use scarce land resources for the cultivation of commercial crops, while in unirrigated area the proportionate area under cash crops is the highest (16.85 per cent) for the small farms and lowest of 3.33 per cent in case of medium farms. There was no significant relationship between proportionate area under cash crops and the size class of farms in unirrigated area. Thus, study has concluded that the proportionate area under cash crops in respect of each size class of farms in irrigated area is higher than the respective size class of farms in unirrigated area. The proportionate area under cereal crops is the highest of 35.62 per cent in case of large farms and lowest of 28.59 per cent for the small farms in irrigated area. While in unirrigated area proportionate area under cereal crops is the highest of 55.66 per cent for large farms and the lowest of 40.08 per cent for small farms. This fact indicates that there is positive relationship between the proportionate area under cereal crops and the size group of farms in irrigated and unirrigated area also. The table also shows that the proportionate area under cereal crops in each size group of farms in unirrigated area is higher than the proportionate area under cereal crops in respective size class of farms of irrigated area. Similarly, in irrigated area the proportionate area under pulses is the highest of 25.07 per cent in case of large farms and lowest of 16.94 per cent in case of medium farms. This fact shows that there was no relationship between the proportionate area under pulses and the size class of farms in irrigated area. In unirrigated area, the proportionate area under pulses is the highest of 43.07 per cent for small farms and the lowest of 33.10 per cent for the large farms. Therefore, there is inverse relationship between the proportionate area under pulses and the size group of farms in unirrigated area. Thus, the study indicates that the proportionate area under pulses in each size group of farms in unirrigated area is higher than the respective size group of farms in irrigated area.

Thus the overall crop pattern shows that irrigation has led to increase in cultivation of high value crops instead of low value crops. Thus, the hypothesis that the irrigation favourably influences the crop pattern, which was substantiated on the basis of macro-data in Chapter V is verified again from the micro study and found to hold ground.

IMPACT OF IRRIGATION ON COSTS AND RETURNS IN THE STUDY AREA

The results of field investigation on costs and returns are discussed in this section. Estimates of different costs (cost A_2, cost B and cost C), gross value of output and indices of farm profit, (i.e. farm business income, returns to family labour and management and net returns) per hectare have been worked out for total farm enterprise for an agricultural year to throw light on the issues of relative efficiency of farms with and without irrigation.

The data about average input costs of cultivation (Cost A_2, cost B and cost C) and the gross value of output per hectare of net sown area in irrigated and unirrigated farms have been presented in Table 10. This table reveals that the overall operational cost, i.e. cost A_2, per hectare of net sown area for all crops in an agricultural year for irrigated farms is higher by Rs. 12,662.61. In case of irrigated farming, overall operational cost (i.e. cost A_2) per hectare of net sown area for all crops is Rs. 15337.87 as against Rs. 2675.26 in unirrigated farming. The per hectare operational cost of irrigated farms is higher on account of excess of associated costs involved in irrigated farming. Similarly, the overall cost B in irrigated farms is found to be Rs. 20,797.76 whereas it is Rs. 3,730.95 for unirrigated farms. This indicates that the overall cost B of irrigated farms is higher by Rs. 17,066.81 or 457.44 per cent over that of unirrigated farms. Further, the overall cost C in irrigated farms is Rs. 21,985.80 as against Rs. 4,260.55 in unirrigated area. Therefore, the overall cost C in irrigated farms is higher to the extent of Rs. 17,725.25 constituting 416.03 per cent, as compared to cost C in unirrigated farms.

Table 10
Different Input Costs of Cultivation and Gross Value of Output (GVO) of the Sample Farms in the Study Area

(Rupees per hectare of net sown area: All crops)

Size group of farms	*Cost A_2*	*Cost B*	*Cost C*	*Gross value of output (GVO)*
(a) Irrigated area				
Small	17398.85	24044.56	26054.79	33995.79
Medium	15061.05	19542.75	19962.22	26140.80
Large	11226.13	15366.66	15755.35	20881.09
Overall	15337.87	20797.76	21985.80	28786.67
(b) Unirrigated area				
Small	2922.58	4043.98	4751.16	5077.42
Medium	2331.44	3329.85	3753.92	4429.64
Large	2432.95	3378.83	3546.01	3548.60
Overall	2675.26	3730.95	4260.55	4614.35

Source: Field Survey.

Across the size of holdings, it is observed that operational cost (i.e. cost A_2) is the highest of Rs. 17,398.85 for the small farms in irrigated area, followed by medium (Rs. 15,061.05) and large farms (Rs. 11,226.13). This fact indicates that cost A_2 decreases with the increase in size class of farms in irrigated area. In unirrigated area, the cost A_2 is the highest of Rs. 2,922.58 for small farms and the lowest of Rs. 2,331.44 for the medium farms. Thus, there is no significant relationship between the cost A_2 and size class of farms in unirrigated area. Thus, the cost A_2 in relation to each size group of farms is significantly higher in irrigated area than the corresponding groups in unirrigated area. It is Rs. 17,398.85, Rs. 15,061.05 and Rs. 11,226.13 in small, medium and large farms respectively in irrigated area as compared to Rs. 2,922.58, Rs. 2,331.44 and Rs. 2,432.95 in the corresponding farms of unirrigated area. In other words, it is higher by Rs. 14, 476.27, Rs. 12,729.61 and Rs. 8,793.18 in small, medium and large farms respectively in irrigated area. In terms of percentage, it constitute 495.32 per cent, 546.00 per cent, 361.42 per cent higher in small, medium and large farms respectively in irrigated area. Thus, the overall cost A_2 is higher in irrigated farms as compared to unirrigated farms. This is on account of the excess of associated costs like sowing, transplanting, use of chemical fertilizers, use of more hired labour and use of irrigation, etc. involved in irrigated farming.

Similarly, cost B of small, medium and large farms in irrigated area is higher as compared to same size group of farms of unirrigated area. It is Rs. 24,044.56, Rs. 19542.75 and Rs. 15366.66 in small, medium and large farms respectively in irrigated area. In contrast, it is Rs. 4,043.98, Rs. 3,329.85 and Rs. 3,378.83 in the corresponding size group of farms in unirrigated area. It is higher by Rs. 20,000.58, Rs. 16,212.90 and Rs. 11,987.83 in small medium and large farms respectively in irrigated area. In other words, it is higher by 494.58 per cent, 486.89 per cent and 354.79 per cent in small medium and large irrigated farms respectively. Further, as regards the cost B in relation to the size of the holding, it is found that it is the highest of Rs. 24,044.56 for the small farms and the lowest of Rs. 15,366.66 for large farms in irrigated area. So there is inverse relationship between the cost B and size class of farms in irrigated area. In unirrigated area, there appears no uniform trend between the cost B and size class of farms since cost B is the highest of Rs. 4,043.98 for small farms, and the lowest of Rs. 3,329.85 for medium farms. This is due to the fact that cost B represents the aggregate of cost A_2 and rental value of own land and inter-size class differences in rental value do not neutralize the corresponding differentials in cost A_2. In the same way, cost C is also higher in small, medium and large farms in irrigated area when compared with the same size class of farms in unirrigated area. It is Rs. 26,054.79, Rs. 19,662.22 and Rs. 15,755.35 accounted for small, medium and large farms respectively in irrigated area. As against it is Rs. 4751.16, Rs. 3,753.92 and Rs. 3,546.01 for the corresponding size class of farms in unirrigated area. In other words, it is higher by Rs. 21,303.63, Rs. 16,208.30 and Rs. 12,209.34 respectively for the small, medium and large irrigated farms respectively. To put it in terms of percentage, it is higher by 448.39 per cent, 431.77 per cent and 344.31 per cent in small, medium and large farms respectively in irrigated area as compared to the corresponding farms of irrigated area. Further as regards the cost C, in relation to size class of farms, it is the highest of Rs. 26,054.79 for the small farms and the lowest of Rs. 15,755.35 for the large farms in irrigated area. In unirrigated area, it is the highest of Rs. 4,751.16 in case of small farms and the lowest of Rs. 3,546.01for the large farms. Thus, this shows that, cost C decreases with the increase in size class of farms both in irrigated and unirrigated farming. However, the cost C in irrigated area is higher as compared to that in unirrigated area. This is because all farms in irrigated area incur more expenditure when compared with the corresponding farms in unirrigated area.

Any way, cost A_2, cost B and cost C in case of each size class of farms in irrigated area are higher than the corresponding costs in each size class of farms in unirrigated area.

The Table 10 also reveals that, per hectare gross income or gross value of output for all crops is Rs. 28,786.67 in irrigated farms as against Rs. 4,614.35 in unirrigated farms. Therefore, the over all per hectare gross value of output in irrigated farms is significantly higher by 6.24 times as compared to per hectare gross value of output in unirrigated farms. In case of gross value of output, taking inter-size group of farms into consideration, it is found that the gross value of output of small, medium and large farms in irrigated area is higher when compared to the same size group of farms in unirrigated area. It is Rs. 33,995.79, Rs. 26,140.80 and Rs. 20,881.09 for the small, medium and large farms respectively in irrigated area as compared to Rs. 5,077.42, Rs. 4,429.64 and Rs. 3,548.60 for the corresponding farms respectively in unirrigated area. In other words, it is 6.69, 5.90 and 5.88 times higher in small, medium and large farms respectively in irrigated area when compared to respective farms in unirrigated area. Thus, irrigation has enabled the farmers to raise their gross value of output when compared with farmers in unirrigated area. It is also seen from the Table 10 that gross value of output decreases with the increase in size of class of farms both in irrigated and unirrigated area. This fact show that as regards gross value of output in irrigated and unirrigated areas, small farms are more successful as compared to medium and large farms. Any way, the gross value of output (per hectare) is higher in irrigated area as compared to that in unirrigated area. This is because the irrigation has largely contributed to increase gross value of output or gross income in irrigated farms. The farm size-wise observation reveals that the gross value of output per hectare of net sown area as the norm for determination of inter -size class relative farm efficiency, then the small farms both in irrigated and in unirrigated conditions would emerge as the most efficient. In other words, small holdings become operationally more viable when compared to large holdings.

MEASURES OF FARM PROFIT

It is the farm profit, but not the absolute size of crop income which is an appropriate indicator of economic efficiency. For this, the details of farm business income, returns to family labour and management and net income or net return with respect to sample farms in both irrigated and unirrigated farming have been separately worked out and are presented in Table 11. It is seen from this table that overall farm business income in irrigated farms is significantly higher than that in unirrigated farms. It is Rs. 13448.80 in irrigated area as against Rs. 1939.09 in unirrigated area. This shows that the overall farm business income is 6.93 times higher in irrigated farms. This is because irrigation has helped to use more inputs resulting in increased production and productivity in irrigated farming. Thus, the farm business income from irrigated lands is found in positive side. Further, the farm business income for the small, medium and large farms in irrigated area is also higher than respective farms of unirrigated area. It is Rs. 16,596.95, Rs. 11,079.74 and Rs. 9,654.96 for the small, medium and large farms respectively in irrigated area as against Rs. 2,154.84, Rs.2,098.20 and Rs.1,115.64 for the corresponding farms in unirrigated area. In other words, it is 7.70, 5.28 and 8.65 times higher for the small, medium and large farms respectively in irrigated area

Table 11
Farm Business Income (FBI), Returns to Family Labour and Management (RFLM) and Net Income (NI) of Sample Farms in Irrigated and Unirrigated Area

(Rupees per hectare of net sown area from all crops per annum)

Size class of farms	*FBI*	*RFLM*	*NI*
(a) Irrigated area			
Small	16596.95	9951.23	7941.00
Medium	11079.74	6598.95	6178.85
Large	9654.96	5514.43	5125.74
Overall	13448.80	7988.91	6800.87
(b) Unirrigated area			
Small	2154.84	1033.44	326.26
Medium	2098.20	1099.78	675.72
Large	1115.64	169.77	2.59
Overall	1939.09	883.40	353.80

Source: Field survey.

than the respective size groups of farms in unirrigated area. This is due to the fact that irrigation has helped to use more inputs resulting in increased production and productivity. Inter-size group of farms comparison revealed that the farm business income is the highest in small farms and the lowest in case of large farms in irrigated and unirrigated areas. Thus, there is inverse relationship between the farm business income and the size class of farms both in irrigated and unirrigated areas. Thus, the small farms both in irrigated and unirrigated conditions as regards the farm business income, would emerge as the most efficient.

Similarly, the overall return to family labour and management is found to be Rs. 7,988.91 in irrigated area as against Rs. 883.40 in unirrigated area. In other words, it is higher by 9.58 times in irrigated area. This fact shows that the overall returns to family labour and management in irrigated farms is much higher than that of unirrigated farms. The size class of farms observation for the returns to family labour and management in both irrigated and unirrigated area also reveals that it is also higher in case of small, medium and large farms in irrigated area when compared to the respective size class of farms in unirrigated area. It is found to be Rs. 9,951.23, Rs. 6,598.05 and Rs. 5,514.43 for the small, medium and large farms respectively in irrigated area. On the contrary, it is Rs. 1,033.44, Rs. 1,099.78 and only Rs. 169.77 for the corresponding farms in unirrigated area. To put it in another way, it is 9.63, 5.10 and 31.89 times higher in small, medium and large farms respectively in irrigated area as compared to the respective farms of unirrigated area. The inter-size class of farms observation also shows that the return to family labour and management also decreases with the increase in size class of farms in irrigated area. It is observed that return to family labour and management is the highest of Rs. 9,951.23 in case of small farms and the lowest of Rs. 5,514.43 for the large farms in irrigated area. In unirrigated area, it is the highest of Rs. 1,099.78 for the medium farms and lowest of only Rs. 169.77 for the large farms. Thus, no clear-cut relationship is found between the return to family labour and management and size class of farms in unirrigated area.

In the same way, overall net return in irrigated area is also significantly higher than that of unirrigated area. It is Rs. 6,800.87 in irrigated area as against only Rs. 353.80 in unirrigated area. In other words, it is 19.22 times higher in irrigated area than that of net return in unirrigated area. This shows that overall net return in irrigated area is much higher than that of unirrigated area. In other words, it is 19.22 times higher in irrigated area than that of unirrigated area. Similarly, the net return of small, medium and large farms in irrigated area is also significantly higher than respective farms of unirrigated area. It is found to be Rs. 7,941.00, Rs. 6,178.58 and Rs. 5,125.74 respectively for small, medium and large farms in irrigated area, when compared to Rs. 326.26, Rs. 675.72 and only Rs. 2.59 for the respective size groups of farms of unirrigated area. In other words, it is 24.34, 9.14 and 1979.05 times higher for the small, medium and large farms in irrigated area as compared to corresponding farms of unirrigated area. The net return or income decreases with an increase in size class of farms in irrigated area. Net return is the highest of Rs. 7,941.00 for the small farms and the lowest of Rs. 5,125.74 for the large farms in irrigated area. As against this, it is independent of its size class of farms in unirrigated area. It is the highest of Rs. 675.72 for the medium farms followed by small farms (Rs. 326.26) and large farms (only Rs. 2.59) of unirrigated area.

Thus, the farm business income, return to family labour and management and net income are significantly higher in irrigated farms when compared with unirrigated farms. This is due to the reason that on account of the irrigation facility, the sample farmers are assured of output resulting in increase of farm income in irrigated farming. On the contrary, the agricultural production and income in unirrigated farming depends on the monsoon which is uncertain and unpredictable. Naturally production suffers resulting in decreased income in unirrigated area.

Incremental Farm Business Income, Return to Family Labour and Management and Net Income

The additional farm business income, return to family labour and management and net income generated by irrigated farms over those of unirrigated farms have been worked out and are presented in Table 12.

Table 12

Excess of Farm Business Income (FBI), Return to Family Labour and Management (RFLM) and Net Income (NI) in Irrigated Farms over Unirrigated Farms

(Rs. per hectare)

Size group of farms	*Excess FBI*	*Excess RFLM*	*Excess NI*
Small	14442.11	8917.79	7614.74
Medium	8981.54	5498.27	5502.86
Large	8539.32	5344.66	5123.15
Overall	11509.71	7105.51	6447.07

Source: Field survey.

This table reveals that the overall farm business income in irrigated farms is higher by Rs. 11509.71 per hectare per annum. This is because irrigated farm operators receive substantially higher amounts of farm business income. Our major hypothesis is that the per hectare of irrigated land is more economically profitable to cultivate rather than per hectare of unirrigated land is substantiated. The size class of small, medium and large farms in irrigated area received substantially higher amount of farm business income of Rs. 14,442.11, Rs. 8,981.54 and Rs. 8,539.32 respectively than that of the respective size class of farms in unirrigated area. Further, while the small farms obtain the maximum excess farm business income (Rs. 14,442.11) and the large farms receive the lowest farm business income (Rs. 8,539.32). The excess of farm business income in case of medium farms lies in between.

Another index of farm operator's welfare is family labour income. The overall incremental return to family labour and management per hectare in irrigated farms works out to Rs. 7,105.51 over unirrigated farms. As regards the returns to family labour and management in case of the small, medium and large farms, it is also significantly higher by Rs. 8,917.79, Rs. 5,498.27 and Rs. 5,344.66 respectively in irrigated area over the corresponding size class of farms in unirrigated area. Further, it is also found that there is the highest increase in return to family labour and management of Rs. 8,917.79 for small farms and the lowest of Rs. 5,344.66 for the large farms in irrigated area.

However, the net return or net income also possess high significance as an index of farmers economic well being. The overall net income is higher by Rs. 6,447.07 per hectare per annum in irrigated farms than that in unirrigated farms. This fact indicates that provision of irrigation facility increases the farm income as compared to farms in unirrigated area. This also establishes support to hypothesis that irrigated farming is more profitable than the unirrigated farming. The net income of small, medium and large farms is found to be considerably higher in irrigated area over the respective size class of farms of unirrigated area. It is Rs. 7,614.74, Rs. 5,502.86 and Rs. 5,123.15 respectively for the small, medium and large farms in irrigated area than the corresponding farms in unirrigated area. As regards the excess of net income, it is found to be the highest of Rs. 7,614.74 for small farms, and the lowest of Rs. 5,123.15 for the large farms in irrigated area.

Thus, the above analysis shows that the provision of irrigation facility increases the farm income of small, medium and large farms as compared to corresponding farms of unirrigated area.

Statistical Significance Test for Farm Business Income, Return to Family Labour and Management and Net Return

The following 't' values (Fisher's 't') for irrigated and unirrigated farm households in each size group of farms and each type of income, i.e. farm business income, return to family labour and management and net income are presented in Table 13.

This table clearly reveals that the 't' values are significant throughout. Therefore, it can be conclusively said that irrigated farm households, on an average, receive significantly higher income than that of unirrigated farm households in the study area. This is true for each size class of farms (i.e. small, medium and large farms) and for all kinds of incomes (i.e. farm business income, return to family labour and management and net

Table 13
't' Values for different Incomes between Irrigated and Unirrigated Farms in each Size Class

(Rs. per hectare)

Size group of farms	*Income*	*Irrigated*	*Unirrigated*	*'t' values (Fisher's 't')*
Small	FBI	16,596.95	2,154.84	9.16**
	RFLM	9,951.23	1,033.44	6.65**
	NR	7,941.00	326.26	5.68**
Medium	FBI	11,079.74	2,098.20	3.30**
	RFLM	6,598.05	1,099.78	2.34*
	NR	6,178.58	675.72	2.36*
Large	FBI	9,654.96	1,115.64	3.90**
	RFLM	5,514.43	169.77	2.91**
	NR	5,125.74	2.59	3.49**
All farms	FBI	13,448.80	1,939.09	9.28**
	RFLM	7,9888.91	883.40	7.08**
	NR	6,800.87	353.80	6.54**

** Significant at 1 per cent
* Significant at 5 per cent

Source: Field survey.

return). Thus, the provision of irrigation facility tends to distribute income in manner favouring the irrigated farms in general as well as farms in each size class of farms in irrigated areas in comparison with unirrigated farms. This study has indicated that irrigated farming leads to regional differences in income distribution between irrigated and unirrigated areas. If this imbalance in income distribution has to be checked in the rural sector, immediate steps should be taken to provide the irrigation facility in unirrigated areas.

OUTPUT–INPUT RATIO

The impact of irrigation can also be analysed from a study of the relative output–input ratios under irrigated and unirrigated conditions. The output–input ratio has been obtained by dividing the gross value of output by different costs of cultivation. The input–output ratios of gross revenue to cost A-$_2$, cost B and cost C for irrigated and unirrigated farms have been presented in Table 14.

Table 14

Ratio of Gross Return (GR) to Cost A_2, Cost B and Cost C

Size class of farms	*Ratio of GR to cost A_2*	*Ratio of GR to cost B*	*Ratio of GR to cost C*
1	2	3	4
(a) Irrigated area			
Small	1.95	1.41	1.30
Medium	1.83	1.34	1.31
Large	1.86	1.36	1.33
Overall	1.88	1.38	1.31
(b) Unirrigated area			
Small	1.74	1.25	1.07
Medium	1.80	1.33	1.18
Large	1.46	1.05	1.00
Overall	1.72	1.24	1.08

Source: Field Survey.

This table reveals that, the overall ratios of gross value of output to cost A_2, cost B and cost C are found to be 1.88, 1.38 and 1.31 respectively in irrigated area as against 1.72, 1.24 and

1.08 respectively in unirrigated area. This indicates that the overall ratios of gross value of output or gross return to cost A_2 cost B and cost C are higher in irrigated area than that in unirrigated area.

As regards the different size group of holdings, output-input ratios are higher in irrigated area. The ratio of gross value of output to cost A_2, cost B and cost C of small farms are 1.95, 1.41 and 1.30 respectively in irrigated area as against 1.74, 1.25 and 1.07 respectively for small group of farms in unirrigated area. Thus, it is observed that, they are relatively higher for the small farms in irrigated area. Similarly with regard to medium farms in irrigated area, the ratios of gross value of output to cost A_2, cost B and cost C are 1.83, 1.34 and 1.31 respectively as against 1.80, 1.33and 1.18 in medium farms of unirrigated area. All the three ratios are higher for medium farms in irrigated area when compared with medium farms in unirrigated area. Further, the ratio of gross value of output to cost A_2, cost B and cost C of large farms are 1.86, 1.36 and 1.33 respectively in irrigated area. On the contrary, they are 1.46, 1.05 and 1.00 respectively for the large farms in unirrigated area. To put it in another way, these ratios are relatively higher for the large farms in irrigated area. Thus, the return per rupee of investment, as indicated by output–input ratio shows that the farming in irrigated area is more profitable than that in unirrigated area. This supports the hypothesis that irrigated crop enterprise is more remunerative than the unirrigated one.

IMPACT OF IRRIGATION ON EMPLOYMENT

Irrigation responds favourably in generation of additional employment opportunities in farm sector. William Sander observes that agricultural modernization primarily due to irrigation development helps to stimulate non-farm employment of a region[6]. Thus, the irrigation also leads to enhanced employment opportunities in activities whose linkages with the agricultural sector are high.

The results of the field investigation about the creation of gainful employment opportunities are presented in Table 15. This table shows the number of man-days of employment per hectare of net sown area per annum for all crop enterprises in irrigated and unirrigated farming condition. The man-days of employment consists of eight hours of work and refers to family labour as well as hired labour. The hired labour in study area are of two types, namely: (a) casually hired labour consisting of male and female workers employed on daily basis, and (b) contract labour or permanently attached labour as employed on an annual basis with cash payment.

Table 15
Man-Days of Employment under Irrigated and Unirrigated Conditions in the Study Area

	Irrigated	*Unirrigated*		
Size group of farms	*Average man-days of employment per hectare of net sown area*	*Average man-days of employment per hectare of net sown area*	*Excess man-days of employment in irrigated area*	*Per cent excess man-days of employment in irrigated area*
Small	144.15	31.18	112.97	362.31
Medium	114.27	27.49	86.78	315.68
Large	95.51	16.58	78.93	476.05
Overall	111.35	24.34	87.01	357.48

Source: Field Survey.

This table reveals that the overall average man-days of employment is 111.35 in irrigated area as against 24.34 man-days in unirrigated area. This fact shows that average man-days of employment in irrigated area is higher than that of unirrigated area. In other words, a hectare of irrigated farm enhances the labour use by 87.01 man-days resulting in 357.48 per cent excess man-days employment. To put in another way, the excess man-days of employment per hectare is registered at 87.01 man-days and constitutes for as high as 357.48 per cent. This employment includes both the family labour as well as hired labour. Thus, the overall average man-days of employment per hectare in irrigated area is higher than that in unirrigated area. This supports the hypothesis that irrigation facility has increased immensely the generation of more employment opportunities in agriculture. It has been stated earlier that such a situation occurs on account of higher intensity, diversification of crop pattern and cultivation of labour intensive crops in the irrigated farming as compared to that in unirrigated area.

As regards the average man-days employment, the size class of farms observation shows that it is also higher for small, medium and large farms in irrigated area as compared to corresponding farms of unirrigated area. The small farms in irrigated area generated 144.15 man-days of employment as against only 31.18 man-days of employment for the small farms in unirrigated area. In other words, there is 112.97 man-days of excess employment (i.e. higher by 362.31 per cent) per hectare in small farms of irrigated area. Further, the medium farms create 114.27 man-days of employment per hectare in irrigated area when compared to 27.49 man-days of employment of medium farms in unirrigated area. To put it in another way, man-days of employment per hectare in medium farms of irrigated area is higher by 86.78 man-days (i.e. 315.68 per cent) than that of medium farms in unirrigated area. Similarly, the large farms in irrigated area also generated 95.51 man-days of employment as against only 16.58 man-days of employment for large farms in unirrigated area. In other words, in large farms of irrigated area per hectare employment was higher by 78.93 man-days (i.e. 476.05 per cent) than that in large farms of unirrigated area. This table also reveals that the average man-days of employment decreases along with an increase in size of holdings in both irrigated as well as unirrigated area. This fact clearly indicates that the small farms are able to generate higher employment opportunities as compared to other size class of farms of both irrigated and unirrigated areas. In brief, the irrigation, thus, has contributed largely to increase farm employment opportunities of sample farms in irrigated area as compared with unirrigated area.

To sum up, the illustrative field study conducted for the irrigated and unirrigated farms in Osmanabad district has positively confirmed the different hypotheses. Therefore, from a micro-level evaluation of the impacts of irrigation on agriculture in study area, the following tentative conclusions have emerged. It has been observed that average size of family is higher for the irrigated sample farms as compared to unirrigated farms. As regards the average size of land holding, it is also higher for the sample farms in irrigated area than that in unirrigated area. The level of literacy (education) of irrigated sample farms is significantly higher when compared with unirrigated farms and which will help in understanding the agricultural problems and quick adopting of innovations taking place in farming business. Further, the study has also observed that there is better land use pattern in irrigated area than that of land use pattern in unirrigated area. The irrigated farmers are more efficient in land utilization than the farmers of unirrigated area. The index of overall crop intensity in irrigated area is significantly higher as compared to unirrigated area. The cropping pattern is also favourable in the irrigated area with more diversification and cultivation of high value crops as compared to unirrigated area. The irrigation has largely contributed to increase in total revenue or gross value of output. The overall per hectare gross value of output is largely higher in irrigated farms when compared with unirrigated farms. In irrigated farming the different costs as well as the gross returns are significantly higher than those in unirrigated farming. The different measures of farm profit (farm business income, return to family labour and management and net return) per hectare are higher in irrigated farming as compared to those of unirrigated farms. The output-input ratios are also found to be comparatively higher in irrigated farms. The average man-days of employment is also relatively higher in irrigated area. Thus, there is no denying of the fact that irrigation has been beneficial for farm economy in sample area and hypotheses developed earlier have been further substantiated by the micro study.

Notes and References

1. Sing Jasbir, An Agricultural Geography of Haryana, 1976, pp. 309-310.

2. Mishra, S., A Comparative Study of the Economics of Minor Sources of Irrigation in Uttar Pradesh (A Report), Oxford and I.B.H. Publishing Co., 1969, p. 39.

3. Gadgil D.R., Economic Effects of Irrigation, Report of Survey of the Direct and Indirect Benefits of Godavari and Pravara Canals, Publication No. 17, Gokhale Institute of Economics and Politics, Pune, 1948, pp. 21-24.
4. Shah S.M., Cropping Pattern in Relation to Irrigation, *Indian Journal of Agricultural Economics,* Vol. XVIII(1), January-March, 1963, pp. 154-60.
5. Krishnan A., Climate Approach to Cropping Pattern Adaptability in Western Rajasthan, In Proceedings of the 'Symposium on Cropping Pattern in India' (ed.) ICAR, Delhi, 1972, pp. 125-71.
6. William Sander, Irrigation Development and Non-farm Employment Changes in Communities in the Philippines, *Indian Journal of Agricultural Economics,* Vol. XXXVIII, No. 1, January-March., 1983, p. 14.

CHAPTER 6

FINDINGS AND POLICY MEASURES

Irrigation plays an important role in agricultural growth and development. It plays a protective role against the vagaries of monsoon. Irrigation acts as a catalytic agent and one of crucial factors in the package of improved inputs and new technology. Green revolution has proved successful only in those areas which have assured irrigation facilities. It is due to irrigation that India has been in a comfortable position with regard to the availability of foodgrain production.

From the launching of the First Five Year Plan till now, the irrigation along with agriculture has been accorded the highest place in our developmental schemes and investment priorities. Therefore, it is necessary to insure that irrigation development creates favourable impact on agriculture and ultimately on the life of the rural households. From this point of view, it is necessary to assess the irrigation impact on agriculture development. The study is undertaken with this view. The district like Osmanabad (in Marathwada region) in Maharashtra state known as drought prone area is purposely selected for the present study. Agriculture is the main occupation of the people in this district and more than 80 per cent of workforce depend on farm sector for their livelihood. After the formation of Maharashtra state and since the Third Five Year Plan, efforts have been made for the development of irrigation in this district and now 17 per cent of gross cropped area is under irrigation. Against such a background, this study was intended the important findings of the present study and their policy implications are discussed below.

FINDINGS

Important findings of the present study are briefly summarised below. All these finding are the results of analysis of both macro and micro–level studies in Osmanabad district. For micro level impact of irrigation on farm economy, the field survey was conducted in study area during year 1999-2000. Use of relevant secondary data collected from different sources pertaining to irrigation development in India, Maharashtra, Marathwada and in Osmanabad district have also helped in drawing some important findings.

Irrigation Development in India

Irrigation has played a vital role in continuous process of agricultural development in India. In successive Five Year plans irrigation development has been given top priority. During the pre-independence period, the emphasis used to be given for developing water resources only as a protective measure against crop failure and famine. In the post-independence area, emphasis was changed to develop irrigation as one of the main productive inputs in agriculture. With the massive investment on irrigation schemes, it became possible to undertake 292 major and 944 medium projects during last 47 years (i.e. 1951 to 1997) in India. The ultimate irrigation–potential of the country has been estimated to be 139.9 m. ha, comprising 75.90 m. ha (54.22 per cent) from surface water and 64.00 m. ha (45.78 per cent) from the ground water resources. Thus, the irrigation facility in India rose from 22.60 million hectares to 91.79 million hectares (i.e. 4 times) during last 47 years. This additional irrigation facility has been provided by completed 158 major and 768 medium and on going 119 major and 176 medium projects along with state sector surface and ground water minor irrigation schemes in India. As compared to just about 18 per cent of the cropped area under irrigation at the time of independence, the irrigation level has since increased to 38 per cent in 1995-96 though there has been an increase of nearly 42 per cent in cropped area.

Irrigation Development in Maharashtra

Before the formation of Maharashtra State, it is found that, position of irrigation development in the state was very poor. However, irrigation development programmes got real boost on inception of the Five - Year Plans, particularly from second plan onwards. Thus, with massive investment in irrigation schemes, it became possible to undertake 125 major, 373 medium and 8130 minor projects during last 46 years (i.e. 1951 to 1997) in Maharashtra State. The ultimate irrigation potential of state has been recently estimated to be 12.6 million hectares by the second irrigation commission (October 2000), comprising, 8.5 million hectares (67.46 per cent) from surface water and 4.1 million hectares, (i.e. 32.54 per cent) from ground water resources. The government of Maharashtra has been provided large amount of money for the irrigation development schemes through successive plans. Therefore, during last 46 years (i.e. 1951-52 to 1996-97), the states irrigation potential has increased from 3.14 lakh hectares to 32.21 lakh hectares. The additional irrigation facility has been provided by the completed 50 major, 182 medium and 2880 minor projects and partial ongoing 49 major, 128 medium and 856 minor projects in the state. It was just about 6 per cent of cropped area was under irrigation at the time of formation of the Maharashtra state (1960). The state's irrigation has since increased to 15.40 per cent in the year 1998–99 though there has been an increase of nearly 20per cent in cropped area. In the study of utilized irrigation potential in India and Maharashtra, it is observed that percentage of utilized irrigation potential in India is near about 90 per cent as against only 40 per cent in Maharashtra state in 1995-96. Thus, the utilized irrigation potential is the series problem in case of Maharashtra State when compared with India.

Macro–level Impact of Irrigation

The study was intended to objectively evaluate the major macro-level impacts of irrigation on agriculture in the study area.

On the whole, the benefits of irrigation development have been found to be positive in the study area. The analysis of area effects of irrigation showed that, during last fourteen years (i.e. 1982-83 to 1995-96), there was gradual increase (4.18 per cent) in net cultivated area, 20.85 per cent increase in both double and gross cropped area in the study area. The impact of irrigation on the extension of cultivated (net, total and double) shows the scope for bringing new lands under plough is limited. The extension of irrigation facilities has led to the expansion of double and gross cropped area. Even though the benefits of irrigation development have not been able to appreciably push up the net area sown in the district, the area effects of irrigation have been significant with increase in the index of crop intensity, resulting from double and multiple cropping. The crop intensity index has increased from 104.08 per cent to 124.93 per cent during last fourteen years in the district. The study has also observed that, there is high correlation between the intensity of irrigation and intensity of cropping in Osmanabad district. The "crop pattern effect" of irrigation has been favourable in the study area, since the irrigation has helped the farmers in shifting cultivated area from low value crops to high value crops. During last fourteen years, there was 5.66 per cent of gross cropped area increase in kharif cultivated area. Kharif jowar was the most favourable crop in 1982 followed by tur, oilseeds, sugarcane, paddy and bajra. But after a lapse of fourteen years oilseeds has become most favourable crop in kharif season. Similarly, there was also increase in cultivated area under tur, sugarcane and decrease in area under jowar (hybrid). This shows that introduction of kharif irrigation has helped the farmers to switch over from low yielding dry crops to high yielding wet crops. There was considerable increase in rabi cultivated area during last fourteen years in the district. In the year 1982, jowar (rabi) was the most important crop in the district followed by oilseeds, grams, wheat, fruits and vegetables. After lapse of fourteen years, jowar (rabi) remains the most favourable crop but there was small decrease (-0.44 per cent of gross cropped area) in area under jowar and increase (+2.67 per cent of gross cropped area) in area under oilseeds. There was also decrease in cultivated area under wheat (-1.60 per cent), gram (-1.01 per cent) and increase in cultivated area under fruits and vegetables (+0.26 per cent) during last fourteen years in the district. The per hectare yield effect of irrigation has too been favourable for both kharif and rabi crops in the district. During last fourteen years, there was considerable increase in per hectare crop yields of kharif and rabi crops in the study area. Thus, as a consequence of the cumulative effects of increased crop intensity, shift in crop pattern and enhanced yield rate, there has been an augmentation in the total volume of agricultural production in the district. The beneficial role of irrigation in bringing stability to crop output is observed. A positive correlation between total irrigated area and total crop production and irrigated area under non-foodgrains and non-foodgrain production is observed during last fourteen years in the district. But correlation between irrigated area under foodgrains and food-grain production is found to be insignificant. This fact also showed that, during last fourteen years, irrigation development is in favour to farmers for the diversification from the traditional cereal crops to commercial crops in the district.

Thus, from the study of macro-level analysis, it can be concluded that, during last fourteen years (1982-83 to 1995-96), because of expansion and intensive utilization of irrigation facilities, Osmanabad district has made rapid strides in agriculture. The macro-level different impacts of irrigation on agriculture have been found to be positive in the district.

Micro-level Impact of Irrigation

From a micro-level evaluation of impact of irrigation on agriculture in the study area, the following tentative conclusions have emerged.

Irrigation and Family Size

In the study of micro-level impact of irrigation on family size in the district, it is observed that, the average size of family is higher in irrigated sample farms as compared to unirrigated farms, the figures being 4.58 and 3.95 respectively. It increases with the increase in size of holding in both irrigated as well as unirrigated farms which shows that, relatively larger farms have more members to support. But when the size of family is considered *vis-a-vis* number of persons per hectare, the opposite trend is noticed. The size of family per hectare is inversely related to the size of land holding that relatively smaller farms had larger members to support as compared to the relatively larger farms. This means land-man ratio is unfavourable to the small farm operators.

Irrigation and Literacy

The overall literacy in irrigated area is (86.85) per cent as against (77.58) per cent in unirrigated area. This showed that, overall literacy in irrigated area is higher when compared with unirrigated area. In the study of level of literacy in relation to the size-group of farms, it is the highest of 92.00 per cent in case of medium farms and lowest of 81.17 per cent for small farms in irrigated area. In unirrigated area, it is the highest of 85.71 per cent in case of medium farms and lowest of 74.19 per cent for small farms. Thus, there was no significant relation between the literacy and size-group of farms in irrigated and unirrigated areas.

Irrigation Impact on Land use Pattern

The landuse pattern in irrigated area is found to be better useful than that of unirrigated areas. It is observed that irrigated farmers are more efficient in land utilisation (i.e. 76.86 per cent) when compared with land utilisation (66.92 per cent) in unirrigated area.

Irrigation Impact on Crop Intensity

The index of crop intensity is found to be 115.58 in irrigated area in the contrast it is 103.14 per cent in unirrigated area. Thus, overall crop intensity in irrigated area is found to be higher than in unirrigated area. It is also true for every size class of farms in irrigated area when compared with corresponding size class of farms in unirrigated area. Further, it is also observed that, crop intensity was the highest of 125.29

per cent in case of medium farms and lowest of 110.16 in case of large farms. In unirrigated area, it was the highest of 105.79 per cent in case of small farms and lowest (101.12 per cent) for the large farms. This showed that, there was no significant relation in between the index of crop intensity and size-group of farms in irrigated as well as unirrigated area.

Irrigation Impact on Cropping Pattern

Field observations indicate that irrigation has induced the farmers in irrigated area to grow cash crops as compared to the unirrigated area. Long duration crop like sugarcane was the most popular cash crop which covers the 28.82 per cent of gross cropped area in irrigated area and followed by groundnut (11.20 per cent), turmeric (1.79 per cent), fruits and vegetables (1.68 per cent) and sunflower (0.47 per cent). On the other hand, a few cash crops like sunflower (8.33 per cent)and groundnut (2.78 per cent) are raised in unirrigated area. This indicates that the cropping pattern in irrigated area is in favour of commercial crops as compared to unirrigated area. Further, it is also found that there is a tendency to take more commercial crops like sugarcane, groundnut, turmeric, fruits and vegetables in case of all size class farms in irrigated area when compared with corresponding size class farms in unirrigated area. In study of grouping crops, it is observed that, irrigation has discouraged the growth of food crops (cereals and pulses) and encouraged to growth of commercial crops. The proportion of area under food-grains (88.89 per cent) is found to be higher in unirrigated area, as compared to proportion of area under food-grain crops (54.83 per cent) in irrigated area. Similarly, the proportion of area under commercial crops (45.17 per cent) is found to be more in irrigated area. Across the size-groups of farms, the proportion of area under commercial crops is the highest 54.19 per cent in small farms and lowest 39.31 per cent for the large farms in irrigated area. Therefore, the proportion of area under commercial crops decreases with increase in size group of farms in irrigated area and no such significant relation is found between proportion of area under cash crops and size group of farms in unirrigated area.

Irrigation Impact on Cost of Cultivation and Farm Income

It is observed from the study of field investigation that, the irrigation has increased the cost of cultivation in irrigated farming. The overall cost A_2 per hectare of net sown area for all crops is found to be higher by Rs. 12,662.61 in irrigated area than in unirrigated area. The per hectare operational cost in irrigated farming is higher on account of excess of associated costs involved in irrigated farming. The overall cost B in irrigated area is of Rs. 20,797.76, whereas it is Rs. 3,730.95 in unirrigated area. This indicates that, the cost B in irrigated area is higher by Rs. 17,066.81 (457.44 per cent) over that of unirrigated area. Further, the overall cost C in irrigated farms is higher to the extent of Rs. 17,725.25 constituting 416.03 per cent as compared to cost C in unirrigated farms. Thus, all the costs i.e. cost A_2, cost B and cost C are found to be higher in irrigated area than that in unirrigated area. This is also true for each size class farms in irrigated area when compared with corresponding size class of farms in unirrigated area. In the study of different costs in relation to size of land holdings, it is observed that, cost A_2 is the highest of Rs.17,398.85 for the small farms and lowest of Rs. 11,226.13 for the large farms in irrigated area. This shows that cost A_2 decreases with increase in size of farms in irrigated area. In unirrigated area, there was no such significant relation between cost A_2 and size of farms. Similarly, cost B is found to be the highest of Rs. 24,044.56 in case of small farms and lowest of Rs. 15,366.66 for large farms in irrigated area. This fact shows that, there was inverse relationship between the cost B and the size of land holding of farm operators in irrigated area. In unirrigated area, it is the highest of Rs. 4,043.98 for the small farms and lowest of Rs. 3,329.85 for the medium farms. Thus, there appears no uniform trend between the cost B and size of farms in unirrigated area. Further, the cost C is the highest of Rs. 26,054.79 in case of small farms and lowest of Rs. 15,755.35 for large farms in irrigated area, whereas it is the highest of Rs. 4,751.16 in case of small farms and lowest of Rs. 3,546.01 for large farms in unirrigated area. Thus, this shows that cost C decreases with increase in size of farms in both irrigated and unirrigated areas.

Irrigation has largely contributed to increase in the gross value of output in the study area. The overall gross value of output per hectare for all crops in irrigated is being Rs. 28,786.67 as against Rs. 4,614.35 in unirrigated area. Therefore, the overall gross value of output in irrigated area is significantly higher (by 6.24 times) than that of unirrigated area. It is also true for each size class of farms in irrigated area when compared with the respective size class of farms in unirrigated area. The gross value of output is highest of Rs. 33,995.79 in small farms and lowest of Rs. 20,881.09 for large farms in irrigated area, whereas in unirrigated area, it is highest of Rs. 5,077.42 for the small farms and lowest of Rs. 3,598.60 for large farms. This shows that gross value of output decreases with increase in size class of farms in irrigated and unirrigated areas.

Irrigation has highly contributed to increase in income such as, farm business income, return to family labour and management and net income in irrigated farming. The overall farm business income in irrigated farms is found to be higher by Rs. 11,509.71 (i.e. 6.93 times) than that in unirrigated farms. This is because that irrigation has helped to use more inputs resulting in increase in production and productivity in irrigated farming. Thus, the farm business income in irrigated farming is significantly higher than that of unirrigated farming. It is also highest in each of the size class of farms in irrigated area when compared with corresponding size class of farms in unirrigated area. It is also observed that the farm business income is the highest of Rs. 16,596.96 for the small farms and the lowest of Rs. 9,654.96 for large farms in irrigated area. Whereas in unirrigated area, it is the highest of Rs. 2,154.84 for small farms and the lowest of Rs. 1,115.64 for large farms. This indicates that, farm business income decreases with increase in size class of farms both in irrigated and unirrigated areas.

Further, the per hectare return to family labour and management in irrigated farming is found to be higher by Rs. 7,105.51 than that in unirrigated farming. As regards the return to family labour and management, in case of small, medium and large farms in irrigated area are also significantly higher by Rs. 8,917.79, Rs. 5,498.77 and Rs. 5,344.66 respectively over the corresponding size class of farms in unirrigated areas. It is also found that there is inverse relationship between the return to family labour and management and the size class of farms in irrigated area. Similarly, the overall per hectare net return in irrigated farms is found to be higher by Rs. 6,447.07 than that in unirrigated farms. It is the highest for each size class of farms in irrigated area as compared to corresponding size class of farms in unirrigated area. It is also observed that net return is the highest of Rs. 7,941.00 in case of small farms and the lowest of Rs. 5,125.74 for the large farms in irrigated land. Thus, there is inverse relationship between the net return and the size class of farms in irrigated area.

Carrying out statistical significant tests, it was observed that 't' values (Fishers 't') were significant throughout, that is for all kinds of farm operators and for all kinds of farm incomes (i.e. farm business income, return to family labour and management and net income) in irrigated area. This conclusively proved that in the study area irrigated farm households on an average received significantly higher income than the unirrigated farm households.

The output-input ratio is computed to show the relative farm efficiency under the irrigated and unirrigated areas. It is observed that the overall ratio of gross value of output to cost A_2, the ratios of gross value of output to cost B and the ratio of gross value of output to cost C are comparatively higher in irrigated area than that in unirrigated area. In study of input-output ratios apart from size class of farms, it is observed that each size class of farms in irrigated area has higher input-output ratios than the corresponding size class of farms in unirrigated area. Further, it is also observed that input-output ratio is the highest in case of small farms and lowest in case of large farms in irrigated area. This shows that input-output ratio decreases with the increase in size class of farms in irrigated area. Therefore, this reveals that in general relatively small farmers in irrigated area have greater efficiency in farm enterprises.

Irrigation Impact on Man-Days Employment

Provision of irrigation has also generated more employment in the study area. The overall excess per hectare man-days of employment in irrigated area is higher by 87.01 man-days over unirrigated area. Thus, irrigation has largely contributed higher employment opportunities in irrigated area, with respect to different size group of farms, the small, medium and large farms generate 362.31 per cent, 315.68 per cent and 476.05 per cent respectively in irrigated area when compared with the respective size group of farms in unirrigated area.

In short, the illustrative field study conducted in both irrigated and unirrigated areas of Tuljapur taluka in Osmanabad district has positively substantiated the different hypotheses of the study. It has been observed that the index of crop intensity in irrigated area is higher than that of crop intensity in unirrigated area. The cropping pattern is also favourable for farmers in irrigated area with more diversification and cultivation of commercial crops as compared to unirrigated area. The per hectare gross value of output in irrigated area is significantly higher than that of unirrigated area. The different costs as well as different measures of farm profits per hectare are significantly higher in irrigated farming as compared to unirrigated farming. The output-input ratios are also comparatively higher in irrigated area. The man-days of employment generated is also considerably higher in irrigated area. Therefore, there is no denying the fact that the impact of irrigation on farm economy has been benefited to farmers in the study area and hypotheses developed earlier have been confirmed substantially by the micro-level field study.

POLICY MEASURES

On the basis of these findings, some relevant policy implications emerging from the study maybe summarised as follows:

(1) Minor irrigation claims priority over major and medium irrigation because of its proven definite and practical advantages. Minor irrigation leads to increase in higher irrigation potential immediately and high

potential utilization as compared to major and medium projects. Hence in irrigation planning, in times to come, more emphasis should be given to the development of minor irrigation.

(2) During last 46 years (1951-52 to 1996-97, inspite of large investment made in irrigation sector, the return to the investment, both in terms of yields and income are very disappointing in India. Since the inception of planning, 292 major and 944 medium projects are undertaken up to 1997, but so far only 158 (54.11 per cent) major and 768 (81.35 per cent) medium projects have been completed in India. Therefore, it is suggested that in order to boost up the irrigation growth, the gestation period of all types of irrigation projects should be substantially reduced, with projects being completed as per schedule time. Secondly, more emphasis should be given to minor irrigation schemes rather than major and medium projects. Because minor projects could be completed quickly which will start yielding benefits almost immediately as compared to major and medium projects.

(3) To ensure faster rate of quantitative expansion of irrigation potential, minor irrigation, particularly ground water resources need to be accorded high priority in irrigation planning of the state.

(4) It is found that there are wide and enormous intrasectoral imbalances in investment allocation between minor irrigation and major and medium irrigation during last 46 years (i.e. 1951-52 to 1996-97) in Maharashtra state. In all the Five Year Plans, higher portion of public investment has gone in favour of major and medium projects in the state. Out of the total expenditure incurred in irrigation sector during last 46 years, major and medium sector accounted for 88.48 per cent and remaining sector viz. minor irrigation schemes, accounting for only 11.52 per cent. Therefore, more efforts have to be made to allocate adequate

resources for the development of minor irrigation in the state.

(5) Even though there are noteworthy achievements in development of irrigation in Marathwada region and Osmanabad district, there is still considerable scope for bringing new cultivable area under assured water supply by taking up more minor irrigation schemes, particularly ground water sources (wells and tube wells) in Marathwada and Osmanabad district. According to Marathwada Agriculture Special Reports (February 1996), there is more scope for drilling wells for irrigation purpose in Marathwada region. So swift measures have to be initiated to bring more dry land under well and tube well irrigation for the benefits of small farmers.

(6) It is observed that utilisation of irrigation potential is a serious problem in Maharashtra state as compared to national level. To make more optimal utilisation of irrigation potential already created in state at huge cost to the public exchequer, field channels need to be provided to all irrigated area at an early date on a priority basis. Government should play more meaningful and positive role in respect of construction of field channels. Secondly, the lack of adequate and timely availability of water is also one of the reasons for low utilisation of irrigation potential. Therefore, project authority should ensure reliable, adequate and timely supply of irrigation water. This can be achieved by systematic planning and proper implementation of planned irrigation programme.

(7) While providing the irrigation facility to farmers, it is also necessary to see that these farmers must utilise the scarce water resources scientifically. Therefore, farmers should be given proper training to make use of available water resources through water management technique so that wasting of water could be avoided effectively.

(8) It is observed that small farmers could not take up the venture of bringing their cultivable land under assured irrigation water for want of financial assistance. Therefore, liberal financial assistance should be provided through institutions like cooperative banks, regional rural banks and commercial banks at concessional rate of interest. Secondly, government should play more positive role in respect of drilling more wells and tube wells in backward region like Marathwada so that poor farmers can take more advantage of such irrigation. This will enable the small farmers to come forward to irrigate their land under assured water.

(9) In low arid district like Osmanabad, the modern methods of irrigation (i.e. drip and sprinkler) are the most useful. Modern methods are the more efficient in utilisation of water and higher productivity. Generally this modern irrigation method can save 30 to 40 per cent water and 20 to 30 per cent increase in crop yields with good quality of farm produce as compared to traditional irrigation method. Further, government is also providing of 50 per cent subsidy for the drip and sprinkler units for the small and marginal farmers. But these methods of irrigation are not found to be so popular both in irrigated and unirrigated area. Therefore, it is recommended that these methods of irrigation should be promoted in irrigated and unirrigated areas by propaganda, demonstrations and training to the farmers.

(10) In agricultural sector, the well infrastructural facilities like electricity, road, transport, communication, marketing, banking are essential and more useful for increasing agricultural production. Further, health and educational facilities should also be improved. Good infrastructural facilities always help for quick transport and easy access to nearby towns for marketing. These improved infrastructural facilities will be helpful to farmers for increasing net returns.

(11) The farmers involvement and participation in irrigation management is very useful for optimal utilisation of irrigation potential. There should be proper linkages among the different organisations along with water users' associations. Active participation of the farmers is a pre-requisite for effective irrigation water management. Therefore, government should take keen interest in creating effective farmers organizations, which would be helpful for better irrigation water management.

Findings of this study and their policy implications are definitely helpful for understanding the important role of irrigation in agriculture development of Osmanabad district. The government should carefully consider these suggestions keeping in view the fact that accelerated expansion of irrigation facility and improvement of irrigation systems are the essential pre-requisites for a prosperous agricultural sector.

Bibliography

Books

Acharya S.S., Lodha N.R. and Solanki A.S., In Water Management Problems and Prospects in Command Areas, edited by Jaspalsing and others, Himanshu Publications, Udaipur, 1999.

Ansari Nasim, Economics of Irrigation Rates: A study in Punjab and Uttar Pradesh, Asia Publishing House, Bombay, 1968.

Ashturkar B.W. and Satpute T.G., Socio-Economic Survey of Purna Command Area, Marathwada Agricultural University, Parbhani, 1992.

Ashturkar B.W. and Satpute T.G., Evaluation Survey of Purna Command Area, Marathwada Agricultural University, Parbhani, 1992.

Azam Syed Farooque, Irrigation and Agricultural Development, B.R. Publishing Corporation, Delhi, 1998.

Basu S.K. and Mukherjee S.B., Evaluation of Damodhar Canal (1959-60), Asia Publishing House, Bombay, 1963.

Bharadwaj Krishna, Production Conditions in Indian Agriculture: A Study Based on Farm Management Survey, Cambridge Press, 1974.

Bhatia B.M. Poverty, Agriculture and Economic Growth, Vikas Publications, New Delhi, 1977.

Bhatia Ramesh and Sinha Baswan Economic Appraisal of Irrigation Project in India, Agricole Publishing Academy, New Delhi, 1982.

Brahme Sulbha, Pore Kumud and Pore S.H., Regional Planning: A Case Study of Marathwada Region, Gokhale Institute of Politics and Economics, Pune, 1975.

Chatterjee Nandini, Irrigated Agriculture: A Case Study of West Bengal, Rawat Publications, Jaipur, 1994.

Clark Colin, The Economics of Irrigation, Pergamon Press, London, 1970.

Dandekar V.M., The Indian Economy 1947-92, Volume I : Agriculture, Sage Publications India Pvt. Ltd., New Delhi, 1994.

Desai Vasant, A Study of Rural Economics, Himalaya Publishing House, Bombay, 1983.

Dhawan B.D., Development of Tube well Irrigation in India, Agricole Publishing Academy, New Delhi, 1982.

Dhawan B.D., Studies in Irrigation and Water Management, Commonwealth Publishers, New Delhi, 1989.

Dhawan B.D., Trends and New Tendencies in Indian Irrigated Agriculture, Commonwealth Publishers, New Delhi, 1993.

Dhawan B.D., Irrigation in India's Agricultural Development, Productivity, Stability and Equity, Sage Publishers, New Delhi, 1988.

Dhawan B.D., Studies in Indian Irrigation, Commonwealth Publications, New Delhi, 1999.

Dhongade M.P., Suryawanshi S.D. and Deshmukh P.D., Farmers Attitude Survey in Khadakwasala Command Area, Mahatma Phule Agricultural University, Rahuri (Maharashtra), 1986.

Eckstein Otto, Water Resources Development: The Economics of Project Evaluation, Harwad University Press, Massachusetts, 1958.

Frankel F. India's Green Revolution-Economic Gains and Political Costs, Oxford University Press, Bombay, 1971.

Gadgil D.R., Economic Effects of Irrigation - Report of a Survey of the Direct and Indirect Benefits of Godavari and Pravara Canals, Gokhale Institute of Politics and Economics, Pune, 1948.

Gosh R.N., Agriculture in Economic Development with Special Reference to Punjab, Vikas Publications, New Delhi, 1977.

Gowda N.K., Agricultural Development, Mangal Deep Publications, Jaipur, 1998.

Gurjar R.K., Irrigation for Agricultural Modernisation, Scientific Publishers, Jodhpur, 1987.

Gulhati N. D. and Smith William Charles, Irrigated Agriculture: An Historical Review, American Society of Agronomy, Madison, Wisconsin, U.S.A. 1967.

Henry Hart, Administrative Aspects of River Valley Development, Asia Publishing House, Bombay, 1961.

Hillel D., Advances in Irrigation, Vol. III. Academic Press, New York, 1985.

Hooja Rakesh and Kavita P.S. (Edited), Planning for Sustainability in Irrigation, Rawat Publications, Jaipur, 1994.

Jai Prakash and Padamchand Jain, Role of Irrigation in Stabilising Agricultural Production, Radha Publications, New Delhi, 1993.

Jha U.M., Irrigation and Agricultural Development, Deep and Deep Publications, New Delhi, 1984.

Kallur M.S., Irrigation and Economic Development, Chugh Publications, Allahabad, 1988.

Kothari C.R., Research Methodology-Methods and Techniques, Wishwa Prakashan, New Delhi, 1990.

Kumar P., Economics of Water Management, Heritage Publishers, New Delhi, 1977.

Malik R.M. and Padhi S.P., Final Report on Irrigation Systems in Orissa: Its Impact on Agricultural Development, Namakrushna Choudhari (Centre for Development Studies), Bhubaneshwar, Orissa, 1995.

Meti T.K., Tungabhadra Irrigation, Strategy and Accelerator of Development, Vol. 1, Karnataka University, Dharwad, 1977.

Mishra K.M., Irrigation and Economic Development, Ashish Publishing House, New Delhi, 1990.

Mishra K.M., A Comparative Study of Economics of Minor Sources of Irrigation in Uttar Pradesh, Oxford and IBH Publishing Co., 1968.

Mishra G.P. and Vivekananda M., Impact of Canal Irrigation in Rural Areas: A Case Study of Bellary District, Himalaya Publishing Company, Bombay, 1979.

Nadkarni M.V., Irrigation Development in Karnataka - An Impact of Irrigation by Tank, Well and Canal, Himalaya Publishing Company, Bombay, 1979.

Nageshwar Rao K., Economics of Water Supply, Himalaya Publishing Company, Bombay, 1993.

Padoshi A.R., Agricultural Development of India, Himalaya Publishing Company, Bombay, 1991.

Pal S.P., Contribution of Irrigation to Agricultural Production and Productivity, NCAER, New Delhi, 1985.

Pandey M.P., The Impact of Irrigation on Rural Development: A Case Study, Concept Publishing Company, New Delhi, 1979.

Patil R.G., Suryawanshi S.D. and Kapse P.M., Socio-Economic Survey of Girna Irrigation Project in Jalgaon District (Maharashtra), Mahatma Phule Agricultural University, Rahuri, 1978.

Pawar C.T., Impact of Irrigation: A Regional Perspective, Himalaya Publishing House, Bombay, 1989.

Rao D. Vasudeva, Rural Development Through Irrigation, Ashish Publishing House, New Delhi,1987.

Rao V.K.R.V. (Ed.) New Seeds Adoption and Yield, Sterilise Publishers Pvt. Ltd., New Delhi, 1979.

Rao V.M., Farming with Irrigation and Irrigated Farming-A Comparative Study in Impact of Irrigation by Tank, Well and Canal, Himalaya Publishing Company, Bombay, 1979.

Reddy N. Bhaskara, Economics of Conjunctive Irrigation in Canal Command Area, Anmol Publications, New Delhi, 1992.

Satpathy T., Irrigation and Economic Development, Ashish Publishing House, New Delhi, 1984.

Scarlett Epestein T., Economic Development and Social Change in South India, Oxford University Press, Delhi, 1962.

Satpute T.G., Irrigation Management in Command Area, Mittal Publications, Delhi, 1988.

Sharma P.M., Bhati R.S. and Shekhawat R.S., Some Magnitudes and Directions of Irrigational Effects on Farm Economy of Shriganganagar District, Rajasthan, In Water Management, Edited by Jaspalsing, Himanshu Publications, Udaipur, 1990.

Tyagi B.P., Agricultural Economics and Rural Development, Jai Prakash Nath and Co., Meerut (Uttar Pradesh), 1990.

Vasanth Desai, A Study of Rural Economics, Himalaya Publishing Company, Bombay, 1990.

Vyas V.S., Foundation of Indian Agriculture, Ed. By Vadilal Vora and Company Publishers Private Ltd., Bombay, 1968.

Waheeduddin Khan and Tripathi R. N., Intensive Agriculture and Modern Inputs-Prospects of Small Farmers Study in West Godavari District, NICD, Hyderabad, 1972.

Articles

Abdul Majid, Crop Pattern and Size of Cultivation Holdings, *Indian Journal of Agricultural Economics,* Vol. XVIII, January-March, 1963.

Abhange G.V., Irrigation Development in Marathwada, Fourteenth Conference of Maharashtra Engineering Service Organization, Aurangabad, 1991.

Alexander A.C., Agricultural Development and Social Transformation, *Journal of Rural Development,* Vol. No. 1, January 1982.

Abhange G.V. and Jadhav R., Future Planning and Problems of Water in Marathwada Region, Maharashtra Sinchan Vikas, January-March, 1999.

Alexander A.C., Agricultural Development and Social Transformation, *Journal of Rural Development,* Vol. No 1, January 1982.

Anand O.P., Some Aspects of Optimum Benefits from Utilisation of Irrigational Potential of Chambal Valley Project, *Indian Journal of Agricultural Economics,* Vol. XV, October-December, 1960.

Azad M.P. and others, Economic Efficiency of Tubewell Irrigation in Kanpur District, Uttar Pradesh (A Case Study), *Indian Journal of Agricultural Economics,* Vol. XXXIX, No. 3, July-September, 1984.

Bashir A. Desai and Thingalaya N.K., Irrigation Factor and Yield Variability in Rice Growing Districts in India, *Indian Journal of Agricultural Economics,* Vol. XX, No. 3, July-September, 1965.

Bharadwaj Krishna, Notes on Farm Size and Productivity, *Economic and Political Weekly,* Vol. V. No. 39, 26th September, 1970.

Bhattacharya C.B., Micro Irrigation in Rural India, *Yojana,* 16th-30th September, 1983.

Choudhary D.K., Disparity in Income in Context of HYV, *Economic and Political Weekly,* Vol. V, No. 39, 26th September, 1970.

Dhawan B.D., How Stable is Indian Irrigated Agriculture, *Economic and Political Weekly,* Vol. XXII, No. 39, 26th September 1987.

Dhawan B.D., Impact of Irrigation on Farm Economy in High Rainfall Areas, the Kal Project, *Economic and Political Weekly,* Vol. XXVII, No. 52-53, December 24-31, 1988.

Dikshit P. and Sing A.K., Impact of Green Revolution and Agricultural Production Structure-A Study of the Changes in Cropping Pattern in Uttar Pradesh, *Agricultural Situation in India,* Vol. 29, 1974.

Ghosh R., Water Resources Development and Management in 2015 A.D. - A Perspective, *Journal of Indian Water Resources Society,* Vol. 13, No. 3 & 4, July-October, 1993.

Giri A.K. and Malik, Some Economic Aspects of Public Source of Irrigation-A Comparison with Private Source of Irrigation, *Indian Journal of Agricultural Economics,* Vol. XXXIX, No. 3, July-September, 1994.

Jawahar Thakur and Praduman Kumar, Comparative Study of Economic Efficiency of Different Irrigation Systems in Western Uttar Pradesh, *Indian Journal of Agricultural Economics,* Vol. XXXIX, No. 3, July-September, 1984.

Jha D., Impact of Irrigation on Employment in Indian Agriculture, Rural India, Vol. 23, No. 7, 1960.

Kahlon A.S., Miglani S.S. and Hanumant Singh, A Comparative Analysis of Dry and Irrigated Farming in Ferozepur District, Punjab, *Indian Journal of Agricultural Economics,* Vol. XXVI, No. 4, 1971.

Moorty T.V. and Mellor John, A Comparative Study of Costs and Benefits of Irrigation from State and Private Tube Wells in Uttar Pradesh, *Economic and Political Weekly,* Vol. XXVIII, No. 4, October-December, 1973.

Patel A.S., Irrigation - Its Employment Impact in the Command Areas of Medium Irrigation Projects in Gujarat, *Economic and Political Weekly,* Vol. XXXVI, No. 4, 1981.

Raghuvanshi C. S., Madhuresh Chandra and Gupta, Socio Economic Impact of Irrigation Management on Employment and Farm Income-An Empirical Study, *Water Management,* Vol. 1, No. 1, July 1991.

Ramakrishna K.S. and Deshpande R.S., Irrigation Impact on Employment and Income, *Agricultural Situation in India,* Vol. XLIV, No. 10, January, 1990.

Regan M.M. and Wietwell E.G., "Economic Valuation of Soil and Water Conservation-Measures and Programmes", *Journal of Farm Economics,* November, 1947.

Renuka C., Irrigation and Rural Development, A Study in Kadam Project of Andhra Pradesh, Ph.D. Thesis, Kakatiya University, Warangal, September, 1990.

Sangle S.T., Economic Impact of Irrigation in Jayakwadi Command Area, Ph.D. Thesis, Dr. Babasaheb Ambedkar Marathwada University, Aurangabad, 1996.

Sharma R.K., Moorti T.V. and Sharma A.K., Resources Use Variability on Irrigated and Unirrigated Farms in Mandi District of Himachal Pradesh, *Indian Journal of Agricultural Economics,* Vol. 69, 1988-89.

Sidhu D.S., Ramesh Chand and Kaul J.K., An Economic Analysis of Various Sources of Irrigation in Punjab, *Indian Journal of Agricultural Economics,* Vol. XXXIX, No. 3, July-September, 1984.

Suryawanshi S.D. and Kapse P.M., Impact of Ghod Irrigation Project on Employment of Female Agricultural Labour, *Indian Journal of Agricultural Economics,* Vol. 40, No. 3, July-September, 1985.

Subramanian and Selvarajan, Economic Impacts of Resource-Use Optimization Augmentation in Farms of Parambikulam Aliyar Project, *Indian Journal of Agricultural Economics,* Vol. XXXVI, No. 1, January-March, 1981.

Thamarajakshi R., National Agricultural Policy, Confusion on Ends and Means, *Economic and Political Weekly,* Vol. 26, September 2, 2000.

Vaidyanathan A., Asha Krishnakumar, Rajagopal A. and Varatharajan, Impact of Irrigation on Productivity of Land, *Journal of Indian School of Political Economy,* Vol. VI, No. 4, October-December, 1994.

Vijaya Shyamala C., Current Approach to Irrigation Management, *Yojana,* Vol. 38, No. 10, June 15, 1989.

William Sander, Irrigation Development and Non-farm Employment Changes in Communities in the Philippines, *Indian Journal of Agricultural Economics,* Vol. XXXVIII, No. 1, January-March, 1983.

Reports

Government of India, Report of Indian Irrigation Commission, 1901-1903, Part I, Superintendent of Government Printing Press, Calcutta, 1903.

Report of the Irrigation Commission, Vol. I, Ministry of Irrigation and Power, New Delhi, 1972.

Water and Related Statistics, Central Water Commission, Ministry of Water Resources and Power, New Delhi, 1998.

Water Resources Development in India (1947-1997), Ministry of Water Resources, New Delhi, 1998.

Report of the National Commission on Agriculture, Vol. V, Resource Development, Ministry of Agriculture and Irrigation, New Delhi, 1976.

Seventh Five Year Plan, Planning Commission, Vol. II (1985-1990).

Government of India, Report on Evaluation Study for CAD Programme, Chambal Irrigation Project, Rajasthan, Ministry of Water Resources, New Delhi, June 1996.

Report of the Irrigation Commission, Vol. II, Ministry of Irrigation and Power, New Delhi, 1972.

Government of Maharashtra, Economic Survey of Maharashtra, Directorate of Economics and Statistics, Planning Department, Government of Maharashtra, Mumbai, 1999-2000.

District Census Handbook Osmanabad, Census of India 1991, Maharashtra Census Directorate Published in 1995.

Report of First Maharashtra State Irrigation Commission, 1962.

Report of the Fact Finding Committee on Regional Imbalance, April, 1984.

Water and Irrigation Commission, Vol. I, June, 1999.

Socio-Economic Review and District Statistical Abstract of Osmanabad District, Directorate of Economics and Statistics, 1982-83, 1986-87, 1990-91, 1995-96.

Annual Report of Irrigation 1997-98, Chief Engineer, Irrigation Department, Aurangabad, 1999.

Districtwise General Statistical Information of Agricultural Department, Part II, Epitome of Agriculture in Maharashtra, 1986-87.

Government of Maharashtra, District Hand-Book of Osmanabad, Osmanabad. Maharashtra Sinchan Vikas, January-March, 1999.

Districtwise Agricultural Statistical Information of Maharashtra, Part II, Commissionerate of Agriculture, Pune, 1995-96.

Epitome of Agriculture Year 1996-97 and 1997-98, Part 1, Commissioner of Agriculture, Maharashtra State, Pune, 1998.

Districtwise Agricultural Statistical Information of Maharashtra, Part II, Commissionerate of Agriculture, Pune, 1997-98.

District Hand Book in Marathwada Region, Chief Engineer, Irrigation Department, Aurangabad, 1999.

Marathwada 2001, Part II, Jaihind Printing Press, Aurangabad, 1987.

Planning for Development of Marathwada, Vol. 1, 1981.